Lecture Notes of the Institute for Computer Sciences, Social Informatics and Telecommunications Engineering 353

More information about this series at http://www.springer.com/series/8197

Enver Ever · Fadi Al-Turjman (Eds.)

Forthcoming Networks and Sustainability in the IoT Era

First EAI International Conference, FoNeS – IoT 2020
Virtual Event, October 1–2, 2020
Proceedings

 Springer

Editors
Enver Ever ⓘ
Computer Engineering Department,
Northern Cyprus Campus
Middle East Technical University
Mersin, Turkey

Fadi Al-Turjman ⓘ
Artificial Intelligence Department
Near East University
Nicosia, Turkey

ISSN 1867-8211   ISSN 1867-822X (electronic)
Lecture Notes of the Institute for Computer Sciences, Social Informatics
and Telecommunications Engineering
ISBN 978-3-030-69430-2   ISBN 978-3-030-69431-9 (eBook)
https://doi.org/10.1007/978-3-030-69431-9

This Springer imprint is published by the registered company Springer Nature Switzerland AG
The registered company address is: Gewerbestrasse 11, 6330 Cham, Switzerland

Preface

We are happy to introduce the proceedings of the 2020 European Alliance for Innovation (EAI) International Conference on Forthcoming Networks and Sustainability in the IoT Era (EAI FoNeS-IoT 2020). This conference brought together researchers, academics, developers and practitioners around the world who are contributing to application areas for advanced communication systems and the development of new services, in an attempt to facilitate the tremendous growth of new devices and smart things that need to be connected to the Internet through a variety of wireless technologies. In addition to this, thanks to the rapid advancement of facilitating technologies, we were also able to accept contributions in the areas of pervasive sensing, multimedia sensing, machine learning, deep learning, unmanned aerial vehicles, and cloud and edge computing, which have the potential to introduce services and business models beyond the traditional mobile Internet.

The technical program of FoNeS-IoT 2020 consisted of 13 full papers, in oral presentation sessions at the main conference tracks. The conference tracks were: Track 1 – IoT and Network Applications; Track 2 – Machine Learning and Distributed Computing; and Track 3 – Cellular Networks and Security. In addition to the high-quality technical paper presentations from our contributors, the technical program also featured a keynote speech from Associate Prof. Ahmed Abdelgawad. Our keynote speaker considered the design and implementation of IoT signal processing systems in his presentation.

Coordination with the steering chairs, Imrich Chlamtac and Fadi Al-Turjman, was essential for the success of the conference. We sincerely appreciate their feedback, support and guidance. It was also a pleasure to work with our organizing committee team, and we would like to thank them for their hard work in organizing and supporting the conference. In particular, the Technical Program Committee, led by our Chair Prof. Huan Nguyen and Co-Chairs Dr. Purav Shah and Dr. Yöney Kırsal Ever contributed the peer-review process of technical papers and made a high-quality technical program. We are also grateful to the Conference Managers, Natasha Onofrei and Eliška Vlčková.

The FoNeS-IoT 2020 conference was able to provide a good forum for researchers, academics, students, developers and practitioners. We sincerely hope that the FoNeS-IoT 2020 proceedings will serve as an important resource and reference, and that future FoNeS-IoT conferences will be at least as successful as the one we organized in 2020.

Thank you.

October 2020

Enver Ever
Fadi Al-Turjman

Conference Organization

Steering Committee

Chair

Imrich Chlamtac   Bruno Kessler Professor, University of Trento, Italy

Member

Fadi Al-Turjman   Near East University, Cyprus

Organizing Committee

General Chair

Fadi Al-Turjman   Near East University, Cyprus

TPC Chair and Co-chair

Huan Nguyen   Middlesex University London, UK

TPC Co-chairs

Purav Shah   Middlesex University London, UK
Yöney Kırsal Ever   Near East University, Cyprus

Web Chairs

Eser Gemikonakli   University of Kyrenia, Cyprus
Sinem Alturjman   Antalya Bilim University, Turkey

Publicity and Social Media Chairs

Yöney Kırsal Ever   Near East University, Cyprus
Ilker Gelisen   Biotechnology Association, Turkey
Murat Fahrioglu   Middle East Technical University, Cyprus

Workshops Chairs

Md. Arafatur Rahman   University of Malaysia Pahang, Malaysia
Krishna Doddapaneni   Amazon Web Services, USA

Sponsorship and Exhibits Chair

Leonardo Mostarda   Camerino University, Italy

Publications Chair

Enver Ever   Middle East Technical University – Northern
                                  Cyprus Campus, Cyprus

Panels Chair

Orhan Gemikonakli   Middlesex University London, UK

Demos Chairs

Ilsun You   Soonchunhyang University, Republic of Korea
Shehzad Ashraf Chaudhry   Istanbul Gelişim University, Turkey

Posters and PhD Track Chair

Kamil Dimililer   Near East University, Cyprus

Local Chairs

Ümit Deniz Uluşar   Akdeniz University, Turkey
Fadi Al-Turjman   Near East University, Cyprus

Technical Program Committee

Technical Program Committee Chair

Huan Nguyen   Middlesex University London, UK

Technical Program Committee Co-chairs

Purav Shah   Middlesex University London, UK
Yöney Kırsal Ever   Near East University, Cyprus

Members

Yaser Jararweh   Duquesne University, USA
Rahib Abiyev   Near East University, Cyprus
Orhan Gemikonakli   Middlesex University London, UK
Ümit Deniz Uluşar   Akdeniz University, Turkey
Shehzad Ashraf   Istanbul Gelişim University, Turkey
Arafatur Rahman   University of Malaysia Pahang, Malaysia
Krishna Doddapaneni   Amazon Web Services, USA
Umar Özgünalp   Cyprus International University, Cyprus
Sertan Serte   Near East University, Cyprus
Hadi Zahmatkesh   Oslo Metropolitan University, Norway
Ramiz Salama   Near East University, Cyprus

Contents

From Traditional House Price Appraisal to Computer Vision-Based: A Survey

Naser Naser[1](✉), Sertan Serte[1], and Fadi Al-Turjman[2]

[1] Department of Electrical and Electronics Engineering, Near East University, Nicosia, Cyprus
nasersmn751@gmail.com, sertan.serte@neu.edu.tr
[2] Research Center for AI and Iot, Near East University, Nicosia, Cyprus
fadi.alturjman@neu.edu.tr

Abstract. Online house price appraisal involved complex and quite challenging task. Several researches have been proposed in the literature, providing various techniques and tools for finding and pricing houses to make the process more efficient, comfortable, and reliable for realtors and clients. Traditional house appraisal approaches focused on the economic and demographic variables and mainly used statistical methods to estimate the houses' values. Even though those estimates provide valuable information, they are extremely unreliable in certain situations. The interior and exterior appearance, which is not considered in the estimation using these techniques, is one of the crucial variables influencing the valuation of a house. Recent advances in digital cameras, machine learning, deep learning, computer vision, and the Internet of Things (IoT) have led to the development of sophisticated house appraisal techniques, taking into account the houses' economic, demographic, and pictorial information. This survey article investigates the current state of the art and future trends in house price appraisal methods.

Keywords: House appraisal · Machine learning · Computer vision · CNN · IoT

1 Introduction

Several studies have been carried out in order to establish reliable and straightforward house pricing platforms for realtors and their clients. Traditional techniques have been used for many years and are still used by some realtors to date. Still, with the evolution of Artificial Intelligence, much simpler and more accurate techniques are being studied, and they demonstrate excellent results. The conventional Hedonic methods, which are statistic-based using econometric and demographic variables, are hectic and rely on many variables; they might also not provide the house's visual features, making it difficult for a client in the house search. Traditionally, econometric and demographic variables are used in house price evaluation by looking at income, repeat sale of property cells, crime rate, population, house size (per square meter), building years, architecture, venue, living costs of carbon emissions, and citizens' well-being, as the visual aspects of the houses are not taken into consideration by these approaches, the knowledge is inadequate to provide

E. Ever and F. Al-Turjman (Eds.): FoNeS-IoT 2020, LNICST 353, pp. 1–10, 2021.
https://doi.org/10.1007/978-3-030-69431-9_1

a detailed assessment [1–10]. In determining the price of houses, there are several factors to be considered, interior features such as the floor, furniture, building quality, paints, decoration design, number of rooms, reception, heating systems, toilets, and bathrooms [11, 12]. External assessment is based on the building quality and street views (Fig. 1), natural landmarks like castles, canals, coast, green areas, and human-made structures like castles, athletic fields (Fig. 2) and the houses external features around [13]. Geographical Information System (GIS) was also used in some house price estimation or prediction research to provide information about the neighborhood base on proximity of house location from some variables like amenities such as school, worship areas, fire stations, hospitals, shopping areas, and road accessibility to the workplace and all, in the GIS methods outstanding performance are also recorded [14–16].

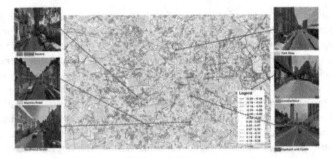

Fig. 1. GIS image house outdoor and street view

Fig. 2. Landscape of areas

2 Reviews

In this review, emphasis will be given more to visual and hybrid house pricing appraisal methods. It gives buyers a clear picture and gives a more efficient prediction of the property based on the house's interior, neighborhood view, and exterior quality. Several classical machine learning techniques are used in house price appraisal prediction or estimation [1, 2]. A Dynamic Model Averaging and Dynamic model Selection was used to estimate houses' prices using state-level all transaction house price index to forecast houses' property prices in 50 states in the United States. In this work, nominal data from the mid-1970s was used to forecast available from the Federal Housing Finance Agency. All-transactions indexes are constructed using repeat-sales and refinancing's on the same single-family properties and are available at a quarterly frequency. [3] made a comparison between Hedonic models with Artificial Neural Network, the house prices in Turkey are examined for the urban, rural and whole country using the 2004 Household Budget Survey Data to determine the price, the variables for pricing the house include size, number of rooms, age of building Heating systems and other structural features, and in the research ANN outperforms the Hedonic methods [4] price prediction using Machine learning techniques was used in predicting the prices of houses in the United States, the RIPPER, Naïve Bayesian, and AdaBoost were compared and the RIPPER outperforms the other two machine learning techniques in terms of accuracy. This shows that the RIPPER can be a good tool for the prediction of the house price. [6] examine the information from the Hedonic and Spatiotemporal method, though machine learning has shown great success with algorithms like SVM and Tree-based techniques, in their research tree technique with bagging show greater performance with the local spatiotemporal method and less performance with global spatiotemporal.

Distributed model with paragraph vector using xgboot to improve the model by missing values, Analytic hierarchy process (AHP), which is one of the Multi-Criteria Decision Analysis (MCDA) methods, is used to reproduce coefficients which would base for real estate valuation, the xgboos improves performance by dealing with missing variables in a data [10]. In [7] sudden house price drop has been predicted using Ensemble Empirical Mode Decomposition (EEMD) from the field of signal processing with the Support Vector Regression (SVR) methodology that originates from machine learning, the performance of the models was compared with a random walk. Random Walk (RW), a Bayesian Autoregressive and a Bayesian Vector Autoregressive model. The dataset record is from 1989-2012 which include real house price, unemployment, real GDP per capita, population, real construction work, etc. [8] several Machine learning techniques like partial least squares (PLS), support vector machine (SVM), and least squares support vector machine (LSSVM) was employed to forecast home values, due to the non-linearity of the data, PLS performance was not as good as SVM and LSSVM. The variables in the data include per capital crime rate of the town. Also, the Hybrid model of Particle Swamp Optimization with regression was used. PSO is used for selection of affect variables and regression analysis is used to determine the optimal coefficient in prediction. The result from this research proved combination regression and PSO is suitable and get the minimum prediction error obtained which is IDR 14.186. the study was based on two years of data, the building coast tends to be stable and the land rate tends to change [5].

Satellite images may be used as instruments for pricing a house depending on the position of the house and the neighborhood, but nominal or time series data are often important in the prediction at the same time [17]. Focus on using satellite and street image to estimate the price of houses in an area, the satellite map gives the geographic location and the street view provide the detail information of the street In which a buyer will decide on base on the research it was observed that using image features from the street like the buildings around, store and schools and GIS information provides distances between the house and amenities which are determining factors in having more accurate prediction of house price compared to the traditional methods of housing prediction that is using age and size. A Deep Neural Network was used to extract features from Google Street View images and Bing aerial images in estimating the house price model, a linear and nonlinear models were used in considering the neighbourhood based on a dataset containing traditional attributes including location, structural and neighbourhood. An Analytic Hierarchy Process (AHP), which is one of the Multi-Criteria Decision Analysis (MCDA) methods, issued to reproduce coefficients which would base for real estate valuation. The AHP and MCDA were integrated with GIS data to predict house prices in an area, a time series data was used In training the models and the houses are located on the GIS map, with this method the prices of houses in the area can be estimated using the GIS platform [14] (Fig. 3).

Fig. 3. Indoors views

As mention earlier, visual features are very important in giving a client a clear picture of the property the client is intending to buy, though, the econometric and demographic data are also important but with the database that can provide both the econometric and demographic data, using supervised learning we can extract features from a scene base and know the price of the objects in the scene base on the labels of the classes of the images and from those features, we can calculate or predict the price of the properties. As research was carried out in evaluating the price of second-hand items and license plate numbers the performance was commendable as the buyer can see the item and the physical status of the item [18, 19]. Poursaeed et al. in [11] employed house external and interior features to evaluate the houses, in their research the impact of the interior features such as the furniture, floors, decoration was considered in extracting the features of Deep Neural Network with DenseNet backbone was used to identify features in a scene, and a loss was calculated at the end of the network between the features price value and the price value obtained from a dataset for house price estimation. Supervised training was performed as the image data was classified into eight levels of luxury (Table 1).

The beauty of the outdoor scene is very important in pricing a house, these views include natural vegetation like mountains, canal coast and lots more, for the man-made

Table 1. Comparison of the proposed method with existing techniques

Reference	Techniques	Data	Predictors	Case study area
(You et al. 2017)	Recurrent Neural Network (RNN)	Images	Visual Features	San Jose, New York
(Risse and Kern 2016)	Dynamic model averaging	Time series	macroeconomic, monetary, demographic	Belgium, France, Germany Italy, Netherland and Spain
(Bork and Møller 2015)	Dynamic model averaging	Time series	macroeconomic and demographic	USA
(Selim 2009)	Hedonic regression, ANN	Time series	Locational and structural characteristic	Turkey
(Park and Kwon 2015)	Naïve Bayesian, Adaptive Boost (AdaBoost) RIPPER	Time series	Locational and structural characteristic	Fairfax country
(Nur et al. 2017)	Regression, Particle Swarm Optimization (PSO)	Time series	Locational and structural characteristic	Malang, East Java, Indonesia
(Pace and Hayunga 2020)	Hedonic, support vector machine (SVM), Classification And Regression Trees (CART)	Time series	Locational and structural characteristic	UK
(Plakandaras et al. 2015)	Ensemble Empirical Mode Decomposition (EEMD), Support Vector regression (SVR)	Time series	Macroeconomic and demographic	USA
(Mu et al. 2014)	SVM, Least square SVM (LSSVM)	Time series	Macroeconomic and demographic	Boston
(Poursaeed et al. 2018)	Deep CNN (ConvNets)	Images and metadata	Image features and home characteristics including size, number of bedrooms	USA

(*continued*)

Table 1. (*continued*)

Reference	Techniques	Data	Predictors	Case study area
(Bency et al. 2017)	Deep convolutional Neural Net-work (CNN)	satellite imagery	Image features and house attributes	London, Birmingham and Liverpool
(Law et al. 2019)	Deep convolutional neural-networks (ConvNets)	Street and satellite images	House attributes; age, size accessibility and visual features	London UK
(Yao et al. 2018)	Convolutional neural network for united mining (UMCNN) and Random Forest	Images and time series	Spatial information, social media data and visual features	Shenzhen, China
(Gu et al. 2011)	Hybrid of genetic algorithm and support vector machines	Time series	Previous selling price	Tangshan city, Chna
(Kuşan et al. 2010)	Fuzzy logic	Time series	Environmental factors	Eskisehir city in Turkey
(Ahmed and Moustafa 2016)	NN, SVM	Images and time series	Visual and textual features	USA
(Milunovich 2020)	Machine learning and deep learning algorithms	Time series	Previous selling price	Australia
(Jiang and Shen 2019)	FFNN and deep learning algorithms	Time series	Previous selling price	Shanghai China
(Liu and Liu 2019)	LSTM and GA	Time series	Residential, economic features and state financial policies	Shenzhen, China
Proposed method	Deep Learning (CNN)	Images & Time series	Image visual features, locational and structural characteristics	Northern Cyprus

structures such as castles, green areas, grasses, and athletic fields were considered in their research [13]. To extract these features a Convolutional Neural Network was used using transfer learning on pre-trained networks such as Alexnet, VGG16, GooglNet and ResNet were employed [19]. Computer vision-based car detection was used using CNN to determine the values of areas in a region in United State, images of care make and models data were in cooperated with demographic and socio-economic data to predict the well-being, income, carbon emission, cost of living and voting power of citizens in the area, with these parameters pricing of houses in the area can be determined though that was not the of the researches, it can cooperate with another computer vision-based housing appraisal techniques to determine the housing price in an area [15]. Spatial Auto Correlation was used to find the correlation between the house and the neighbourhood and Deep Convolutional Neural Network was used to perform the feature extraction base on transfer learning to extract features from the GIS maps, with the concatenation of house-level explanatory variables such as neighbourhood infrastructure, number of longitude and latitude, rooms and receptions, stores, worship areas, fire station, social and cultural sites and at the end of the network three regression techniques where used, linear, random forest and Multi-Layer Perceptron (MLP) Regression to have the best prediction of the house price as shown Fig. 4.

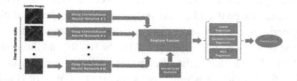

Fig. 4. The architecture of deep convolutional neural network

Furthermore, Koch et al. [12] uses CNN with AlexNet backbone to predict the building condition of a house for pricing, several patches of the houses are being trained to determine the quality of a building, this will help buyer to assess the buildings externally and with that, the asking price of the house can be compared with the estimated price base on the building quality as to how in Fig. 5. The use of Unmanned Ariel Vehicle can also be used to determine the price of a house appraisal, by using cameras on them to extract features from the scene, but the major challenge is privacy low and hard to maintain, but it the feature it might be possible [20].

very good   good   poor

Fig. 5. Outdoor view of houses

3 Enabling Technologies

In most of the computer vision-based approach, the data are stored in clouds, and personal computers, for a client to know the price of the house, he has to contact the realtor if the agent does not provide a web platform, the client can access a web platform in which it has access to the data stored and process in the cloud, due to the limitations of the points mentioned earlier, internet of things can provide a solution by providing high capacity storage, big data analysis, and a better communication protocol.

In IoT we have Infrastructure as a Service (IaaS) in which a realtor has the ability of web hosting, the realtor can install applications and operating systems, while Platform as a Service (PaaS) realtor can install, build and control applications and Software as a Services (SaaS) realtor can access and use the software at a remote location using a web browser. The benefits of cloud computing are that it doesn't require you to maintain or manage it (no need to have an IT expert), the realtor does not need to worry about capacity and data is accessible at any time. The protocol of the IoT addresses the issue of data speed, encoding, addressing, the exchange between devices and retransmission of lost package. The end device is embedded systems like computers and phones. For the IoT, we have the end devices such as computers, tablets, phones, sensors, printers, VR and AR, barcode scanners, gadgets which provides the realtor and the client information they seek regarding a house, the media of communication of the network can be either using copper wire, fibre optics or wireless networks such as Wifi or Bluetooth, the end devices and the media are connected via intermediary network devices like switches, repeater and so on. Efficient data communication is very important to achieve computer vision-based house prizing appraisal and to have efficient information about the property.

4 Discussions

Predicting or pricing a house is not an easy task, it is a task that requires a lot of variables to be looked at, with e evolution of computer vision-based housing price prediction, this will be easier for both the realtor and the client to find the house price in any location, neighbourhood, or base on the interior and exterior features of the house, the review in the previous section shows that there is a great performance from the visual techniques, easy understanding of properties by having the visual information unlike the traditional econometric and demographic methods, but still, the neighbourhood satellite images can also provide the location price base on the methods used in evaluating the neighbourhood, both the traditional time series data and the image data must be in use for an efficient house pricing. To ease the prediction and finding the prices of houses for both the realtor and the client, IoT as an emerging technology can address the issue by providing reliable, fast, efficient and user friendly devices that can exchange data at any point and location in time.

5 Conclusions

The future of computer vision-based in the industry of real estate is very bright because with computer vision information from a scene can be extracted and be used for the purpose intended, in house pricing appraisal, internal, outdoor, external and satellite information of a house can be known and base on that a good estimate of the house could be known. Also, it is easier for the client to have a clear insight of what they are intending to buy and them realtor can estimate the house price base of the asking price of the property. In conclusion, more efforts should be given to the area of computer vision in housing pricing and there are lots to be more like setting up datasets for the intended purpose and more algorithms to be developed since most of the works carried out uses transfer learning base on pre-trained networks.

References

1. Risse, M., Kern, M.: Forecasting house-price growth in the Euro area with dynamic model averaging. North Am. J. Econ. Financ. **38**, 70–85 (2016)
2. Bork, L., Møller, S.V.: Forecasting house prices in the 50 states using dynamic model averaging and dynamic model selection. Int. J. Forecast. **31**(1), 63–78 (2015)
3. Selim, H.: Determinants of house prices in Turkey: hedonic regression versus artificial neural network. Expert Syst. Appl. **36**(2), 2843–2852 (2009)
4. Park, B., Kwon, J.: Expert systems with applications using machine learning algorithms for housing price prediction: the case of Fairfax County, Virginia housing data. Expert Syst. Appl. **42**(6), 2928–2934 (2015)
5. Malang, C.S., Java, E., Febrita, R.E.: Modeling house price prediction using regression analysis and particle swarm optimization, no. January (2017)
6. Pace, R.K., Hayunga, D.: Examining the information content of residuals from hedonic and spatial models using trees and forests (2019)
7. Plakandaras, V., Gupta, R., Gogas, P., Papadimitriou, T.: Forecasting the U. S. real house price index. Econ. Model. **45**, 259–267 (2015)
8. Mu, J., Wu, F., Zhang, A.: Housing value forecasting based on machine learning methods. Abstr. Appl. Anal. **2014**, 1–7 (2014)
9. Peterson, S., Flanagan, A.B.: Neural network hedonic pricing models in mass real estate appraisal. J. Real Estate Res. **31**(2), 147–164 (2009)
10. Vargas-Calderón, V., Camargo, J.E.: A model for predicting price polarity of real estate properties using information of real estate market websites. arXiv:1911.08382v1 [cs.LG]. arXiv Computer Science (2018)
11. Poursaeed, O., Matera, T., Belongie, S.: Vision-based real estate price estimation. Mach. Vis. Appl. **29**(4), 667–676 (2018). https://doi.org/10.1007/s00138-018-0922-2
12. Koch, D., Döller, M., Zeppelzauer, M.: Visual estimation of building condition with patch-level ConvNets, pp. 12–17 (2018)
13. Seresinhe, C.I., Preis, T., Moat, H.S.: Using deep learning to quantify the beauty of outdoor places. R. Soc. Open Sci. **4**(7), 170170 (2017)
14. Yalpir, S.: Forecasting residential real estate values. In: Proceedings People, Buildings and Environment Conference, no. 2014, pp. 694–706 (2014)
15. Bency, A.J., Rallapalli, S., Ganti, R.K., Srivatsa, M., Manjunath, B.S.: Beyond spatial auto-regressive models : predicting housing prices with satellite imagery (2017)
16. Kisilevich, S., Keim, D., Rokach, L.: A GIS-based decision-support system for hotel room rate estimation and temporal price prediction: the hotel brokers context (2012)
17. Law, S., Paige, B., Russell, C.: Take a look around: using street view and satellite images to estimate house prices. ACM Trans. Intell. Syst. Technol. **10**(5), 1–19 (2019)
18. Chow, V.: Predicting auction price of vehicle license plate with deep recurrent neural network. Expert Syst. Appl. **142**, 113008 (2020)

19. Gebru, T., et al.: Using deep learning and google street view to estimate the demographic makeup of neighborhoods across the United States. Proc. Natl. Acad. Sci. U.S.A. **114**(50), 13108–13113 (2017)
20. Xifilidou, A., Kaimaris, D.: Viewing valuations from the sky: UAVs in the appraisal industry. Int. J. Real Estate Land Plann. **1**, 35–41 (2018)

Active Noise Cancellation for IoT-Driven Electronic Stethoscope: A Comparative Study of Adaptive Filters

Erdinc Turk[✉], Umit Deniz Ulusar, Guner Ogunc, Murat Canpolat, and Muhittin Yaprak

Akdeniz University, Antalya, Turkey

{erdincturk,umitulusar,ogunc,canpolat,yaprakm}@akdeniz.edu.tr

Abstract. A key application for IoT based technologies in the field of healthcare is wireless medical sensors that can be used to monitor patients' physiological information such as heartbeat, bowel activity and lung sounds. Real-time detection of bowel motility after major abdominal surgery has significant importance for the patients' healing process. Due to temporal cessation of intestinal motility after the surgery, a period of fasting is commonly practiced, and patients are fed with fluids following the recovery of bowel motility. Many studies have been conducted to monitor intestinal motility and automatically detect bowel activity. Detection and identification are challenging because of the ambient noise in clinical environments. Active noise cancellation methods remove unwanted signals by using adaptive filters. In this paper, active noise cancellation simulations were performed in order to remove ambient noise from gastrointestinal auscultation recordings. The simulation setup was created based on a previously developed IoT-driven electronic stethoscope by our group. Five widely used adaptive filter algorithms: Least Mean Squares, Normalized Least Mean Squares, Affine Projection, Recursive Least Squares, and Adaptive Lattice were tested, and performance evaluations are reported.

Keywords: Adaptive filters · Active noise cancellation · Bowel activity detection

1 Introduction

Auscultation is the typical means of observing internal body sounds using a simple tool called a stethoscope and commonly performed in clinical environments. Gastrointestinal auscultation is necessary for diagnosing diseases such as irritable bowel syndrome and sepsis. This technique is also used for detecting the recovery of bowel activity of patients who had major abdominal surgery. Real-time detection of bowel motility is significantly essential for the patients' healing process. Due to temporal cessation of intestinal motility after the surgery, a period of fasting is commonly practiced, and patients are fed with fluids following the recovery of bowel motility [1].

© ICST Institute for Computer Sciences, Social Informatics and Telecommunications Engineering 2021
Published by Springer Nature Switzerland AG 2021. All Rights Reserved
E. Ever and F. Al-Turjman (Eds.): FoNeS-IoT 2020, LNICST 353, pp. 11–24, 2021.
https://doi.org/10.1007/978-3-030-69431-9_2

For long term bowel activity monitoring, we developed electronic stethoscope designs in our previous studies [2–4]. The duration of a single bowel sound (BS) is typically between 0.02 and 0.1 s [5–7]. The intensity of the intestinal activity and the sound generated from the activity are observed in direct proportion. The sound generated by intestinal activity is observed as non-stationary short-term signal often mixed with heartbeat, movement, and breathing noises [5, 7].

In the auscultation recordings obtained in clinical environments, various other noises can be observed as a result of the operation of nearby devices, which makes the automatic detection of bowel sounds challenging. As a preprocessing step, filtering such noises increases the success of the BS detection algorithms. Adaptive filters are widely used for active noise cancellation (ANC) in biomedical applications for the attenuation of interfering ambient noises [8–14].

In this study, ANC simulations were performed in order to remove ambient noises from bowel activity auscultation recordings. The simulation setup was created based on a previously developed IoT-driven electronic stethoscope that has two microphones [2]. Four different simulation scenarios are designed to generate synthetic auscultation data. Noises are generated using the White Gaussian Noise (WGN) model since it is the basic noise model used to represent many random noises that occur in nature [15]. Five widely used adaptive filter algorithms: Least Mean Square (LMS), Normalized LMS (NLMS), Affine Projection (AP), Recursive Least Squares (RLS), and Adaptive Lattice (AL) were tested for ANC. Each simulation was performed 100 times in order to obtain accurate results, and performance evaluations are reported.

2   Background

2.1   Adaptive Filters

Adaptive filters are digital filters whose coefficients change to make the filter converge to an optimal state. Adaptive filters are widely used in signal processing applications such as noise cancellation, system identification, inverse modeling, prediction, etc. Fig. 1 shows the block diagram of the adaptive filter environment. An adaptive filter has two main substructures: a digital filter and an adapting algorithm. The digital filter operates the input signal and produces an estimate of the desired signal [16, 17].

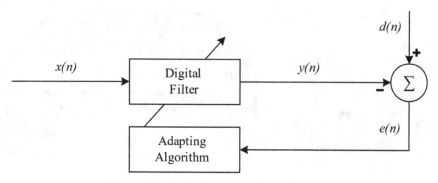

Fig. 1. The block diagram of the adaptive filter

Adaptive filter's output signal $y(n)$ is the multiplication of the digital filter's coefficients $w(n)$ and the input signal $x(n)$ (see Eq. 1). The error signal $e(n)$ is the difference between the desired signal $d(n)$ and output signal $y(n)$ (see Eq. 2). Digital filter's coefficients are updated iteratively by the adapting algorithm to minimize the mean square error (MSE) (see Eq. 3). When the error is minimized, the filter reaches an optimal state [16, 17].

$$y(n) = w^T(n)x(n) \qquad (1)$$

$$e(n) = d(n) - y(n) \qquad (2)$$

$$w(n + 1) = w(n) + f(e(n)) \qquad (3)$$

The main difference between adaptive algorithms is the filter update rule of the digital filter coefficients. In this study, following five widely used adaptive filter algorithms [16, 17] are tested for active noise cancellation:

- The Least-Mean-Square (LMS) Algorithm
- The Normalized LMS (NLMS) Algorithm
- Affine Projection (AP) Adaptive Filter
- The Recursive Least-Squares (RLS) Algorithm
- Adaptive Lattice (AL) Filter.

2.2 IoT-Driven Electronic Stethoscope

We developed an IoT-driven electronic stethoscope (see Fig. 2) to collect, monitor, and detect bowel activity signals in our previous studies [2, 3]. An electret microphone is located in the stethoscope's chest piece in order to observe bowel sounds. Often, ambient noise in clinical environments is observed and classified as bowel activity. Thus, a second microphone, placed in the opposite direction, is utilized to observe ambient noise, and active noise cancellation is applied to attenuate interfering noise on the bowel activity auscultation.

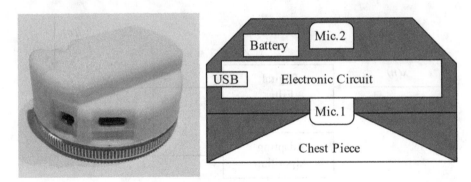

Fig. 2. The IoT-driven electronic stethoscope

A wireless microcontroller (JN5168–001-M00, NXP) is utilized for digitization and wireless data transmission. Signals are sampled with 10-bit ADC at 5 kHz sampling frequency and transmitted wirelessly to the receiving device. The electronic stethoscope is also equipped with a battery that powers the system for up to 18 h in the communication state. Thus, the patients can move freely during the operation of this device, and it allows real-time bowel sound monitoring.

3 Materials and Methods

In this section, ANC experiments are performed in order to compare performances of the selected adaptive filters. Synthetic auscultation data was generated to perform different simulations. The block diagram of the ANC application for the electronic stethoscope is shown in Fig. 3.

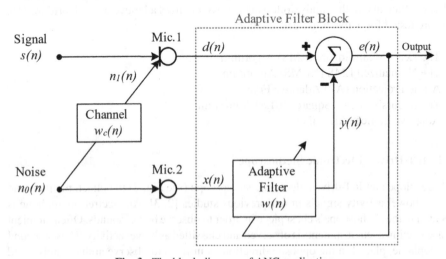

Fig. 3. The block diagram of ANC application

For our IoT-driven electronic stethoscope, the first microphone (Mic.1), which is located inside the chest piece to observe BSs, was assigned as the desired signal $d(n)$ of the adaptive filter. The second microphone (Mic.2) observes only ambient noise and was assigned as the input signal $x(n)$ of the adaptive filter. Due to the shape, orientation, and structure of the chest piece, the first microphone observes noise different from the second microphone. This difference is represented with the Channel block in Fig. 3. In order to generate synthetic auscultation data, this response was identified.

The desired signal $d(n)$ consists of BS signals $s(n)$, ambient noise $n_1(n)$ and background noise $w_1(n)$ (see Eq. 4). The input signal $x(n)$ consists of ambient noise $n_0(n)$ and background noise $w_0(n)$ (see Eq. 5). The ambient noise observed with the first microphone $n_1(n)$ is correlated with the ambient noise observed with the second microphone $n_0(n)$ (see Eq. 6). The background noise (BN) caused by electronic hardware, digitization.

$$d(n) = s(n) + n_1(n) + w_1(n) \tag{4}$$

$$x(n) = n_0(n) + w_0(n) \tag{5}$$

$$n_1(n) = n_0(n)w_c(n) \tag{6}$$

3.1 Electronic Stethoscope System Identification

The filter that represents the amplitude and morphological transformation of the source signal observed in different microphones is shown with the Channel block in Fig. 3. In this section, Channel's frequency response is identified to generate synthetic data for ANC simulations. In order to estimate the Channel's properties, we used the RLS adaptive filter with the unknown system identification setting. The reason for using the RLS adaptive filter is its high performance and convergence rate over the other adaptive filters [16]. Since the Channel's identification is performed offline, the computational cost of the RLS algorithm, which is significantly higher than the other adaptive filters, is not a concern.

We placed the electronic stethoscope on the subject's abdomen and applied 1-s long signals comprising 0.2 s long impulsive noise (IN) with the power of 20 dB from a distance of 50 cm away. INs are created using the WGN model since it is a basic model to represent any random noise that occurs in nature [15]. In this case, ambient noise obtained with the second microphone $n_0(n)$ is used as the adaptive filter input $x(n)$, and altered ambient noise obtained with the first microphone $n_1(n)$ is used as the desired signal $d(n)$.

In order to discover the optimal response model, different lengths (8, 16, 32, 64, 128, 256) of FIR filters, also called the number of taps, were tested. The test was performed 10 times and the average of system response parameters was used as the final model. The power of the error signal $e(n)$, the correlation between the output signal $y(n)$ and the desired signal $d(n)$, and computation times were calculated to evaluate convergence performance. The results were reported as mean value and standard deviation $(\mu \pm \sigma)$ in Table 1. Lower power value and high correlation value mean better convergence.

Table 1. Average performances of adaptive filters for *Channel* identification

Filter length (N)	Computation time (s) t	Power of error signal (dB) $P_{e(n)}$	Correlation $Corr(y(n), d(n))$
8	0.0367 ± 0.0035	9.0865 ± 0.6128	0.6696 ± 0.0237
16	0.0398 ± 0.0040	7.3568 ± 0.6298	0.7906 ± 0.0189
32	0.0428 ± 0.0043	4.8317 ± 0.6827	0.8875 ± 0.0131
64	0.0684 ± 0.0049	1.7899 ± 0.7969	0.9450 ± 0.0088
128	0.2686 ± 0.0192	0.6299 ± 0.8502	0.9574 ± 0.0079
256	0.4604 ± 0.0299	0.5223 ± 0.8156	0.9582 ± 0.0078

The performance of adaptive filter increased by the filter length. The adaptive filters with the lengths of 8, 16, 32, 64 showed poor convergence performance. The 128-tap adaptive filter showed optimal performance since the average power of the error signal was lower than 1 dB and the correlation between its output and desired signal was more than 0.95. The 256-tap adaptive filter showed slightly better performance than the 128-tap adaptive filter, but its computation time was substantially higher than the others.

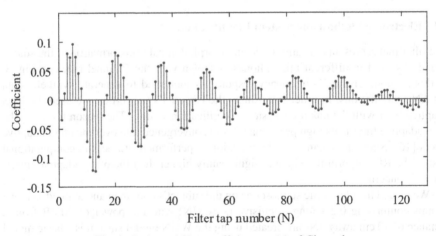

Fig. 4. Estimated filter coefficients $w_c(n)$ of *Channel*

Estimated average FIR filter coefficients $w_c(n)$ were extracted for further ANC simulations (Fig. 4). Figure 5 shows the magnitude and the phase response of the Channel. Some signals up to 500 Hz were amplified and others were attenuated. This frequency response is especially suitable for observing BSs and explains why bell-shaped chest pieces are used, since bowel activity signals happen to be between 100 and 500 Hz.

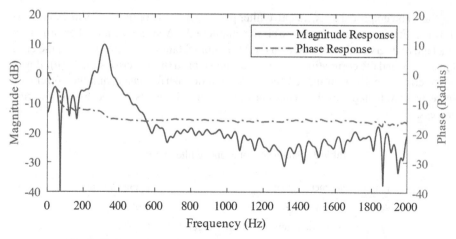

Fig. 5. Estimated magnitude response and phase response of *Channel*

3.2 ANC Simulation

For this study, we performed ANC simulations with five widely used adaptive filter algorithms: LMS, NLMS, AP, RLS, and AL. Four different simulation scenarios were designed to assess ANC performances of the adaptive filters in different situations. For each simulation, different synthetic auscultation signal was generated for both microphones. A single burst bowel sound signal was extracted from a real auscultation record and was used as the BS signal. Ambient noise $n_0(n)$ was designed as zero-mean IN and generated using the WGN model. Altered ambient noise $n_1(n)$ was obtained by filtering original ambient noise $n_0(n)$ using FIR coefficients that represents electronic stethoscope frequency response. Finally, zero-mean additive WGN is used as BN. In these simulations, signal parameters were determined based on the observations of real auscultation recordings taken with the developed electronic stethoscope (Table 2).

Table 2. Signal parameters of synthetic data generation

Symbol	Parameter name	Parameter value
f_s	Sampling frequency	5000 Hz
P_s	Power of BS signal	~20 dB
t_s	Duration of BS signal	0.04 s
P_n	Power of IN	20 dB
t_n	Duration of IN	0.2 s
P_w	Power of BN	−5 dB

Based on empirical tests, adaptive filter parameters were optimized as in Table 3. As shown in Fig. 3, the error signal $e(n)$ is the output of the ANC application. Performances of adaptive filters evaluated based on the MSE, computation time, the power of the error signal $e(n)$, and the correlation between desired signal $d(n)$ and error signal $e(n)$. Power of the error signal was evaluated for noise reduction performance, and the correlation value was evaluated for observing corruptions in BS signals caused by the filtering process.

Table 3. Parameters of adaptive filter algorithms

Symbol	Parameter name	Parameter value
N	Length of digital filter	128
μ_{LMS}	Adaptation step size of LMS algorithm	0.00003
μ_{NLMS}	Adaptation step size of NLMS algorithm	1
μ_{AP}	Adaptation step size of AP filter	1
L_{AP}	Projection order of AP filter	8
λ_{RLS}	Forgetting factor of RLS algorithm	1
λ_{AL}	Forgetting factor of AL filter algorithm	1

Table 4 shows generated signal content for each simulation. These ANC simulations were performed 100 times, and for each of them, synthetic auscultation signals were randomly generated. The results were reported as mean value and standard deviation $(\mu \pm \sigma)$ in the results section.

Table 4. Synthetic auscultation signal content for each type of simulation

Sim. Nr.	Simulation name	Signal duration	# of BS	# of IN	BN exists
1	Single IN	0.2	0	1	No
2	Multiple IN	60	0	10	Yes
3	Multiple IN and BS	60	30	10	Yes
4	Multiple IN and BS without BN	60	30	10	No

Descriptions of four ANC simulations are as follows:

Simulation 1 (Single IN): In this simulation, 0.2 s long input signal $x(n)$ and desired signal $d(n)$ were generated, as shown in Fig. 6. These signals consist of only one IN. BN and BS signals were not used. Then, ANC applications using selected adaptive filters were performed. This simulation was performed to compare convergence speed from the MSE performance of selected adaptive filter algorithms.

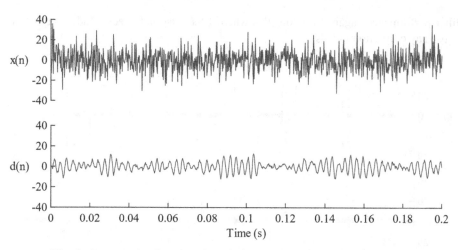

Fig. 6. An example of generated synthetic auscultation data in Simulation 1

Simulation 2 (Multiple IN): In this simulation, 60 s long input signal $x(n)$ and desired signal $d(n)$ were generated, as shown in Fig. 7. A dedicated number of INs were randomly located, and BN was also added. Then, ANC applications using selected adaptive filters were performed. The purpose of this simulation was to compare adaptive filter performances against random INs where BSs do not exist.

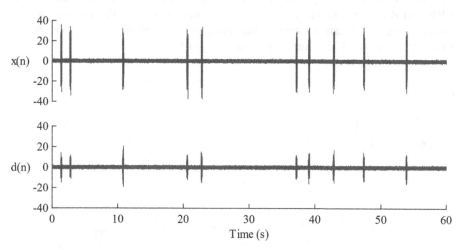

Fig. 7. An example of generated synthetic auscultation data in Simulation 2

Simulation 3 (Multiple IN and BS): In this simulation, 60 s input signal $x(n)$ and desired signal $d(n)$ were generated, as shown in Fig. 8. A dedicated number of INs and BSs were randomly located, and BN was also added. Then, ANC applications using selected adaptive filters were performed. The purpose of this simulation was to compare filter performances against random INs where BSs exist and check if adaptive filters cause any corruption in BSs.

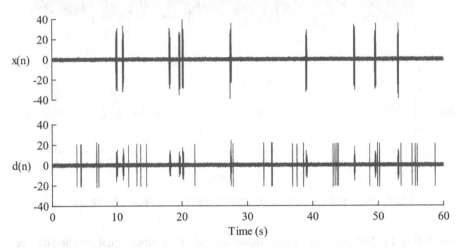

Fig. 8. An example of generated synthetic auscultation data in Simulation 3

Simulation 4 (Multiple IN and BS without BN): In this simulation, 60 s input signal $x(n)$ and desired signal $d(n)$ were generated as shown in Fig. 9. A dedicated number of INs and BSs were randomly located. No BN was generated. The purpose of this simulation was to compare filter performances against random INs where BN is absent and check if adaptive filters cause any corruption in BSs.

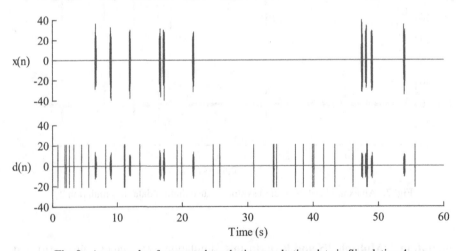

Fig. 9. An example of generated synthetic auscultation data in Simulation 4

4   Results and Discussion

This section shows the results for four different ANC simulations. Each ANC simulation was performed 100 times in order to obtain accurate results. Performance results of adaptive filters were reported as mean ± standard deviation. Fig. 10 shows the average MSE for the first simulation. RLS and AL algorithms reached the minimum MSE value after 150 samples, NLMS and AP algorithms reached around 500 samples, and LMS reached around 1000 samples.

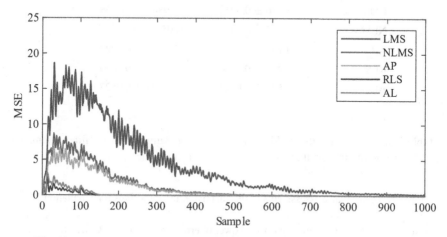

Fig. 10. Average MSE performance of adaptive filter algorithms for Simulation 1

Mean power and standard deviation of the average MSE values were calculated and utilized for evaluation as in Table 5. Small power and standard deviation values mean faster convergence. RLS and AL adaptive filters converged faster than other adaptive filters. Although RLS filter performed better, it had a significantly higher computational cost than AL filter.

Table 5. Performance assessments of the adaptive filter algorithms for Simulation 1

Adaptive filter	Computation time (s) t	P_{MSE} (dB)	σ_{MSE} (dB)
LMS	0.0248 ± 0.0372	16.2237	4.9100
NLMS	0.0209 ± 0.0055	8.0090	2.1511
AP	0.2350 ± 0.0386	5.6985	1.6476
RLS	0.4716 ± 0.0802	−11.1466	0.2640
AL	0.1809 ± 0.0293	−6.5609	0.4442

Table 6 shows the results for simulation 2. LMS and AL algorithm attenuated ambient noise significantly better than the others. Although the computational cost of LMS filter lower than the AL filter, the AL filter performed more stable considering standard deviation values.

Table 6. Performance assessments of the adaptive filter algorithms for Simulation 2

Adaptive filter	Computation time (s) t	Power of Error Signal (dB) $P_{e(n)}$
LMS	0.0270 ± 0.0019	-3.9845 ± 0.0758
NLMS	0.0332 ± 0.0016	0.0056 ± 0.1334
AP	5.6195 ± 0.0954	-0.0245 ± 0.1222
RLS	13.0457 ± 0.5606	-3.4346 ± 0.2039
AL	2.3526 ± 0.0440	-3.9927 ± 0.0527

Table 7 shows the results for Simulation 3. In this simulation AL filter attenuated ambient noise while preserving bowel signals better than others.

Table 7. Performance assessments of the adaptive filter algorithms for Simulation 3

Adaptive filter	Computation time (s) t	Power of error signal (dB) $P_{e(n)}$	Correlation $Corr(s(n), e(n))$
LMS	0.0272 ± 0.0014	0.9603 ± 0.0908	0.9620 ± 0.0038
NLMS	0.0333 ± 0.0017	4.4116 ± 0.2302	0.6464 ± 0.0172
AP	5.7599 ± 0.1087	4.4308 ± 0.2469	0.6441 ± 0.0171
RLS	13.1852 ± 0.4335	1.1337 ± 0.1146	0.9432 ± 0.0102
AL	2.3666 ± 0.0484	0.9445 ± 0.0909	0.9639 ± 0.0033

Table 8 shows the results for Simulation 4. In this simulation LMS filter attenuated ambient noise while preserving BS signals better than others. It can be seen from the tables that BN effected the performance of the LMS adaptive filter, but the AL filter performed more stable overall.

Table 8. Performance assessments of the adaptive filter algorithms for Simulation 4

Adaptive filter	Computation time (s) t	Power of error signal (dB) $P_{e(n)}$	Correlation $Corr(s(n), e(n))$
LMS	0.0254 ± 0.0016	-0.5568 ± 0.1334	0.9763 ± 0.0046
NLMS	0.0326 ± 0.0012	-0.2078 ± 1.0882	0.9441 ± 0.0728
AP	5.4839 ± 0.1508	-0.2032 ± 0.4351	0.9393 ± 0.0381
RLS	13.3520 ± 0.2913	$0.63955 \pm .0381$	0.9288 ± 0.2169
AL	2.3464 ± 0.0402	-0.1796 ± 2.0064	0.9522 ± 0.1361

5 Conclusion

Continuous monitoring of bowel activity is desirable to perform research on healing enhancement after surgery. Noise in clinical environments creates an additional challenge for automated bowel sound detection systems. In this paper, we evaluated the performances of adaptive filters and performed simulations for the electronic stethoscope that was developed by our group. The findings of this study showed that AL and LMS filters perform better than others. In terms of computation, the LMS algorithm is less demanding. The downside of the LMS is it does not have an adaptive step size control and sometimes converges to unstable filter coefficients that result in outlier values. As a result, the AL filter algorithm is selected for ANC for bowel activity detection applications due to its high noise reduction performance and moderate computational cost. For future studies, the AL filter will be implemented in C language and run using the developed device in clinical environments.

References

1. Lewis, S.J., Egger, M., Sylvester, P.A., Thomas, S.: Early enteral feeding versus "nil by mouth" after gastrointestinal surgery: systematic review and meta-analysis of controlled trials. BMJ **323**, 773–776 (2001). https://doi.org/10.1136/bmj.323.7316.773
2. Ulusar, U.D., Turk, E., Oztas, A.S., Savli, A.E., Ogunc, G., Canpolat, M.: IoT and edge computing as a tool for bowel activity monitoring. In: Al-Turjman, F. (ed.) Edge Computing. EICC, pp. 133–144. Springer, Cham (2019). https://doi.org/10.1007/978-3-319-99061-3_8
3. Türk, E., et al.: Wireless bioacoustic sensor system for automatic detection of bowel sounds. In: 2015 19th National Biomedical Engineering Meeting (BIYOMUT), pp. 1–4 (2015). https://doi.org/10.1109/BIYOMUT.2015.7369458.
4. Ulusar, U.D., Canpolat, M., Yaprak, M., Kazanir, S., Ogunc, G.: Real-time monitoring for recovery of gastrointestinal tract motility detection after abdominal surgery. In: 2013 7th International Conference on Application of Information and Communication Technologies, pp. 1–4 (2013). https://doi.org/10.1109/ICAICT.2013.6722654.
5. Dimoulas, C., Kalliris, G., Papanikolaou, G., Petridis, V., Kalampakas, A.: Bowel-sound pattern analysis using wavelets and neural networks with application to long-term, unsupervised, gastrointestinal motility monitoring. Expert Syst. Appl. **34**, 26–41 (2008). https://doi.org/10.1016/j.eswa.2006.08.014

6. Ranta, R., Louis-Dorr, V., Heinrich, C., Wolf, D., Guillemin, F.: Digestive Activity Evaluation by Multichannel Abdominal Sounds Analysis. IEEE Trans. Biomed. Eng. **57**, 1507–1519 (2010). https://doi.org/10.1109/TBME.2010.2040081

7. Ulusar, U.D.: Recovery of gastrointestinal tract motility detection using Naive Bayesian and minimum statistics. Comput. Biol. Med. **51**, 223–228 (2014). https://doi.org/10.1016/j.com pbiomed.2014.05.013

8. Yin, Y., Yang, W., Jiang, H., Wang, Z.: Bowel sound based digestion state recognition using artificial neural network. In: 2015 IEEE Biomedical Circuits and Systems Conference (BioCAS), pp. 1–4 (2015). https://doi.org/10.1109/BioCAS.2015.7348364.

9. Jatupaiboon, N., Pan-ngum, S., Israsena, P.: Electronic stethoscope prototype with adaptive noise cancellation. In: 2010 Eighth International Conference on ICT and Knowledge Engineering, pp. 32–36 (2010). https://doi.org/10.1109/ICTKE.2010.5692909.

10. Mirza, A., Kabir, S.M., Ayub, S., Sheikh, S.A.: Impulsive noise cancellation of ECG signal based on SSRLS. Proc. Comput. Sci. **62**, 196–202 (2015). https://doi.org/10.1016/j.procs. 2015.08.440

11. Djendi, M., Gilloire, A., Scalart, P.: Noise cancellation using two closely spaced microphones: experimental study with a specific model and two adaptive algorithms. In: 2006 IEEE International Conference on Acoustics Speech and Signal Processing Proceedings, pp. III–III (2006). https://doi.org/10.1109/ICASSP.2006.1660761.

12. Suzuki, A., Sumi, C., Nakayama, K., Mori, M.: Real-time adaptive cancelling of ambient noise in lung sound measurement. Med. Biol. Eng. Comput. **33**, 704–708 (1995). https://doi. org/10.1007/BF02510790

13. Bai, Y.-W., Lu, C.-L.: The embedded digital stethoscope uses the adaptive noise cancellation filter and the type I Chebyshev IIR bandpass filter to reduce the noise of the heart sound. In: Proceedings of 7th International Workshop on Enterprise networking and Computing in Healthcare Industry, HEALTHCOM 2005, pp. 278–281 (2005). https://doi.org/10.1109/HEA LTH.2005.1500459.

14. Asada, H.H., Jiang, H.-H., Gibbs, P.: Active noise cancellation using MEMS accelerometers for motion-tolerant wearable bio-sensors. In: The 26th Annual International Conference of the IEEE Engineering in Medicine and Biology Society, pp. 2157–2160 (2004). https://doi. org/10.1109/IEMBS.2004.1403631.

15. Vaseghi, S.V.: Advanced Digital Signal Processing and Noise Reduction. Wiley, Hoboken (2008)

16. Haykin, S.: Adaptive Filter Theory. Pearson (2013)

17. Diniz, P.S.R.: Adaptive Filtering: Algorithms and Practical Implementation. Springer, Heidelberg (2020). https://doi.org/10.1007/978-3-030-29057-3

Design of a Navigation System for the Blind/Visually Impaired

Adedoyin A. Hussain[1,5], Fadi Al-Turjman[2,5], Eser Gemikonakli[3,5],
and Yoney Kirsal Ever[4,5(✉)]

[1] Computer Engineering Department,
Near East University, Nicosia, Mersin 10, Turkey
hussaindoyin@gmail.com

[2] Artificial Intelligence Engineering Department,
Near East University, Nicosia, Mersin 10, Turkey
fadi.alturjman@neu.edu.tr

[3] University of Kyrenia, Kyrenia, Mersin 10, Turkey
eser.gemikonakli@kyrenia.edu.tr

[4] Software Engineering Department,
Near East University, Nicosia, Mersin 10, Turkey
yoneykirsal.ever@neu.edu.tr

[5] Research Centre for AI and IoT,
Near East University, Nicosia, Mersin 10, Turkey

Abstract. Since individuals with needs in the general public increased, the work introduced is a navigation system that will give a solid and durable obstacle detection and environmental imager and navigation for the user. It provides minimal cost system to permit navigation. The obstacle detection is to distinguish the deterrent and guide the visually impaired (VIP) about a suitable pathway. The framework utilises sensor based obstacle detection, and sends back buzzer or audio sound as a reaction that warns the VIP about position. The primary technique utilised by each blind or visually impaired is the strolling stick for identifying deterrent in which its functionality is restricted, it doesn't secure territories close to the head let alone all obstacle. This framework acquires data about impediments close to the head and provides the right pathway for the VIP. When utilised with a mobile stick, the VIP is completely ensured against a snag, and the route is made simple. The environmental imager and navigation mode is the sound and visual guide for the VIP which permits users to just touch a button and proposed destination to the caregiver. This includes GPS and live video feed direction. The general system is versatile and can be conveyed by a VIP. The accuracy achieved for the system differs from 94.15% to 99.72%. The percentage rate of the snag discovery for either indoor or outside varies from 95.40% to 99.67%. This examination will Increase the VIP mobility significantly.

Keywords: Audio guidance · Real-time · Navigation · Visually impaired · Sensor-based detecting system

© ICST Institute for Computer Sciences, Social Informatics and Telecommunications Engineering 2021
Published by Springer Nature Switzerland AG 2021. All Rights Reserved
E. Ever and F. Al-Turjman (Eds.): FoNeS-IoT 2020, LNICST 353, pp. 25–45, 2021.
https://doi.org/10.1007/978-3-030-69431-9_3

1   Introduction

Visually impaired, can likewise be referred to as vision loss, it is a decrease in the capacity to see, it causes non-fixable issues as standard methods, similar to glasses. It likewise incorporates those with diminished capacity to have a reasonable vision since they probably won't approach glasses or focal points. Visual debilitation causes challenges for individuals with ordinary day by day exercises, for example, driving, strolling, mingling, and perusing. Vision hindrance is a significant issue that wean a human being of approximately 80–90% and is a genuine effect on experts social, and individual life [1]. The WHO measures the visually impaired (VIP) to be 285 million; most are more than 50 years old, although, in ongoing social orders, the information on visual impairment and requirements are ineffectively identified for VIP, whereas, Fig. 1 depicts a pie chart illustrating the global cause of blindness. Detecting obstacle is one of the significant highlights which have been considered in the improvement of versatility assistive gadgets for the old. Present-day portability assistive gadgets are furnished with this capacity as a hindrance finder during strolling either in the indoor or open condition. Identification of impediments on the pathway is imperative to prevent a crash with deterrents which can make the client experience a fall. Thus, falls are a major issue in a maturing populace. CDC expressed that 1 out of 3 grown-ups which are 65 years of age and more, falls every year and of the individuals who fall, about 20% to 30% endure moderate to extreme wounds that make it difficult for them to live or to get around autonomously [2].

Another choice that gives the best travel help to the visually impaired is the dog guide. Given the advantageous interaction between the VIP and his canine, the preparation and the relationship to the dog are the keys to progress for this strategy. The canine can identify complex circumstances like cross strolls, steps, possible risk, and more [3]. The client can feel the mentality of his canine, investigate the circumstance, and provide him fitting requests. However, dogs are still a long way from being moderate, because it's around the cost of a decent vehicle, and their normal life span is restricted, with a minimum of 8 years. Thus, a visually impaired individual utilising a guide dog, which must be more aware of signs from the pooch than an individual utilising a stick. Then again, the white stick can just distinguish obstacles up to the abdomen level. Thus, there are a few sorts of impediments that the white stick can't identify because of its measurement, shape, or restriction. Also, the canine won't advise the visually impaired person about the need to go amiss from hindrances over the abdomen level. Notwithstanding, when contrasted with the white stick, the canine is progressively compelling while managing deterrents underneath the abdomen level. Outwardly, blind individuals can't do visual assignments in day to day life. This makes life hard for individuals who have this medical issue. Generally, VIP utilises a stick to go to anyplace or to discover a path. For this situation, they face numerous issues while navigating in a jam-packed spots.

In any case, utilising numerous technologies, their life turns out to be simple, free, and agreeable. These advances incorporate an Electronic Travel Aid (ETA), route frameworks and so on, these innovations have some downside [4,5].

Regular individuals visit numerous spots like shopping centres, businesses, and so on. On the other hand, those spots are obscure, in which they follow a map that is available at passages. Individuals can see that map outwardly however the VIP can't see that map. This paper assists the VIP to overcome these challenges. Utilising this proposed system, VIP can without no much effort move on grounds of any shopping spots, universities, or enormous enterprises. For example, in outdoor circumstances, handheld GPS frameworks for the visually impaired are currently accessible. These apparatuses are not useful for neighbourhood navigation, path arranging, and crash avoidance [6]. This paper portrays a system for a navigation apparatus for the VIP's. All things considered, there is a lot of augmentations for it, for instance slants instead of steps, handrails, lifts, etc. In any case, improvements are limited to express spots and it is difficult for the VIP to live in most of the propositions spots at present. Especially for daze personals who have no visual information, there is a lot of difficulties in the standard day by day circumstances. These people have a lot of issues to acquire common information. Moreover, obstacles that are not dangerous to basic people can get hazardous to them. Even though they use sticks to secure this information, it is as yet hard for them to walk around in most of the spots. A lot of studies have not been really up a structure to helps these people.

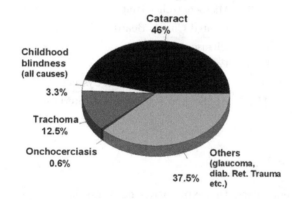

Fig. 1. Diagram illustrating the global cause of blindness [7].

This paper presents a corresponding solution of deterrent discovery for visually impaired individuals and an answer for outwardly blind individuals. Utilising this proposed framework, VIP can undoubtedly move in different spots, shopping malls, universities, or huge businesses. In this work, our contribution and proposition is as the following, an overview of related works about visually impaired navigation system is evaluated. Key plan factors that are required in adding to this framework are put forth. We depict the proposed sensor and Global Positioning System (GPS) receiver for outdoor and indoor navigation respectively. We outline the accuracy and impact of the proposed framework. Lastly, we portray design issues and difficulties in this paper.

Given the reason for this work, its structure and content of the paper is introduced as follows. With the introduction of comparative studies, it adds to the idea of the situation, likewise, we additionally assess the systems and methods utilised which are introduced in Sect. 2. Though, in Sect. 3 we discuss the strategy just as the materials utilised. In Sect. 4, we set forth the outcome gotten from the examination. Finally, Sect. 5 concludes the end and discussion of the contribution introduced in this paper. Moreover, Table 1 gives a rundown of the abbreviation utilised and its definition.

Table 1. Abbreviations.

Terms	Meaning
VIP	Visually Impaired Persons
GPS	Global Positioning System
ETA	Electronic Travel Aid
WHO	World Health Organisation
CDC	Centre of Disease Control
RFID	Radio Frequency Identification
GPRS	General Packet Radio Service
MCU	Microcontroller Unit
PCB	Printed Circuit Board
US	Ultrasonic Sensor
PSD	Position Sensitive Detector
GIS	Geographic Information System
API	Application Programming Interface

2   Literature Review

In the most recent years, the exploration networks have attempted to create arrangements to tackle or limit issues presented from deterrents when a visually impaired individual is moving all around. Authors in [8] propose an answer that incorporates glasses with an installed camera and an array that holds 400 terminals and it is associated with the glasses using an adaptable link. Glasses catch ongoing pictures and pictures are planned into the array depicting dark scale. The white level has a solid incitement, the dim stage has a medium incitement and the dark level has no incitement by any means. In any case, this arrangement is obtrusive and requests a major timeframe for adjustment. Authors in [9] presented an extended white stick that can distinguish objects at foot level, leg level, and chest level, or even at the head level by using ultrasound sensors. Dissimilar to past arrangements the Ultracane is incredibly ergonomic, however it is excessively costly. On the other hand, authors in [10] deduced a convenient gadget that supplements the long white stick by identifying boundaries up to 2,5 ms and reports them through acoustic signs or buzzer. Beam is an answer more affordable than Ultracane yet it needs consistent utilisation of one of the visually impaired client's hands. As we would like to think this is certainly not a decent arrangement since utilising the Ray gadget and a white stick, two hands of the visually impaired individual are hoarded. Different arrangements attempt to control clients outside [11–13] or inside [14–17] however they are not carefully situated for snag location. These arrangements ordinarily use GPS for outdoors and an instrumented domain for inside. In contrast to every one of these arrangements, analysts of the SmartVision venture have built up a framework that joins the utilisation of GPS mix with Radio Frequency Identification Technology (RFID) to gauge the area of the client. With the help of an exceptionally structured Geographic Information System (GIS), thus, this framework can tell the client about relevant data, similar to the nearness of deterrents or administrations in the region. The framework is additionally ready to compute courses with explicit goals considering the client's constraints. The interface with the RFID is made through a peruser set on an explicitly evolved white stick. This white stick instrument interfaces with a cell phone using Bluetooth. However, the interface with the client is created by haptic innovation and text-to-discourse [18,19]. So also, Blind Guide is focused on both indoor and outdoor situations. It is non-obtrusive and it does not need the client's hands to be conveyed. Authors in [20] plan an inventive indoor route and data framework for any spots, such as shopping centres dependent on existing innovations. This will be an agreeable and accommodating framework for blind individuals in shopping centres. This proposition framework depends on the user's advanced cell and remote sensors. Whereas, in [21] they proposed a framework that gives data utilising sound signs. This framework makes VIP self-subordinate. VIP application can be used after an effective login by the client utilising it with speech recognition. Authors in [22] structured a wearable framework for outdoor use which permits the VIP to recognise and stay away from hindrances. However, in [23] the authors gives a route and area determination framework for the VIP utilising an RFID. However, each RFID labeled is customised after establishment with spatial directions and data depicting the close by places. Authors in [24] structured a smart stick which is utilised for brilliant route finding for disabled individuals in indoor and outside condition separately utilising camera. Authors in [25] depict the engineering and execution of a framework that will assist with exploring outdoor movement for the VIP. In this framework, GPS and obstacle detection were deduced for the VIP guide.

3   Methodology

This section involves the behavior, structure, and more perspectives on the framework. The description is formal and it depicts the proposed system in general, unionised such that it supports thinking which incorporates the structures and behavior. The engineering of the system comprises of components of the system and the development of the system that will work hand in hand while using the general framework. An outline is given in Fig. 2.

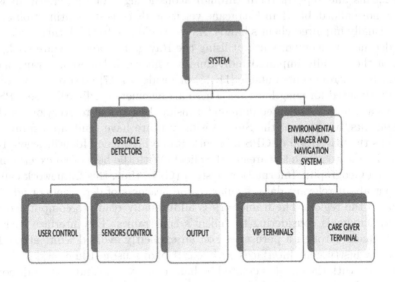

Fig. 2. The system architecture.

3.1 System Description

Fundamentally, a visually impaired individual utilises a stick as a guide for them to secure themselves against obstruction. Practically all region is secured with the stick, for the most part, territories close to the ground like steps and so on. The proposed framework is explicitly intended to watch the region to the head and close to his legs. The framework is intended to give full, absolute route and path planning to the VIP about the environment. It manages the person along snag freeway and gives data about suitable or obstructed way, including separation between impediments, with the utilisation of sensors. It likewise as a Tele-help/Tele-direction framework which is a human guide, in which the VIP utilises a camera and GPS to help and make a constant path planning. The proposed system is developed in two modules, obstacle detection, and environmental imager module. The obstacle detection can also be referred to as the first step of Electronic Travel Aid (ETAs), while the environmental imager can be sub-classed into VIP's and caregiver's terminal which is the second and third step of ETAs that is Environment Imager and Orientation & Navigation Systems (ONS).

Obstacle Detection. This module is the subset of the first step of ETAs which is obstacle detection and is a device worn by visually impaired it scans the environment and surroundings in closed spaces. The devices are tasked with assisting

VIP by intercepting objects placed in their path. It is compulsory that the prototype proposed has to comply with the size suitable for the VIP for installing it successfully and for data collection and testing. Thus, the layouts designed for both printed circuits boards can then be prolonged to add interconnection with multiple layers suitable following the components for the system. The logical structure of our system is segmented to this precise sector and is depicted in Fig. 3. This Section comprehends the activities for hardware installation. The main components which are ultrasonic sensors and the microcontroller will be discussed in detail. The next few sections describe the development of hardware and designing of the system, it also includes discussions compilation of all other components needed for the system. The module will also possess some of these characteristics to the user:

- Will be able to detect obstacles.
- Will be able to detect the distance between users and obstacles.
- Will be able to provide a good pathway to the user.
- Will also make the user interact with his surroundings.

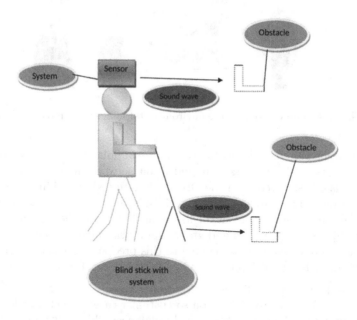

Fig. 3. The system description of obstacle detection.

Environmental Imager and Navigation System. This module is the subset of the second and third classes of ETAs which are Environment Imagers and Orientation & Navigation Systems (ONS) which scan the surrounding in close and near spaces. This system comprises of getting distanced spaces and acquires data

Fig. 4. The system description of the environmental imager and navigation system.

through a larger base distributed networks for example Digital Maps, GPS, and expanded access to the wireless communication networks and the internet. The innovative class associated with the ONS is determined on guiding the visually impaired through a remote human guide which is known as Tele-assistance/Tele-guidance systems. They are given the assignment to assist the visually impaired to cut off objects on their path and grants appropriate path planning. The logical structure of our system is segmented to this precise sector and is depicted in Fig. 4. The module will also possess some of these characteristics to the users:

- Users will have a speed dial to call customer care.
- Users will have a locator (GPS) on so customer care can get user location.
- Customer care will navigate the user through a satellite view and appropriate path planning.
- Users will also have a camera so customer care can see in real-time.

3.2 System Component

In this section, we describe both modules components and how these components are used to provide the desired functional capabilities.

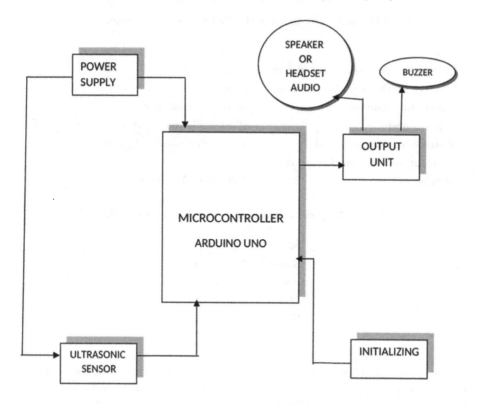

Fig. 5. Block diagram of the obstacle detection system.

Obstacle Detection Component. This module comprises of the user Control, sensor Control, and output. User control entails switches which will allow the visually impaired to select the System?s operation mode. The mode of operation is through Audio and buzzer. These operations are offered to the VIP in taking output by himself on his own accord. Meanwhile, it might not be preferable for him in getting the output in one mode he can rely on the other mode. Likewise, when more of the noise presents itself in the surrounding the buzzer operation might not be portable for him. Another switch which is also controlled, that is the initialising switch. Initialising switch can be pressed when the visually impaired wants to terminate the operation.

This sensor control decides when to alert the sensor to place a measurement, also receives the output value from the given sensor and simplifies it, and controlling the sensor value. Essentially, that is creating a sensor module. Therefore, that is making use of an ultrasonic sensor (US) to detect and provide an appropriate path. The primary intuition is to evade the obstacle using the simplest route. Table 3 shows the specification of the ultrasonic sensor used.

Lastly, the output is given to the visually impaired consists of the indication when the user meets obstacles and provide an appropriate path to the VIP. They

Table 2. Specifications of the obstacle detection system.

Item	Specification
Effective distance of obstacle detection	1.5 m
Effective width for walking pathway	0.5 m
Sensing Environment	Indoor and outdoor
Types of obstacle	Plastic, Plywood, Concrete, Glass, Wood
Shapes of obstacle detected	Circle, Rectangular, Cylinder
Minimum size of obstacle detection	6 cm
Alerting medium	Vibration, Audio message

Table 3. Specifications of the ultrasonic sensor used.

Sensor	Ultrasonic
Range	0.15–6.45 m
Resolute	2.54 cm
Width	$\pm 30°$
Mass	4.3 g

are two output modes, buzzer mode, and audio mode. Users as the privilege to pick any modes of preference concerning the convenience of the VIP. Sometimes buzzer is preferable, mostly when there is more noise into the surrounding. Audio is mostly used relatively when environmental noise is minima and whereas buzzer might irritation to the VIP. Figure 5 illustrates the block representation of the system. There are specific functionalities completed by these components. Table 2 shows the specifications of the obstacle detection system.

The environmental imager and navigation system comprises of two modes, VIP and caregiver?s terminals. In the VIP terminal, the visually impaired initiates a call from the application installed on his phone to the configured caregiver if he needs support. The visually impaired gets guidance by voice instruction using headphones. The VIP will be able to initiate a video call when the teleguidance session starts and start the video live stream which the caregiver can see from is terminal. The caregiver will get the notification about call initiation and termination. This system comprises of the smartphone, camera, headphones, and a cane.

The caregiver terminal can make use of a tablet or a workstation as a terminal. Thus, it gets and initiates the call and live stream from the mobile device given to the VIP and gets VIP?s real-time location coordinates with the use of GPS. VIP can utilise one or more personals as his caregiver, this system grants caregivers to be able to mediate time and load in the assistance by the availability of status info. Thus, it will be studied if there will be an adequate need for the caregiver to override the visually impaired at a particular instance.

3.3   Experimental Process

During the test stage, before utilising the system, the modules undergo individual tests as an integrated system. The advantage of the ultrasonic sensor is its sharp line of sight and small beam angle. As the ultrasonic sensor executes a principle based on echo, studies on its reflective characteristics are very important. The reflection properties were studied on different surfaces, such as, on a concrete wall, wood, metal, and static human body. Smooth surfaces were detected at a maximum range of the ultrasonic sensors. Metal surfaces generate the highest reflections followed by the concrete walls, the wood, and then the human body. In the system evaluation, a test method was proposed. By covering the user's eye, the difficulties in navigation were simulated. Any movement by the individual with the system is protected from surrounding obstacles. A walking stick is used in securing the areas below the head and the areas close to the head are protected by obstacle sensing in the system. To make complete programming we use microcontrollers and then it is simulated on Proteus to find the efficiency. There is a low cost in the system by using efficient yet cheap components like a simple buzzer and an audio module because the majority of the visually impaired belongs to the lower class of income. There is a distinct goal in the proposed system, and that is obstacle detection and sending an alert to the VIP through means such as a buzzer and an audio message. Figure 6 depicts the flow chart of the systems process. These algorithms for the full process of the system is analysed as follows:

- Start.
- Initialization of port.
- Microcontroller
  - Call to read the US.
- If US $\geq$ 200 (value of threshold)
  - If Yes, then go to 5.
  - If No, return to 3.
- US enabled by Microcontroller.
- US is ready to detect an obstacle or threshold.
- MCU gets signals dished from sensors and then calculates US sensor distance.
- The microcontroller ADC converts the analog distance value or threshold into a digital value.
- The digitised data (distance) or threshold are being sent by the MCU to the wireless transmitter module.
- A module which is the wireless transmission read the code and send data in digital form.
- The receiver gets the soften signal and does a form of demodulation, which is then passed to the microcontroller.
- Decoding and conversion of the value of the distance to TTL logic level data are being done by the microcontroller.
- The distance value is being displayed by the microcontroller and initiates the alarm with the value of the given distance.

- Alarms are being triggered by the microcontroller (buzzer or audio) based on the individual interest.
- End.

While the environmental imager and navigation system, in testing the ability to use the system, we will be experimenting by covering the user eyes as this is part of the experimental study with the system and also analysing the camera images and GPS component. Figure 7 depicts the communication process of the systems. Testing the process is as follows:

- **1st step:** VIP starts a phone guidance session then gets voice instruction from the remote caregiver to navigate by the click of a button on the application installed his phone. A speed dial will be initiated. The VIP says is intended destination.
- **2nd step:** VIP initiates a live stream and the location of VIP will be sent to the caregiver.
- **3rd step:** VIP follows the guidance in which the caregiver navigates with adequate path planning.
- **4th step:** User terminates the call.

  Testing caregiver:

- **1st step:** Firstly, the caregiver receives a tele-guidance call from the VIP and guides him by instructions. He checks VIP to confirm VIP. And tell VIP to turn on is a smart device.
- **2nd step:** The remote caregiver guides VIP and navigates the user through the right path. And gets the VIP location and navigates him to his desired destination. Through satellite view and live stream with the help of his smart mobile device.
- **3rd step:** Caregiver gets an indication of call termination.
- **Test step:** The caregiver acknowledges termination.

Considering the requirements like user criteria, the performance, and the ability, usefulness, and economic feasibility, thus it can as well be said that the system considers most of them. In concern with the last requirement that is economic feasibility, it is clear that the cost is low including the hardware used. This system can be managed on a large scale were the only disadvantages will be the lack of connectivity.

3.4   Visualisation

The fundamental point of representation or visualisation is to display all the results graphically or in a tabular form for easy understanding. Imagining this information graphically with the help of the system, just so the outcomes of the experiment are exhibited instinctively. The information perception process is portrayed as getting and investigating the information, information representation, structure determination, show the outcome, conclusion, and lastly, the procedure of representation is refined.

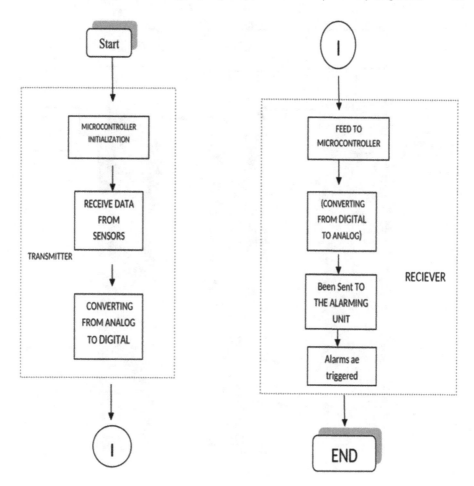

Fig. 6. The obstacle detection system process.

3.5   Computational Environment

The experiments carried out in this paper were implemented physically and using simulation software like Proteus, Arduino interface, and android studio. These are open source and it propels the utilisation of various strategies. They are also a no-pay and a standard programming condition consisting of a solid suite of instruments for information examination and factual methods. It takes a shot on multiple platforms like Windows, macOS, or Linux, and with this, current highlights can be included. The testing and simulation operation was evaluated on a pc with, 2.6 GHz and 8 GB RAM. Whereas, the physical experiment was carried out in both outdoor and indoor conditions.

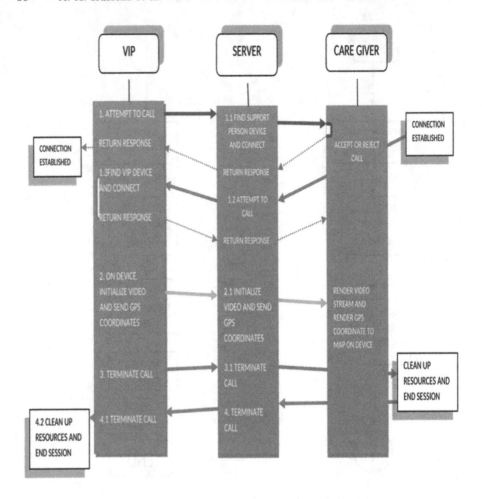

Fig. 7. The environmental imager and navigation system process.

4   Results

As stated in earlier chapters, the performance of the system and the accuracy of the obstacle detection system built is dependent of all the hardware components that serve as the transmitter and the receiver for the obstacle detection module while on the other hand both the caregiver and VIP are required for the environmental imager module.

Following the specifications, the system detects obstacles present on the pathways to get the alarms activated for the output in the receiving end. At this stage of this report, the proposed system has been completely designed and is fully functioning so here we will take you through the outcome of the complete system and highlight the specifications and uniqueness of the system.

Table 4. Obstacle detection system sensibility towards different angles and distance.

Distance (cm)	Measured distance in cm with corresponding angles						
–	120°	110°	100°	90°	80°	70°	60°
30	28.56	28.7	29.15	29.98	29.24	28.65	28.43
50	30.1	45.24	48.62	49.98	48.88	46.1	30.15
70	–	65.2	69.94	70.02	69.62	64.9	–
90	–	75.34	88.56	89.86	88.24	76.2	–
110	–	–	105.22	108.42	104.78	–	–
130	–	–	124.98	137.84	12370	–	–
150	–	–	144.34	148.68	143.84	–	–
170	–	–	–	168.55	–	–	–

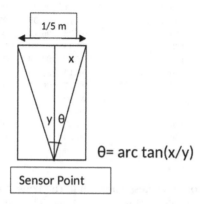

Fig. 8. The measurement for the distance using an ultrasonic sensor.

Table 4 shows the outcomes uncovered from the sensor, it can identify deterrents from 30 cm to 170 cm when confronting 90° edges. At the point where the deterrent is at 10° to one side and left of 90°, then the sensors can distinguish the conceivable impediment up to 150 cm. The sensors can in any case distinguish obstructions at more extensive points for separations under 110 cm. Thus, it is demonstrated that the framework is sufficient to recognise all prospects of hindrances that are present along the normal pathway of 50 cm. In light of 50 cm of way width, the conceivable point of snag discovery can be resolved utilising the trigonometry condition as represented in Fig. 8.

The sensor accuracy is steady for either outdoor or indoor situations as appeared in Table 5 and Table 6 for various colours and different sizes of deterrents. The level of identification is exceptionally trustworthy for the sensor at decided situation changing from 50 cm to 150 cm where it has a 20 cm span for every estimation. The identification score accomplished for each separation fluctuates from 94.15% to 99.72%. Thus, the normal percentage rate of the obstacle discovery for the surface shades for either indoor or outside differs from 95.40%

Table 5. Sensors accuracy and average accuracy towards obstacle surface colour.

Surface colour of obstacle	Initial distance (cm)	Accuracy (%)		Accuracy average (%)
		Indoor	Outdoor	
Black	50	99.92	98.84	99.38
	70	94.8	96.23	95.52
	90	97.19	99.72	98.46
	110	95.29	95.75	95.52
	130	97.77	94.83	96.3
	150	96.54	94.33	95.44
Yellow	50	97.56	95.96	96.76
	70	98.43	99.94	99.19
	90	98.53	99.72	99.13
	110	97.08	98.13	97.61
	130	95.86	94.83	95.35
	150	96.05	94.33	95.19
White	50	99.84	98.84	99.34
	70	97.51	99.94	98.73
	90	98.17	97.39	97.78
	110	98.98	98.13	98.56
	130	97.43	94.83	96.13
	150	97.07	94.33	95.7
Red	50	98.14	98.84	98.49
	70	95.97	96.22	96.1
	90	98.59	99.72	99.16
	110	96.6	95.75	96.18
	130	96.43	94.83	95.63
	150	96.56	94.33	95.45

to 99.67%. These rates of exactness show that the sensor could distinguish the hindrance accurately for each setting separations. The rate distinction between the recognition of indoor and outside condition is under 0.05% for the sensor. This is for each decided separations dependent on a wide range of colour and sizes of hindrances.

The precision of the sensor towards various states of obstruction has marginally diminished for various situations at decided intervals. In any case, the normal level of precision toward various deterrent shape is as yet in worthy range as shown in Table 7. The exact outcomes express that the normal recognition towards football at 150 cm of good ways from the client is 90.78%. Thus, the football-size utilised in the estimation is 10.54–10.86 cm, were is viewed as little, yet the sensor can in any case recognise it. The general exhibitions of the sensor to distinguish the deterrent are acceptable paying little heed to their size, shapes, and color of the obstacle.

Every strategy of the experimental coordination is clarified, including the calculation and programming setup like in Figs. 9 and 10. All experiments are effectively performed. The aftereffects of every one of the experiments are recorded, shown, and talked about in detail. Thus, the key discoveries of the effort in this part spread the systems execution, precision, and investigation. From the estimation part of the system, the usefulness and affectability of the sensor are of

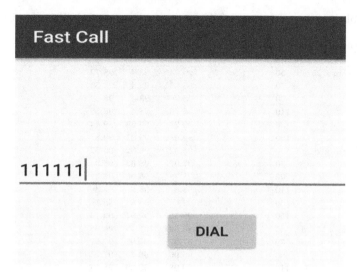

Fig. 9. The experimental coordination as the calculation.

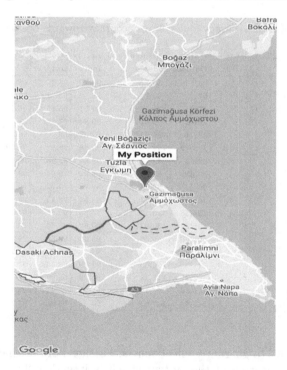

Fig. 10. The experimental coordinationas programming setup.

extraordinary significance and are examined in detail. To confirm this, the deliberate outcomes are contrasted. The outcome demonstrates that the programming

Table 6. Sensors accuracy and average accuracy towards obstacle size.

Obstacle size	Initial distance (cm)	Accuracy (%)		Accuracy average (%)
		Outdoor	Indoor	
15 cm × 25 cm	50	99.04	98.4	98.72
	70	98.63	98.4	98.52
	90	98.78	98.4	98.59
	110	98.76	98.4	98.58
	130	99.23	99.65	99.44
	150	99.68	99.91	99.8
10 cm × 20 cm	50	96.52	96.52	96.52
	70	97.97	98.63	98.3
	90	98.78	95.96	97.37
	110	98.8	98.8	98.8
	130	99	98.4	98.7
	150	99.55	99.91	99.73
6 cm × 14 cm	50	96.52	97.44	96.98
	70	97.97	97.97	97.97
	90	95.96	98.78	97.37
	110	96.98	99.29	98.14
	130	97.69	99.65	98.67
	150	99.91	99.91	99.91

Table 7. Sensors accuracy and average accuracy towards obstacle shape.

Obstacle shape	Initial distance (cm)	Distance measured (cm)		Accuracy (%)		Accuracy average (%)
		Outdoor	Indoor	Indoor	Outdoor	
Rectangular	50	48.7	50.42	99.16	97.4	98.28
	70	67	69.15	98.79	95.71	97.25
	90	87.2	90.44	99.51	96.89	98.2
	110	107.2	109.82	99.84	97.45	98.65
	130	127.4	130.04	99.97	98	98.99
	150	148.19	149.97	99.98	98.8	99.39
Circle	50	52.02	49.42	98.84	95.96	97.4
	70	69.95	69.95	99.94	99.94	99.94
	90	90.25	90.25	99.72	99.72	99.72
	110	107.94	110.54	99.51	98.13	98.82
	130	123.28	123.28	94.83	94.83	94.83
	150	136.29	136.03	90.69	90.86	90.78
Cylinder	50	50.25	49.96	99.92	99.5	99.71
	70	69.79	73.64	94.8	99.7	97.25
	90	91.21	92.53	97.19	98.66	97.93
	110	108.87	115.18	95.29	98.97	97.13
	130	125.62	127.1	97.97	96.63	97.3
	150	145.44	147.81	98.54	96.96	97.75

stage is imperative to guarantee effectiveness. Further work at that point incorporates the investigation of the system which is intentionally intended to be enacted when the impediment is identified. Various movement styles of walking were also considered, this employment is additionally muddled and tested, particularly in the parts of the human body and the appropriateness of alerts types. Results from both limited component examination and trial works have demonstrated that the sensors are fit for distinguishing different kinds of hindrances materials, surface color, and size of impediments. In this way, the results show the accuracy and effectiveness of the system.

5   Conclusion

In the introduced paper, we presented and depicted a safe system for the mobility of the visually impaired people/ blind. One of the focal points of the system is, it makes the user mindful about hindrances of the right side, left side, and front side adequately. We are utilising the benefits of the blind stick and recognition by sensor investigation. The system gives a total and all-out route and the correct pathway. We made the incorporation of a mobile stick into the system since it is supposed to be the most widely recognized method of walking for VIP with the goal that it tends to be extremely helpful for them. The system can give precision in recognising hindrances of right, left, and front, with comfort for the user assuring protection from both head and ground level, it is also low in cost and an exceptionally low power utilisation. The environmental imager and navigation system are settled with the possibility that the individual can be rendered help by audio information from a caregiver which gets an actual lifestream video from the camera of the VIP. In this manner, the utilisation of the full system for the VIP and caregiver are all presented and tested. The quantitative assessment to explore the demeanour given by the VIP including route planning were put forth. The accuracy accomplished for the system varies from 94.15% to 99.72%. The percentage rate of the snag discovery for either indoor or outside varies from 95.40% to 99.67%. This assessment will increase the VIP versatility essentially at whatever point being thought of. This paper is without a doubt a groundbreaking experience that empowers acing a far-reaching range related to designing abilities and skill. Given the measures during the study, future exploration is to be considered to give intelligent guidance utilising AI, also utilising a neuro-fuzzy control calculation into programming the microcontroller is strongly recommended, joining the framework with RFID, battery observing circuit can be introduced in the framework. Low flexibly of current will influence the precision of the sensor. Finally new gadgets for detecting, advances coordinated chips can be introduced in the system created.

References

1. Bourne, R.R.A., et al.: Magnitude, temporal trends, and projections of the global prevalence of blindness and distance and near vision impairment: a systematic review and meta-analysis. Lancet Global Health **5**, e888–e897 (2017)
2. Spaniolas, K., Cheng, J.D., Gestring, M.L., Sangosanya, A., Stassen, N.A., Bankey, P.E.: Ground level falls are associated with significant mortality in elderly patients. J. Trauma-Inj. Infect. Crit. Care **69**, 821–824 (2010)
3. Asati, C., Meena, N., Orlando, M.F.: Development of an intelligent cane for visually impaired human subjects. In: 2019 28th IEEE International Conference on Robot and Human Interactive Communication (RO-MAN), Orlando, pp. 1–5. IEEE Press (2019). https://doi.org/10.1109/RO-MAN46459.2019.8956328

4. Hussain, A.A., Bouachir, O., Al-Turjman, F., Aloqaily, M.: AI techniques for COVID-19. IEEE Access **8**, 128776–128795 (2020). https://doi.org/10.1109/ACCESS.2020.3007939

5. Al-Turjman, F., Karakoc, M., Gunay, M.: Path planning for mobile DCs in future cities. Ann. Telecommun. **72**(3), 119–129 (2017)

6. Redmon, J., Divvala, S., Girshick, R., Farhadi, A.: You only look once: unified, real-time object detection. In: IEEE Conference on Computer Vision and Pattern Recognition (CVPR), pp. 779–788 (2016)

7. Susan Boyer, K.: Global initiative for the elimination of avoidable blindness. Vidyya Med. News Serv. **2**(29) (2001)

8. BrainPort Technologies. BrainPort V. 100 (2015). http://www.wicab.com/en_us/v100.html

9. Ultracane (2015). http://www.ultracane.com/

10. CareTec (2015). http://www.caretec.at/Mobility.148.0.html?&cHash=a82f48fd87&detail=3131

11. Holland, S., Morse, D.R., Gedenryd, H.: Audio GPS: spatial audio in a minimal attention interface. In: Proceedings of the 3rd International Workshop on Human-Computer Interaction with Mobile Devices, Lille, France, 10 September 2001, pp. 28–33 (2001)

12. Sanchez, J., Oyarzun, C.: Mobile assistance based on audio for blind people using bus services. In: New Ideas in Computer Science Education, pp. 377–396. Lom Ediciones, Santiago, Chile (2007). (in Spanish)

13. Sanchez, J., Saenz, M.: Orientation and mobility in external spaces for blind apprentices using mobile devices. Mag. Ann. Metrop. Univ. **8**, 47–66 (2008)

14. Hub, A., Diepstraten, J., Ertl, T.: Design and development of an indoor navigation and object identification system for the blind. In: Proceedings of the ACM SIGACCESS Conference on Computers and Accessibility, Atlanta, GA, USA 18–20 October 2004, pp. 147–152 (2004)

15. Hub, A., Hartter, T., Ertl, T.: Interactive localization and recognition of objects for the blind. In: Proceedings of the 21st Annual Conference on Technology and Persons with Disabilities, Los Angeles, CA, USA, 22–25 March 2006, pp. 1–4 (2006)

16. Pinedo, M.A., Villanueva, F.J., Santofimia, M.J., López, J.C.: Multimodal positioning support for ambient intelligence. In: Proceedings of the 5th International Symposium on Ubiquitous Computing and Ambient Intelligence, Riviera Maya, Mexico, 5–9 December 2011, pp. 1–8 (2011)

17. Sonnenblick, Y.: An indoor navigation system for blind individuals. In: Proceedings of the 13th Annual Conference on Technology and Persons with Disabilities, Los Angeles, CA, USA, 17–21 March 1998, pp. 215–224 (1998)

18. Fernandes, H., et al.: The SmarVision navigation prototype for blind users. J. Digit. Content Technol. Appl. **5**(5), 351–361 (2011)

19. Fernandes, H., Faria, J., Lopes, S., Martins, P., Barroso, J.: Electronic white cane for blind people navigation assistance. In: Proceedings of the World Automation Congress 2010, Kobe. World Automation Congress (2010)

20. Duarte, K., Cecilio, J., Sá Silva, J., Furtado, P.: Information and assisted navigation system for blind people. In: Proceedings of the 8th International Conference on Sensing Technology, 2–4 September 2014 (2014)

21. Nandish, M.S., Balaji, M.C., Shantala, C.P.: An outdoor navigation with voice recognition security application for visually impaired people. Int. J. Eng. Trends Technol. (IJETT) **10**(10), 500–504 (2014)

22. Shin, B.-S., Lim, C.-S.: Obstacle detection and avoidance system for visually impaired people. In: Oakley, I., Brewster, S. (eds.) HAID 2007. LNCS, vol. 4813, pp. 78–85. Springer, Heidelberg (2007). https://doi.org/10.1007/978-3-540-76702-2_9

23. Willis, S., Helal, S.: RFID information grid for blind navigation and wayfinding. In: Ninth IEEE International Symposium, Wearable Computers (2005)

24. Ramprabu, J., Gowthaman, T.: Smart cane for visually impaired people. Int. J. Comput. Sci. Inf. Technol. 4(1), 24–28 (2013)

25. Gawari, H.: Voice and GPS based navigation system for visually impaired. Int. J. Eng. Res. Appl. 4(4), 2248–9622 (2014)

6G Applications and Standards - An Overview

Suleiman Abdullahi[1]([⊠]) and Fadi Al-Turjman[2]

[1] Faculty of Engineering, Research Center for AI and IOT, Near East University, Nicosia, Mersin 10, Turkey
Suleemanc@gmail.com
[2] Research Center for AI and IoT, Near East University, Nicosia, Mersin 10, Turkey
fadi.alturjman@neu.edu.tr

Abstract. Reliable data access is essential to an increasingly smart automated and pervasive digital environment. Mobile networks are very important in a fully connected smart digital world, everything needs to be linked, from people to vehicles, sensors, things, cloud services and even robotic agents. 5 G wireless networks currently being deployed offer significant enhancements beyond LTE, but may not satisfy the full networking requirements of the growing digital society. This paper outlines technology which are intended to convert the sixth-generation 6 G wireless network and which we consider to be an enabler for several potential cases of 6 G use. We offer a detailed system-level perspective on 6 G scenarios and specifications, frameworks, standards, research activities and 6 G technology that can either be addressed by enhancing the 5 G architecture or implementing entirely new communication paradigms.

Keywords: 6G · Applications · Standardization · Research activities · Capacity · B5G · Network 2030 · Wireless communications

1 Introduction

While 5 G has been promoted worldwide, research organizations and universities are expected to expand beyond 5 G and 6 G into green networks providing high quality service and energy efficiency. Significant improvements in mobile network architecture are needed in order to meet potential applications' demands. The 6 G strategy is to undergo incomparable breakthroughs and merge existing traditional mobile networks with the newly emerging space, air and submarine networks aim of providing worldwide internet connectivity [1].

In other words, the number of new IoE facilities is increasing exponentially, examples include augmented reality technologies, telehealth, 3D touch, aerial vehicle, brain-computer systems and self-connected devices like virtual reality, mixed reality, extended reality and augmented reality. These applications, undermine the original 5 G target of promoting fast package URLLC services [2].

In other words, a wireless infrastructure must have high reliability, low latencies and faster data speeds for uplink and downlink devices in order to work effectively using

E. Ever and F. Al-Turjman (Eds.): FoNeS-IoT 2020, LNICST 353, pp. 46–56, 2021.
https://doi.org/10.1007/978-3-030-69431-9_4

IoE technologies like XR and autonomous, connected systems. There will be a range of unique challenges to addressing this new generation of services, from categorizing a fundamental rate-reliability-latency balance controlling their efficiency to exploiting frequencies above sub6 GHz to transforming wireless networks into an autonomous, smart network infrastructure that provides to orchestrate communication-related control location flexibly [3].

In order to address these obstacles, an ambitious 6 G wireless network must be developed, based on the demand and technical trends of IoE applications. The 6 G drivers are a mix of existing developments in emerging technology, modern technologies such as fitness trackers, smartwatches, implants, Artificial intelligence, X Reality devices, and more. Latest trends include densification, higher speeds and longer antennas.

This article's main contribution is a positive, forward-looking 6 G technology vision outlining the requirements, applications, developments and emerging new technologies that will guide the 6 G revolution. This project also outlines the latest 6 G services and sets out a detailed research roadmap and guidelines that will make the leap from current 5 G systems to 6 G easier.

The rest of this article is arranged as follows; section one is introduction, Sect. 2 is summarizing the literature review, Sect. 3 Mobile communications development. Section 4 provides a detailed description of 6 G: Enabling Technologies. Section 5 provides a brief overview of 6 G Driving Applications & Metrics, and Sect. 6 explains standardization and research activities. Section 7 discusses challenges and future 6 G research guidelines. This study is finally concluded in Sect. 8.

2   Literature Review

Authors [4] outlined a vision for 6 G mobile networks capable of meeting IoE's growing needs. They start with a 6 G sketch from the perspective of frequency and space resource utilization. Then they talked about some attractive recent solutions that could bring the dream closer to reality. Finally, a number of challenges have been addressed in the 6 G Communication network, which will hopefully serve as a guideline for their future development. We note that their flexibility and versatility are key features of 6 G networks and the design of 6 G networks is a truly multidisciplinary field of science. They did not cover the effect of 6 G in the fields of medical imaging, semiconductor, spectroscopy, chemistry and even biotechnology.

Authors [5] outlined a vision for 6 G mobile networks capable of meeting IoE's growing needs. They start with a 6 G sketch from the point of view of time, frequency and space resource utilization. Then they talked about some interesting recent solutions that could bring the dream closer to reality. Finally, a number of challenges have been addressed in the 6 G Communication network, which will hopefully serve as a guideline for their future development. We note that their flexibility and versatility are key features of 6 G networks and the design of 6 G networks is a truly multidisciplinary field of science. The impact of 6 G in the fields of medical imaging, semiconductor, spectroscopy, chemistry, and even biotechnology was not covered.

This paper [6] recommends a study on wireless use of 6 G in green networks. They begin with the introduction of the 1 G to 5 G wireless network, which implies a growth trend of 6 G to some extent. Then there are three entirely new developments in the latest technological paradigm shift, including terrestrial and non-terrestrial network convergence, the genuinely smart connections made possible by the omnipresent AI and an improved network protocol stacking structure. Finally, the emphasis is on technology that is evolving. New spectrum technologies, such as THz communication and VLC, as well as new communication paradigms including molecular and quantum communication, have been discussed which are expected to boost data rates significantly and become key elements in a stable society. Innovations in key technology, including the introduction of the bloc chain, flexible and intelligent materials and environmentally sensitive communication, are also clarified. This project also describes the new 6 G technologies and provides a comprehensive research road map and guidance, which will help you move from 5 G to 6 G systems (Table 1).

Table 1. Comparison of previous research.

References	Design factors	6G Drivers	Standards	Spectrum	Applications	R&D groups
[7]	✓		✓	✓		
[8]	✓				✓	✓
[9]	✓	✓		✓	✓	
[10]		✓			✓	✓
[11]	✓		✓			✓
[12]		✓		✓	✓	
Proposed study	✓	✓	✓	✓	✓	✓

3   Development of Mobile Communication

Telecommunications technology seems to have progressed over many decades after first generation began in 1980, next generation began in 1992, 3 G started in 2001, 4 G started in 2011 or LTE Long Term Evolution, and the lastly 5 G network is expected in 2020 [6]. 4 G supports 1 Gbit/s for low mobility and 100 Mbit/s for high mobility at present. The last 5 g has a 10 GBit/s rating for low mobility and a 1 GBit/s rating for high mobility and a 15 ms latency of 4 G and a predicted 5G rating of approximately 1 ms [13].

The first mobile generation Telecommunications technology seemed to have evolved on the basis of the analogue system over the decades of contact in the 1980s. The most common analogue 1 G systems in the United States are the Advanced Mobile Phone System (AMPS). Nordic Mobile Telephone (NMT), TACS and a range of analogue devices have also been on the European market in the 1980s. Both 1 G standards use speech signal frequency modulation techniques. The cell spectrum was divided into a range of channels not efficient in terms of the available radio spectrum, thereby limiting the number of calls received at any point. Analogue systems are based on circuit technology and communicate only voice and data [14].

Second generation was launched at the end of the 1990s. Wireless technology is used by second generation mobile phones. With a data rate of up to 64 kbps, GSM was the first second generation system to be used for voice communication. Because of the low power radio signals, the 2 G cell phone battery lasts longer. Services such as SMS Short message Service and email are also offered. GSM, Code Division Multiple Access CDMA and IS-95 were the main technologies [15].

The third generation (3 G) wireless networks offer 2 G and 2.5 G backwards compatibility. The 3 G technology was initially developed for high-speed Internet connectivity and different forms of web surfing applications. The 3 G standard offers some attractive facilities, one of which is video conferencing, which allows several parties to communicate face to face even though they are at a long distance. This service is beneficial for business sectors where video conferencing takes place at different conferences. 3 G also offers multimedia, video, gaming and internet connectivity facilities at a very high data rate [16].

4 G provides mobile networking opportunities to provide quicker and improved connectivity experiences for mobile broadband and to continue to expand, providing more flexibility in communication and secure and real-time connections. The air interface represents a significant advance of 4 G and has implemented a streamlined All-IP network architecture. This is a fundamental benefit over 3G since the functionality of the RNC, and the BSC Base Station Controller is distributed between the Evolved Node B (eNB), servers and gateways. However, since the 4 G architecture enables interoperation between various wireless technologies, the networks have a more significant effect on network efficiency and security [17].

The fifth generation of mobile communications, the goal of 5 G, is to bring about revolutionary changes in data speed, latency, network stability, energy efficiency and significant convergence. It not only utilizes the latest spectrum of microwave bands (3.3–4.2 GHz) but also makes the most of the most revolutionary use of the millimetre-wave band, substantially high speeds (up to 10 Gbps). 5 G applies innovative access technology, including the Beam Multiple Access Division (BDMA) and the Dual Carrier Filter Bank (FBMC). Many new technologies are implemented into 5 G to increase network performance: big MIMO capacity enhancement, network mobility software-defined networks (SDNs), spectral quality system (D2D), network traffic reduction Information-Centric Networking (ICN) and rapid roll-out of various services [12]. IMT 2020 proposed three major 5 G scenarios for implementation: improved eMBB broadband network, ultra-reliable and low-latency (URLLC) communications, and mass-server-style mMTC communications [18].

Over the last two decades, cellular networking technology has evolved steadily from the 2 G Global Mobile System (GSM) to the 4 G Long Term Evolution-Advanced (LTE-A) system. The primary reward was more bandwidth and less latency. Although the actual rate of data transmission is throughput, latency depends primarily on how fast each data stream moves. Some related parameters, such as jitter, inter channel interference, connectivity, scalability, energy consumption and compatibility with legacy networks, are also taken into account when developing new mobile technologies along with throughput-based efficiency improvements [13] (Table 2).

Table 2. Comparison of 4G, 5G & 6G.

Features	4G	5G	6G
Time	2010	2020	2030
Spectrum	2–8 Ghz	3–300 GHZ	95 GHz to 3 THz
Data rate	100 MBS	20 Gbs	1 Tbs
Mobility	350 km/h	500 km/h	>1000 km/h
Bandwidth	1.25–20 MHZ	0.25–1 Ghz	Up to 3 THz
AI integration	No	Partial	Fully
Automation integration	No	Partial	Fully
Xr	No	Partial	Fully

4 Sixth Generation Enabling Technologies

In order to facilitate and ensure the quality of the above-listed services, it is essential to integrate a cohort of new disruptive technologies into 6 G. Small cells to small cells: the need for higher data rates and SEEs in patterns 1 and 2 everywhere motivates exploration of higher frequency bands above 6 GHz in 6 G in any case. This includes advanced mm-wave technology to make handheld mm waves possible in early 6 G systems. As 6 G advances frequencies beyond the mm waves, the Terahertz (THz) band may have to be used. The scale of 6 G cells must be decreased from small to microcells by using higher waves and THz frequencies [19].

Every generation up to 5 G will continue to be subject to the three basic dimensions: spectral spectrum, spectral efficiency and spatial reuse: 6G. RF technology can increase power in low bands and allow better use of spectrum. There is a chance that the spectrum will be increased at least tenfold by using terahertz frequency bands. The use of MIMO bands will increase spectral efficiency not only in centimeter wave but also in millimeter wave MM Wave bands as we switch from analogue to hybrid to digital beams in the lower mm-Wave bands. With huge MIMO costs dropping, even larger arrays can be deployed to improve spectral efficiency further.

Network densification will undoubtedly continue to grow – not only because of capacity but also to have more excellent coverage at higher frequency ranges, higher data rates and greater reliability.

Much broader spectrum access is also available; sharing between operators with already licensed SDR-powered spectrum and AI/ML-powered spectrum will allow much higher reuse of spectrum. Effective reuse of spectrum is especially important in lower bands as they have strong non-linear optical propagation characteristics (NLOS), and their spectrum resources are limited [20] (Fig. 1).

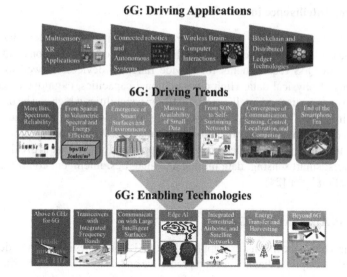

Fig. 1. 6G main Applications, trends, and technologies [21]

4.1 Terahertz Communications

The terahertz frequency band, the last radio spectrum range, is 0.1 to 10 THz and is considered to be a terahertz distance. The Terahertz strip is designed to offer exceptionally high performance, low latency and brand new devices up to the data speed of Tbps. In mill metric wavebands where network bandwidth is seldom 1 GHz, this might not be feasible. The first IEEE 802–100 Gbps project, IEEE 802.15d, was authorized in March 2014, although there was no standard business plan available. The Terahertz range offers a variety of wireless communication advantages, including broad bandwidths >50 GHz, allowing Tbps links, higher frequency, short wavelengths with wide resolution and short time-domain pulses for high resolution sensing and positioning [22].

In other words, Terahertz communication is designed as a key 6 G technology that requires 100+Gbps data rate, one-millisecond latency and other performance metrics. THz would fuel a number of groundbreaking emerging technologies as a robust wireless network, including advanced WLAN networking systems such as Tera-WLAN, Terahertz network backhaul and other long-awaited new paradigms. While the carrier's change to higher frequencies is noticeable, it is still difficult for mm-wave systems to consider a TBP data rate that is limited by the overall precision of the usable bandwidth of less than 10 GHz. Next door to the mm-wave band, with four strengths: 1) tens to 100 GHz broad resource band; 2) second-level pic symbol length; 3) thousands of antennas with a long integration sub-millimeter; 4). Extreme interference without legacy THz (0–10 GHz) has demonstrated its ability as the key wireless technology to fulfil future 6 g wireless device requirements [23].

4.2 Artificial Intelligence in 6G

The architecture of six G networks is enormous, multi-layered, complex, diverse and heterogeneous. Also, 6 G networks will facilitate smooth communications and provide a wide range of QoS requirements for a wide range of devices, as well as process large amounts of physical data. High computational capacities, cognitive capabilities, optimization of expertise and intelligent recognition capabilities which can be used in 6 G networks to intelligently optimize performance, discover knowledge, advanced learning, organization of systems and complicated decision making. With the aid of AI, we present the intelligent 6 G network architecture that is supported by AI. That is divided mainly into four layers: smart sensing, data mining and analytics, intelligent control layer and smart application layer [24].

4.3 Big Data Analytics for 6G

Big Data Analytics is the first natural application of AI. Four types of 6 G analytics can be used, namely descriptive, diagnostic, and predictive and drug analysis. Descriptive analytics provides an overview of network performance, traffic profile, channel conditions, user perspectives and so on in historical data. It dramatically increases the perception of the situation of network operators and service providers. Diagnostic analytics allows the independent detection of network faults and malfunctions, the detection of root causes of network anomalies and the subsequent improvement of network reliability and protection. Predictive analytics uses data to predict future events, including traffic patterns, user locations, and user behavior and preferences, as well as resource availability. Prescriptive analytics uses predictions that include resource management, network slicing and virtualization, caching, edge computing, etc. Note that a wide-ranging collection and analysis of data raises concerns about data privacy, security, ethics and ownership. The 6 G architecture and protocols are also designed to preserve data security, privacy and dignity. At the same time, it is equally necessary that legislation and regulations be formulated in the sense of 6 G to address data ethics and ownership, taking into account the need for a fair risk and profit balance [25].

4.4 Holographic Communications

Holographic communication is one of the glamor of the 6 G period Hologram is a Three-dimensional technology that tries to manipulate beamed light rays to the target and then uses a recording instrument to capture the resulting interference pattern. Indeed, 3D images are not sufficiently transmitted without a stereo voice to demonstrate the characteristics of the presence. The 6 G era will motivate the development of a platform for the capture of multiple physical presences in each configuration by reconfigurable stereo audio. In other words, entities have the freedom to interact and modify the holographic and video data received if necessary. Holographic data should be supplied by secure network connections, with high bandwidth [26].

5   6G Driving Applications and Metrics

Innovative technologies power every new generation of cell systems. 6 G is nothing but the groundbreaking development of innovative new technologies and technical developments to shape their efficiency targets while redefining 5 G standard services. 6 G is no exception. In this segment, we will introduce the main applications which will inspire 6 G implementation, followed by technical developments, goal performance indicators and the new service requirements. Although traditional applications, including live multimedia streaming, remain central to 6 G, four new applications will be fundamental driving forces for system success [19].

5.1   Multisensory XR Applications

Innovative technologies power every new generation of cell Cross Reality will create a range of AR/MR/VR 6 G killer spectrum applications. Since it cannot have very low latencies for data-intensive XR applications, all sensory inputs are still not completely capable of being received in the next 5 G networks. A real immersive AR/MR/VR experience calls for a comprehensive specification that covers not only wireless, computer, storage but also human senses, cognition and physiological perception requirements. For this reason, it must also take into account minimum and maximum perceptive parameters and limitations during the development process (computing, encoding) in order to combine the physical parameters of the user with the conventional.

5.2   Orbital Angular Momentum Communication

A broad analysis was performed on an orbital angular momentum (OAM) called the electromagnetic wave vortex. The phase-turning factor of the radio vortex signals is exp(-jl) relative to the conventional electromagnetic (PE) wave-based plane. The key advantages of OAM are the electro-magnetic wave characteristics associated with beam vorticity and phase specificity, which have an infinite number of own states (i.e. orthogonal modes) that improve transmission capability and theoretical spectral efficiency over a wide range of channels. OAM has opened up a new layer of electromagnetic wave multiplexing, which will provide a new way to significantly increase spectrum efficiency and is expected to be introduced for future 6 G wireless communication networks [22].

5.3   Tele-Operated Driving

Telecommunicated driving is a remote operating system that enables car remote control. The Smart Transportation System (ITS) refers to this concept. This application needs to satisfy the requirements, namely extremely low latency, highly reliable connection and the highest level of safety. In order to support this feature, vehicles must also enhance collision prevention by combining the sensors on a specific avoidance algorithm. The concept will be used in several segments, starting with the industrial and the military ends [27].

5.4 Robotics and Autonomous Systems

A variety of automotive technology experts are currently studying vehicles and wired cars. The 6 G systems are used for the attachment of robots and the implementation of autonomous systems. The UAV drone delivery system is an example of this kind of system. An automated 6 G wireless communication vehicle will radically change our everyday life-styles. The network of 6 G is intended to contribute to the development of self-propelled cars (stand-alone automobiles and non-driving vehicles). A self-driving vehicle looks to the world through a combination of different sensors including light-sensing and light-spectrum, compass, radar, GPS, vibration, odometer and inertial measurement units [28].

6 Standardization and Research Activities

A short overview of 6 G research and standardization activities is given in this section. Overall, manufacturing organizations and governments launched 6 G activities with a view to evolving and defining the 6-G system and modifying the framework in addition to the wireless business model.

The FCC expanded the scope to establish in the United States a new category of experimental licenses of 95 GHz to 3 THz. IEEE introduced the IEEE Future Network under the banner of "Enabling 5 G and beyond." In order to meet the service requirements of future networks by 2030 ITU-T Group 13 also has established an ITU-T Focus Group Innovation Network 2030. In order to develop key technologies for 6 G mobile networks, Samsung Electronics has opened a research and development facility. In order to speed up the production of solutions and standardize 6 G, Samsung carries out extensive cellular technology research, with the next-generation telecom research team being turned into a Centre.

The 6 G research activities under Finland's flagship program were initiated at Oulu University. 6 G Flagship research is grouped into four common research components: wireless networking, distributed computing, infrastructure and applications. For important technical components of 6 G systems, scientific innovations will be made. ITU-R's ITU Radio Communications Sector 5 G standardization activities were based on IMT-2020. ITU-R is therefore expected to release IMT-2030, which will summarize possible mobile communications requirements by 2030.

A successful first 6 G wireless summit was held in Lapland, Finland, in March 2019. Academics, industry experts and suppliers from all over the world conducted a wide and successful debate. The summit was attended by leading wireless networking researchers. The summit was also attended by the world's leading telecommunications firms. The Summit will open discussions on key topics such as the motivation behind 6 G, the move from 5 G to 6 G, the evolving 6 G market and technology support.

7 Challenges and Future Research Direction

To incorporate 6 G communication systems effectively, a range of technical challenges must be overcome. Some possible problems are briefly discussed below.

Terahertz Band: the THz band is the largest wireless 6 G limit. Although high levels of data are obtained, high frequencies are a major challenge in resolving high road losses. For long-distance communication, atmospheric absorption and transmission losses are very high. This is an exciting subject to explore. The massive bandwidth means that new Multi-Path models need to be designed to solve the frequency dispersion problem.

Network Security The wireless 6 G network links not only smartphones but also intelligent automation, AI and XR. It should therefore be considered modern security techniques using advanced cryptographic methods, including physical layer safety techniques and low-cost network protection techniques, low complexity and too high security.

8 Conclusions

The rising demand for 5 G telecommunications technology in 2030 has not been met. Research in 6 G should also be undertaken to achieve its objectives by 2030. New features in 6 G and future applications and technologies to be implemented in 6 G are presented in this report. The fundamental problems in 6 G technologies are discussed here. It is concluded that 6 G will improve network power, merge various technologies and enhance the QoS offering a super-smart company with the entire network connected.

Ultimately the 6 G network can hit terabit speeds per second and an average of 1000 plus. Instant holographic networking in wireless nodes is always available everywhere in 10 years (2030-). The future will become an utterly data-driven society in which people and objects (thousands of seconds) are almost instantaneously connected.

Acknowledgement. This research was supported by Jamhuriya University of Science and Technology, Faculty of engineering, department of electrical and electronics.

References

1. Mendes, L.L., Gontijo, J.G.S., Brito, J.M.C.: Brazil 6G project - an approach to build a national-wise framework for 6G networks. In: 2nd 6G Wireless Summit (6G SUMMIT), Levi, Finland (2020)
2. Matinmikko-Blue, M., Ahokangas, P., Yrjölä, S.: How could 6G transform engineering platforms towards ecosystemic business models? In: 2020 2nd 6G Wireless Summit (6G SUMMIT), Levi, Finland (2020)
3. Elmeadawy, S., Shubair, R.M.: 6G wireless communications: future technologies and research challenges. In: 2019 International Conference on Electrical and Computing Technologies and Applications (ICECTA), Ras Al Khaimah, United Arab Emirates (2019)
4. Wikström, G., et al.: Challenges and technologies for 6G. In: 2nd 6G Wireless Summit (6G SUMMIT), Levi, Finland (2020)
5. Kato, Y., Sakamaki, R., Horibe, M.: Electromagnetic measurement techniques for materials and device used in 6G wireless communications. In: 2nd 6G Wireless Summit (6G SUMMIT), Levi, Finland, 2020, Levi, Finland (2020)
6. Alves, H., López, O.A., Shehab, M., Osorio, D.P.M., Latva-Aho, M., Mahmood, N.H.: Six key features of machine type communication in 6G. In: 2nd 6G Wireless Summit (6G SUMMIT), Levi, Finland (2020)

7. Zhao, Y., et al.: 6G mobile communication networks: vision, challenges, and key technologies. SCIENTIA SINICA Informationis **49**(8), 963–987 (2019)
8. Gupta, A.K.: A study of wireless network: 6G technology. In: National Conference on Recent Innovation in Emerging Technology & Science (2018)
9. Lu, X.Y.: 6G: a survey on technologies, scenarios, challenges, and the related issues. J. Ind. Inf. Integr. **19** (2020)
10. Chowdhury, M.Z., et al.: 6G wireless communication systems: applications, requirements, technologies, challenges, and research directions. IEEE Open J. Commun. Soc. **1**, 957–975 (2020)
11. Long, Q., et al.: Software defined 5G and 6G networks: a survey. Mob. Netw. Appl. **2019**, 1–21 (2019). https://doi.org/10.1007/s11036-019-01397-2
12. Yaacoub, E., Alouini, M.-S.: A key 6G challenge and opportunity - connecting the base of the pyramid: a survey on rural connectivity (2020). https://doi.org/10.36227/techrxiv.118288 08.v1
13. Mansoor, A.M., Idris, M.Y.I., Al-Namari, M.A.: A brief survey on 5G wireless mobile network. Int. J. Adv. Comput. Sci. Appl. **8**, 52–59 (2017)
14. Agrawal, J., et al.: Evolution of mobile communication network: from 1G to 4G. Int. J. Multidiscip. Curr. Res. (IJMCR) **3**, 1100–1103 (2015)
15. Gupta, A.: A survey of 5G network: architecture and emerging technologies. IEEE Access **3**, 1206–1232 (2015)
16. Ahmed, A.M., et al.: Comparison between cellular generations. Int. J. Eng. Appl. Manag. Sci. Paradigms **22**(01), 1–10 (2015)
17. Kaddoum, G., Matar, G., Mavoungou, S.: Survey on threats and attacks on mobile networks. IEEE Access **4**, 4543–4572 (2016)
18. Mitra, R.N., Agrawal, D.P.: 5G mobile technology: a survey. ICT Express **1**, 132–137 (2016)
19. Saad, M.W: A vision of 6G wireless systems: applications, trends, technologies, and open research problems. IEEE Access **34**(3), 134–142 (2019)
20. Viswanathan, H., Mogensen, P.E: Communications in the 6G era. IEEE Access **8**, 57063–57074 (2020)
21. https://www.arxiv-vanity.com/papers/1902.10265/
22. Yuan, Y., et al.: Potential key technologies for 6G mobile communications. Sci. China Inf. Sci. **63**, 1–19 (2020)
23. Han, C., et al.: Terahertz communications (TeraCom): challenges and impact on 6G wireless systems. Computer Science, Engineering, Mathematics ArXiV (2019)
24. Yang, H., et al.: Artificial intelligence-enabled intelligent 6G networks. arxiv (2019)
25. Letaief, K.B., et al.: The roadmap to 6G: AI empowered wireless networks. IEEE Commun. Mag. **57**, 84–90 (2019)
26. Alsharif, M.H., et al.: Sixth generation (6G) wireless networks: vision, research activities, challenges and potential solutions. Symmetry **12**, 676 (2019)
27. Yastrebova, A., et al.: Future networks 2030: architecture & requirements. In: 2018 10th International Congress on Ultra Modern Telecommunications and Control Systems and Workshops (ICUMT) (2019)
28. Chowdhury, M.Z., et al.: 6G wireless communication systems: applications, requirements, technologies, challenges, and research directions. Arxiv (2019)
29. Elmeadawy, S., Shubair, R.M.: 6G wireless communications: future technologies and research challenges. In: International Conference on Electrical and Computing Technologies and Applications (ICECTA), Ras Al Khaimah, United Arab Emirates (2019)

IOT Based Energy Monitoring of PV Plants - An Overview

Ahmad Rasheed[1]([✉]) [iD] and Fadi Al-Turjman[2] [iD]

[1] Electrical and Electronics Engineering Department, Eastern Mediterranean University, Famagusta, TRNC, Mersin 10, Turkey
ahmad.rasheed@emu.edu.tr
[2] Department of Artificial Intelligence, Research Center for AI and IoT, Near East University, Nicosia, Mersin 10, Turkey
fadi.alturjman@neu.edu.tr

Abstract. With the increasing demand of electric power and pressure of mitigating GHG emissions, electric utilities are inclined towards increasing the renewable capacity in their electricity mix. Solar photovoltaic systems, being one of the major contributors in sustainable energy production, cover a vital portion of global cumulative installed renewable capacity. To ensure the optimal efficiency and avoid any forthcoming outage, monitoring of photovoltaic plants is an essential element of integrating renewable into current generation systems. Authors review the types of photovoltaic plants based on configuration and the parameters that are optimal for energy monitoring. It also includes the measuring techniques for the different parameters of monitoring. Familiarity with these parameters and their measuring techniques is essential in development of an efficient photovoltaic energy monitoring system. Various components of these monitoring systems are exposed to extreme weather conditions which reduce their life span. In addition, the efficiency of the photovoltaic modules degrade over time and the cost and complexity of energy monitoring systems limits their usage at a larger scale.

Keywords: Energy monitoring · Photovoltaic plants · Grid-connected · IoT

1 Introduction

As the energy demand increases, electric utilities are under high pressure for incremental production as well as finding new and reliable resources for power generation. With the current global warming crises, utilities are more inclined towards finding sustainable power resources. The use of fossil fuels for electricity production seems inevitable in foreseeable future, but renewable energy seems to be digging a strong foundation for long term utilization along with the help of material sciences laboring to reduce the carbon footprint [1]. Renewable energy can be defined as any persistent and repetitive energy source naturally available in environment, whereas the non-renewable energy can be defined as the underground non-replenishable static sources of energy extracted by humans [2]. Importance of renewable energy can be realized from different factors

E. Ever and F. Al-Turjman (Eds.): FoNeS-IoT 2020, LNICST 353, pp. 57–64, 2021.
https://doi.org/10.1007/978-3-030-69431-9_5

measured in our local or global environment. Carbon Dioxide and other Green House Gas concentration in atmosphere is increasing rapidly every year. CO_2 abundance in atmosphere has up surged to more than 410 ppm in the beginning of year 2020 from 360 ppm almost two decades ago. Moreover, other GHGs have also increased to 1.6 annual GHG index, making the CO_2 equivalent concentration of GHG up to >500 ppm in the atmosphere today [3]. In addition to that, radiative forcing of carbon dioxide has increased almost 60% in last three decades [4]. Energy consumption for the year 2019 saw the highs of 627 quad BTUs, which is projected to increase to 910 quad BTUs with in next three decades [5]. With the set pathway that is being followed, the climatic risk are unavoidable and global warming is inevitable. This calls the attention towards utilization of clean and environmental friendly energy resources, to avail the renewable resources present in local environment for the better future.

Another way to cope with this increasing demand of energy is the efficient use of energy on each and every node from production till consumption. Efficient use of energy saves up tonnes of GHGs, and is projected to be one of the far-reaching contributor in the measures taken for climate change mitigation [6]. One of the key factors in the effective implementation of efficient energy usage is energy monitoring. Energy monitoring is an efficacious technique practiced by utilities and consumers.

Solar energy, first in the line of renewable energy resources, is an abundant and sustainable energy source used since ancient times to harness energy has evolved a lot in recent times and used in multiple ways to produce energy such as photovoltaic, thermal electricity, and solar fuels [7]. In the light of its contribution towards healthier energy production, government of various countries have provided subsidies to consumer and utilities for adding solar energy into their energy mix, which has led to a global increase of cumulative installed capacity of solar panels to more than 620 GW in 2019 [8]. With this constant increase in the solar energy, it is now necessary to monitor the photovoltaic energy production to predict and resolve unwanted circumstances [9].

2 Photovoltaic Energy Monitoring

In addition to the global increase of installed photovoltaic energy capacity, to overcome the global climate crises industrialists have taken a step towards photovoltaic energy, which forecasts a skyrocketing rise in photovoltaic plants in coming years [10]. Therefore monitoring is necessary to achieve desired results in photovoltaic energy as a number of factors affect control the optimal outcome of generation. For instance, partial shadowing of photovoltaic panels cause somewhere around 10–20% energy loss annually [11]. Consequently, different monitoring technologies have been developed to sense undesirable events, such as production loss due to climatic or geographical conditions etc. and tackle them to achieve optimal potential of photovoltaic panels [12]. With the increase in solar energy installation, the monitoring systems are becoming more and more sophisticated with a lot of research and development being labored to yield an effective and low cost monitoring system. This section provides an overview of photovoltaic monitoring systems.

The basic elements of photovoltaic monitoring system includes sensors, signal conditioning unit, personal computer, and system control unit. First and foremost element

of monitoring system 'sensors' measure the variables in real time which are then fil-
tered, amplified, and processed by signal condition unit. The microcontroller in this unit
transmits the conditioned signal to a computer which instructs the system control unit
based on analysis and user commands [10].

2.1 Classification of Photovoltaic Systems

Photovoltaic systems can be categorized based on various factors which includes configuration, connection type etc. Among these categories grid connected and stand-alone
photovoltaic systems are the major configurations, whereas they can be connected to
hybrid systems and other utilities. The major classifications of these systems based on
their configurations are further explained as follows.

Stand-Alone Photovoltaic Systems. Stand-alone photovoltaic systems, also known as
direct coupled photovoltaic systems, as the name suggests are directly connected to
load. These systems are subcategorized based on their availability of battery connection.
With the absence of storage element, these systems are functional only during the day
light, provide optimal output energy when used with maximum power point tracking.
These systems, when used with storage element, require some additional components
for battery safety such as charge controller to prevent any damage by disconnecting the
generation and load side during faulty conditions [13].

Grid Connected Photovoltaic Systems. Grid connected photovoltaic systems comprises of photovoltaic panels, power conditioning unit, and distribution panel. The DC
power generated by the panels is converted to AC power by the power conditioning unit.
The major function of the conditioning unit is the conversion of DC to AC with respect to
the requirements imposed by the connected grid. As the name suggests, that these photovoltaic modules are connected to grid, so functionality of conditioning unit is to mind the
voltage, frequency and power impositions of the connected grid. A bi-directional interface is provided by a distribution panel between the output of power conditioning unit
and grid/on-site load. These on-site distribution panel allows the electricity provision
directly to AC load and/or grid system [14].

In addition to these major categories of photovoltaic systems, there are hybrid systems as well which include Wind-Photovoltaic and Diesel-Photovoltaic hybrid system.
These systems are integration of photovoltaic with wind turbines, or diesel generators
which can have multiple configuration topologies in accordance with the aforementioned
configuration schemes.

2.2 Energy Monitoring Variables

The sporadic nature of solar energy does not allow regular power output and the fluc-
tuations may result into grid stress [15]. The richness of monitoring system can be
contemplated by the selection of variables to be measured which are to be selected
based on British Standard BS IEC 61724 [16]. Regardless of the configuration topology
of photovoltaic panels, some of the most important monitoring variables include solar

radiation, ambient and module temperature, and the panel's voltage and current. Table 1 enlists the essential variables that are covered by a photovoltaic energy monitoring system, whose measurement techniques will later be discussed in detail.

Table 1. Energy monitoring variables for photovoltaic panels.

Configuration system	Variables	
Stand-alone system	i Output: Voltage, Current, Power	
Grid connected system	i Output: Voltage, Current, Power, Energy ii Current & Power: To and from utility grid iii Grid Voltage	i Irradiance ii Temperature: Ambient air, PV Module iii Wind: Speed, Direction, Humidity, Atmospheric pressure

2.3 Measurement of Variables

Measurement of the monitoring variables is a sensitive and crucial part of energy monitoring systems. These variables depict the conditions of photovoltaic systems and the atmosphere around it, which help maintaining the stability of system and preventing it from any forthcoming faulty conditions. The parameters of photovoltaic modules and the atmosphere that reflect the major contribution, such as current, voltage, temperature, and solar radiation of monitoring system are mentioned in Table 2. Current measurement plays an important role in the stability of the system and can be measured with a number of different methods which follow discrete working principles [17]. Voltage measurement of photovoltaic plants is dependent on the type of configuration, to measure different level of voltages at different nodes of generation and transmission system. An estimate of 45% increase in electricity demand is forecasted within next two decades [5].

With such expected high demands, when grid connected photovoltaic capacity increases, inevitably the stress on the grid system will increase with the variation in the voltage level. Consequently, it is of utmost importance that the voltage levels of the photovoltaic plants should be monitored to forecast any system outage [18, 19]. In addition to these, measurement of solar radiation at the site of photovoltaic plant is of crucial importance as it determines the generation potential of any photovoltaic panel [20]. Furthermore, the temperature measurement of the photovoltaic panel and the atmosphere around it is a key factor in achieving the optimal efficiency as vital portion of the solar radiation received by the photovoltaic panel results into its higher temperature [21]. Table 2 also mention different classifications and methods of measuring these variables.

Table 2. Photovoltaic energy monitoring variables.

Measurement variable	Working principal	Method
Current	Ohm's law	Shunt resistor Trace resistance shunting
	Faraday's law of induction	Rogowski Coil Current Transformer
	Magnetic field effect	Hall effect Magneto resistance effect
	Faraday effect	Polarimeter detection Interferometer detection
Voltage		Resistive potential divider Potential transformer Capacitive coupled voltage transformer Electro-optical voltage sensor
Solar Radiation	Thermoelectric Thermos-mechanical Photoelectric Calorimetric	Radiation sensor
Temperature		Thermocouple Resistive temperature detector Thermistor Silicon temperature sensor

3 Components of Monitoring Systems

A wide range of instruments are used for measuring the variables of monitoring systems mentioned above. Selection of these instruments is a process of precision, as these functional limitation of these components define the efficiency and reliability of the monitoring system. Selection of these components is dependent on various factors including scale of photovoltaic plant, cost limitations, location, and environmental restrains etc. some of the major components used in the development of measuring unit of monitoring system are mentioned as follows.

Sensors: Current, Voltage, Temperature, Solar radiation, Wind speed, Hygrometer, and Barometer.

Data: Acquisition, transmission, storage, and analysis system.

4 Challenges of Photovoltaic Energy Monitoring Systems

Solar energy harvesting have seen its peak in this decade and photovoltaic systems are gradually becoming more and more sophisticated. With this advancement, trailblazing energy monitoring systems are following the path along with which comes hindrance due to the wide range of instruments used in the practical application. As mentioned previously, different sensor and components, installed on-site bear harsh climatic conditions.

These environmental conditions such as high temperature, long exposure to sunlight, and corrosive environment etc. may result into short lifespan or inaccurate measurements, eventually the reliability of the sensors and other components reduce over time.

With this reduced reliability of sensors, the timely transmission of measurements can also be questioned, as delayed transmission consequently results into delayed analysis, processing, and commanding the system. One of the major challenge faced by the researcher is the degradation of photovoltaic modules and the system as a whole, as different parts of the energy conversion system, under different environmental conditions, have different effects on the power output of the module and this degradation continues over time.

5 Discussion

Working condition vary for each and every individual site of photovoltaic plant, which results into discrete selection of sensors and other components for particular photovoltaic plant. Depending on the scale of PV plant, shunt or Hall-effect sensors are used widely for current measurements. Former sensor is low cost but inaccurate at high current values, whereas the latter is a high cost, high accuracy sensor. Other sensors are either costlier or have practical constraints which allows usage in particular situations only. Voltage measurement is carried out with the help of potential divider, potential transformer, and capacitive coupled voltage transformers, which are used for low, medium, and high voltage measurement respectively. Solar radiation sensors are used based on the working principle required such as conversion of solar heat into electric signal or measurement of diffused radiation etc. Lastly, for the temperature measurement of the modules or the air ambient temperature on-site of plant, thermocouples and resistive temperature detectors are examples of widely used sensors. Former has the tendency of inaccuracy and non-linearity with temperature, whereas the latter has high accuracy and varies linearly.

6 Proposed Protective Measures

With the rapid research and development, energy monitoring systems are becoming more futuristic. From the measurement of monitoring parameters to data processing, till the handling of forecasted events, every step has a room for improvement. The outdoor sensors exposed to extreme conditions, especially in sunlight can have face over temperature inside the equipment for which the high endurance against temperature must be ensured for optimal efficiency and reliability. In-person visual checks should be performed more often to make sure of the accurate conversion system operation. Table 3 mentions few protective measures that should also be followed to ensure operation of outdoor equipment against corrosive environment.

Table 3. Suggested measures for protection of monitoring systems.

Parameters/Components	Suggestion
Cables	Use of protective cable boots to increase endurance against harsh climate and corrosion
Calibration	End to end calibration must be carried out to avoid offset errors in outdoor environment
Temperature	Sensors and other components which are directly exposed to sunlight should have high endurance rating against intense temperature
Measuring Errors	Ensure the precision and omission of measurement errors to acquire true value from sensors
Measuring Individuals	High frequency of data acquisition, in other terms larger data set with short recording intervals should be ensured for early forecasting of failures
Examining Interval	In-person visual checks should be performed more often to ensure the accurate operation of in/out-door equipment

7 Conclusion

An extensive overview of types of photovoltaic plants, their energy monitoring systems which include the parameters to be measured for efficient monitoring and the sensors used for the measurement of given parameters are detailed. Covering each and every individual sensor is improbable due to complexity and time constraints. Overview can be further expanded to cover the different case studies which have followed mentioned working principles, and comparison can be made in the efficiency results of individual sensors. Hopefully the collective information covered in article can come in handy while developing an efficient photovoltaic energy monitoring system.

References

1. Chu, S., Chu, Y., Liu, N.: The path towards sustainable energy. Nat. Mater. **16**(1), 16–22 (2017)
2. Twidell, J., Weir, T.: Renewable Energy Resources. Routledge, London (2015)
3. Butler, J.H., Montzka, S.A.: The NOAA Annual Greenhouse Gas Index (AGGI), National Oceanic & Atmospheric Administration, Boulder, CO (2020)
4. NOAA: Trends in Atmospheric Carbon Dioxide. National Oceanic & Atmospheric Administration, Washington, DC (2020)
5. U.S. EIA: International Energy Outlook 2019 with projections to 2050. U.S. Energy Information Administration, Washington, DC (2019)
6. Infield, D., Freris, L.: Renewable Energy in Power Systems. Wiley, Hoboken (2020)
7. Singh, G.K.: Solar power generation by PV (photovoltaic) technology: a review. Energy **53**, 1–3 (2013)
8. IEA: Photovoltaic Power System Programme Annual Report 2019. International Energy Agency, Lausanne (2019)

9. Benghanem, M.: Low cost management for photovoltaic systems in isolated site with new IV characterization model proposed. Energy Convers. Manag. **50**(3), 748–755 (2009)
10. Madeti, S.R., Singh, S.N.: Monitoring system for photovoltaic plants: a review. Renew. Sustain. Energy Rev. **67**, 1180–1207 (2017)
11. Hanson, A.J., Deline, C.A., MacAlpine, S.A., Satauth, J.T., Sullivan, C.R.: Partial-shading assessment of photovoltaic installations via module-level monitoring. IEEE J. Photovolt. **4**(6), 1618–1624 (2014)
12. Davarifar, M., Rabhi, A., El-Hajjaji, A., Dahmane, M.: Real-time model base fault diagnosis of PV panels using statistical signal processing. In: 2013 International Conference on Renewable Energy Research and Applications (ICRERA), Madrid (2013)
13. Fara, L., Craciunescu, D.: Output analysis of stand-alone pv systems: modeling, simulation and control. Energy Procedia **112**, 595–605 (2017)
14. Arulkumar, K., Palanisamy, K., Vijayakumar, D.: Recent advances and control techniques in grid connected PV system – a review. Int. J. Renew. Energy Res. **6**(3), 1037–1049 (2016)
15. Ahmad, A., Subhani, M.J., Arshad, N.: A strategy to reduce grid stress through priority-based inverter charging. Energy Procedia **134**, 555–566 (2017)
16. International Electrotechnical Commission, IEC 61724, photovoltaic system performance monitoring e guidelines for measurement, data exchange and analysis. 1st ed., Geneva: IEC: International Electrotechnical Commission (1998)
17. Patil, T.G., Asokan, A.: A proficient solar panel efficiency measurement system: using current measurements. In: 2016 International Conference on Communication and Electronics Systems (ICCES), Coimbatore (2016)
18. Moghe, R., Lambert, F.C., Divan, D.: Smart "stick-on" sensors for the smart grid. IEEE Trans. Smart Grid **3**(1), 241–252 (2011)
19. Ramljak, I., Bago, D.: Influence of PV plant connection on voltage quality parameters considering connection point in distribution grid. In: 2018 First International Colloquium on Smart Grid Metrology (SmaGriMet), Split, Croatia (2018)
20. Nespoli, L., Medici, V.: An unsupervised method for estimating the global horizontal irradiance from photovoltaic power measurements. Sol. Energy **158**, 701–710 (2017)
21. Ferreira, R.A.M., Pottie, D.L., Dias, L.H., Filho, B.C., Porto, M.P.: A directional-spectral approach to estimate temperature of outdoor PV panels. Sol. Energy **183**, 782–790 (2019)

Student Grade Prediction Using Machine Learning in Iot Era

Adedoyin A. Hussain[1,3]([⊠]) and Kamil Dimililer[2,3]

[1] Computer Engineering Department, Near East University, Nicosia, Mersin 10, Turkey
`hussaindoyin@gmail.com`
[2] Electrical and Electronic Engineering Department, Near East University,
Nicosia, Mersin 10, Turkey
`kamil.dimililer@neu.edu.tr`
[3] Research Centre for AI and IoT, Near East University, Nicosia, Mersin 10, Turkey

Abstract. The work proposed in this paper is the application of machine learning techniques in recognizing patterns and predicting student success rate on the bases of their performance on their previous grades in this IoT era. With this, using machine learning algorithms improves predicting student grade efficiently. This method is implemented with their previous academic data for students present in the tertiary institution. However, the education system of students in Portugal have enhanced during the past decades. Precisely, the inadequate achievement of success in critical courses like the Portuguese language and also Mathematics is a grave issue. In this paper, we intend to analyze student's success in tertiary institutions using ML techniques. Real-world raw data were received by using existing data from the school. The two core courses were modeled, also four ML techniques were tested. The results gotten shows that student success rates can greatly be instigated by their previous performance. With the direct outcome of the research, a more adequate predicting tool can also be developed, which improves education quality and enhances resource management for schools. This study is said to increase student performance greatly if taken into consideration.

Keywords: Educational system · Linear regression · Machine learning · Support vector machine · Neural networks · K-nearest neighbors

1 Introduction

Tertiary institutions are priority stations for greater knowledge. Reservation of Students' concerning an institution is a matter of soaring interest [1]. Some studies have been carried out in universities sitting out dropout rates of students, this problem highly increases in the early year due to support lacking, during their undergraduate course. A first-year undergraduate is referred to as a year of Make or Break because of this [2]. Without support with regards to student course or complexity, this may lead to demotivating the student and can be a cause of withdrawer for that particular course [3]. There will be an important aspect to deploy a way in supporting students to be retained

E. Ever and F. Al-Turjman (Eds.): FoNeS-IoT 2020, LNICST 353, pp. 65–81, 2021.
https://doi.org/10.1007/978-3-030-69431-9_6

at a higher education institution [4, 5]. Prediction grades early is a way out that as the potential in monitoring the progress of these students concerning their degree courses which are taken at the university and this will give rise to the student process of learning base on grades being predicted.

Recognition of pattern has these functions. a) The extraction of features (measuring and selecting properties representation of input raw data in a form that is reduced). b) Matching patterns (comparing input patterns in referencing patterns with the use of distance measuring). c) Memory reference template (the input pattern is compared against it). d) Making decisions (in finding out the closest nearest reference template to the given input pattern) [6]. Amongst the entire stated unit, the more crucial component is a matching pattern, which locates the best coordinate and the distance-related between the reference designs and the obscure test input. Patterns are a discrete sequence of real numbers, sequence index is usually being defined at times [7–9]. The rate of success relies mostly on how the pattern test is close to the templates reference [10]. Moreover, due to the noise and distortion given while handling the pattern test, this similarity desired may deteriorate, whereas consequently the process may lapse in that one and may begin making mistakes in matching.

However, with this, institutions need to make advancement in developing an educational model that asserts on the implementation of ICT (information and communication technologies), this could offer a high functioning tool inequality in social responsibility and opportunities, and also encourages knowledge construction process [11]. Technology-enhanced learning (TEL) is known as applying technology to the processes of teaching-learning. Using digital technology in having the goal of enhancing the experience of teaching-learning, is what this term is coined from. TEL relevance has increased due to the emerging number of huge technological resources which aids in the development of student critical thinking [11]. TEL incorporates a large number of emerging technologies like, LMS (learning management systems), mobile applications learning, augmented and virtual interventions, services learning in the cloud, networking, etc. [12].

Some of the related techniques stated above, if they are applied, will have a huge impact on the educational system, it will also manage and generate a large number of data far and wide as present [13]. Text mining, big data, data mining, and intelligent data are some specific new technologies in fulfilling data analysis tasks. The merging of these technologies in association with the educational systems will give rise in analyzing the data, also transforming it into fruitful and meaningful information [14].

In examining the establishment's information we utilize, learning investigation, and educational data mining (EDM). These are the developing criteria used for guidance. The analysis are made possible through various statistical techniques and tool including DM and also ML. This is one of the objectives leading to analytics learning, this provides the analysis of the given data originated from the educational archive [15].

Based on some of the stated principles, the main objective is recognizing a pattern while predicting student grades following several attributes in regards to their performance academically. This is proven formidable by individual student tracking, by subject, area, and so on. The significance of this tracking is to minimize the rate of dropout and as well as providing follow up for students for educational system improvement.

Student retention rate is a term that implies the student rate in a cohort whose studies has not been abandoned for another institution. This term is highly significant for university admin because this affects the rate of graduation directly [16]. Once the identity of the student is provided to the prediction technique, it becomes easier to give closer attention to prevent them from leaving their studies untouched. Moreover, some early admonition method could be studied and implemented to help the presentation pace of understudies [17].

In this work, the contributions are as follows.

- We overview the literature about grade predictions in detail.
- We summarize key design factors that are required and the collection of real-world data.
- We categorize the different procedures for ML techniques in predicting the grades.
- We outline patterns gotten during the predictions.
- We summarize issues and challenges in this paper.

The paper is presented as follows. Presentation of similar studies which adds to the concept of the situation, also we evaluate the methodologies and techniques used which are presented in Sect. 2. Whereas, in Sect. 3 we describe the method as well as the materials used. In Sect. 4, we put forth the result and pattern gotten from the experiment. Finally, Sect. 5 presents the conclusion and discussion of the contributions presented in this paper. Also, Table 1 provides a summarization of the abbreviation used and its definition.

Table 1. Abbreviations used

Terms	Meaning
ICT	Information and communication technologies
EDM	Educational data mining
LMS	Learning management systems
TEL	Technology-enhanced learning
SVM	Support vector machine
DEWS	Dropout early warning systems
MF	Matrix factorization
FM	Factorization machine
PLMR	Personalized multi-linear regression
ML	Machine learning
NN	Neural networks
LR	Linear regression
SL	Supervised learning
VS	Virtual studio

2 Literature Review

Some research works in student's performance prediction comes to facilitate planning of degree or pinpoint students at risk. They've been a stretch range of works related to EDM, where many tool were put forward with the aim of knowledge discovery, decision making, and the provision recommendations. In [18] is a study concerning big data application in the educational system, it is said that it aids big data techniques while some analytic learning can be supported, such as attrition risk detection, performance prediction, visualization of data, feedback intelligence, the recommendation of courses, estimation of student skills, grouping and collaboration of student and behavior detection, amid others. In the study, the prediction analysis functionality is emphasized, which is circled in predicting the behavior of student, performance, and skills.

University of Northern Taiwan was used as a case study in [22], educational big data approaches and analytic learning were used in predicting and for the calculation of the course. This paper applies the principal regression component in predicting the final academic performance of students. In this paper, some attributes extraneous to the problem, like the behavior of video-gaming, behavior of outside class practice, quiz, and assignment score, including after school tutorials, were also added.

A study carried out concerning factors impacting software correction [23], it is concluded that when using educational environments and data mining, it presents two methods of data analysis generally used. This is based on a descriptive model and of the premise of the prediction model. The predictive approach generally uses the supervised learning technique in estimating the foreign values of the dependent variables [24]. In contrast, the descriptive model mostly uses unsupervised learning for it to recognize a pattern that interprets its structure of data being extracted [25].

The collaborative filtering method is a common technique in predicting the future performance of students in their academic year, which is dependent on student grades. In the sector of education, the collaborative filtering technique is on the premise that the performance of students which prediction is done is gotten from the previous grades completed successfully. In [26] the future prediction of the evaluation grade for the academic year, using the collaborative filtering method on the bases of factorization probabilistic Bayesian models and matrix.

In another paper [27], a collaborative filtering application method was described, the aim is in predicting student performance from the start of the student's year, based on the student grades. This implementation is on student learning representation from the grades based on courses taken by the student, for it to align students with attributes they have in common. The information system of Masaryk University was used as a case study using its stored historic data. The gotten results show an effective approach just like using common machine learning methods, just like SVM.

In other papers, the researchers proposed the evolution of techniques that make use of previous data of course by grades, having the aim of predicting the success of students [28]. The idea is based on using a linear model and factorization low-range matrix. The paper gave an evaluation of the technique using data gotten from Minnesota university, which content is previous grades of close to twelve and a half years working period. The method shows when focusing on a specific course, the accuracy improves in predicting grades.

In [29], presents a peculiar method which makes use of a recommendation system for the extraction of education data, mostly when predicting students' performance. Invalidating this approach, the recommendations system technique is being compared with the traditional method of regression, such as linear regression or logistics. In addition to the contribution of works done in applying the system recommendation techniques, just like factorization of a matrix in the system of education, for future grade prediction.

With big data, the benefit and opportunity it brings to the education system are regularly being researched. The relationship, scrutiny between the education environment and also big data are discussed in [30]. This paper overviews different tools, methods, big data algorithms, and methods implemented in the education system to gain knowledge of its impacts which includes the learning and teaching progress. The analysis gotten from the paper recommends that the fusion of a way based on big data is very important. This path contributes automatically by improving the process of studying, for its process must be aligned accurately in the system of education. A smart system for some e-learning courses based on big data is discussed in [32]. In this paper, the approach of the association of rules is implemented to discover the relationship gotten between academic activities in which the student carries out. Based on the extracted rules, the accurate price catalog is gotten following the preferences and behavior of the student. Lastly, the result derived shows the effectiveness and scalability of the expected recommendation system.

The last grade expectation dependent on the restricted introductory information of students and courses which is a difficult errand because of the vast majority of the understudies are roused in the primary semester. Yet, as the time went there may be an abatement in inspiration and execution of the student. The calculation can be utilized in both regression and classification settings to anticipate students' presentation in a course and arrange them into two gatherings. The authors in [33] used supportive in representing a calculation to foresee the last grade of an individual understudy when the normal precision of the forecast is adequate. The authors in [34] considered relapse models with variable choice and variable conglomeration way to deal with anticipating the presentation of graduate understudies and their totals. The examination likewise showed that the ideal forecast of the presentation of every understudy would permit educators to intercede in like manner. They have utilized a dataset of 171 understudies from Eidgen"ossische Technische Hochschule (ETH) Zürich, Switzerland. According to their findings, the undergraduate performance of the students could explain 54% of the variance in graduate-level performance. By analyzing the structure of the undergraduate program, they assessed a set 3 of students' abilities. Their results can be used as a methodological basis for deriving principle guidelines for admissions committees (Table 2).

Table 2. Systematic Summary of some Literature.

Ref	Study purpose	Dataset	Methods/techniques	Relevant findings
[35]	Factorization approaches to predict student performance	Two real-world datasets from KDD Cup 2010	Matrix Factorization	MF technique can predict performance by guessing
[36]	Matrix factorization models	2 real-world datasets From KDD Cup 2010	Matrix Factorization and Tensor based Factorization	MF techniques are useful for sparse data to predict the performance
[37]	Build a dropout early warning system	2006–2007 of grade7 cohorts	Early Dropout Warning Systems (DEWS)	DEWS predicts dropout rate
[38]	Predict students' course grades for the next enrolment term	33000 GMU students' data of fall 2014	Factorization Machine	FM models have a high level of prediction with no error
[39]	Predict next term course grades and within-class assessment performance	30,754 GMU, 14,505 UMN and 13,130 SU Students' data	Personalized Multi-Linear Regression models (PLMR)	PLMR and MF, predict next term grades with lower error
[33]	Predict the grades of individual students in traditional Classrooms	700 UCLA undergraduate Student's data	Regression and classification	In-class evaluations enable the timely identification of weak students

3   Materials and Methodology

In this paper, a guided methodology like in Fig. 1 is put forward.

- The data cleansing and collection of historic dataset of the grades taken from students, takes effect.
- The technique of machine learning is selected.
- The model for student grade prediction is gotten from the previous data being processed.
- The obtained results are visualized and analyzed.

3.1   Description of the Data

The data utilized in the paper is poised of the instructive information of 355 students. The total of the previous record of grades for the students' is 6359, this correlates to courses of the students. The dataset is for student accomplishment in tertiary education of two

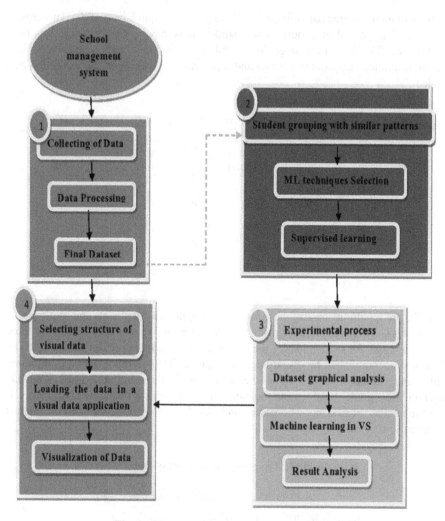

Fig. 1. Diagram of the proposed methodology.

different courses. The attribute of these data includes grades of student, demographic, school, and socially relevant features, and it was gathered by making use of data from the school. Two different sets of data are put forward regarding their achievement in two definite courses, which are Mathematics and Portuguese. In [33], both data were shaped with regression and classification exercise. However, more importantly, the mark attribute is G3 which has a firm interrelationship with the attribute G1 and G2. This is so because of G3 being the final academic year grade, whereas, G2 and G1 correlate with 2nd and 1st-grade period. It will be tedious in predicting G3 without having G1 and G2, this predicting scheme is highly beneficial. Additionally, the information is being gotten from the establishment's instruction framework and are put away in a CSV file system format. The data was repeatedly collected in the tertiary institution and stored in the form of an integrated data repository. Table 3 shows a quick case of the dataset with its attribute. To prevail in a course, every student must have a good pass mark in their G1, G2, and G3 which are first grade, second grade, and last grade respectively. This method is applied fairly to the courses and it is a circular method in the institution as a whole.

Table 3. Dataset samples.

	G1	G2	G3	Study time (hours)	Failures	Absences
0	5	6	6	2	0	6
1	5	5	6	2	0	4
2	7	8	10	2	3	10
3	15	14	15	3	0	2
4	6	10	10	2	0	4

In the pre-handling phase of the information, duplicated documents and invalid value in attributes G1, G2, and G3 were discarded. Another significant task was to make some data anonymous for it to abide by the international standards of data protection. The phase was accomplished by discarding the personal data information like ID number, names, and surnames. Table 4 shows the grade classification. In Fig. 2 and 3, it depicts the cumulative grade variables and the cumulative pass and fail variable respectively. It cites the number of students who passed and failed and also the grade with the highest value and lowest value.

Table 4. The grade classification system.

	Excellent	Good	Satisfactory	Sufficient	Fail
Score	16–20	14–15	12–13	10–11	0–9
Grades	A	B	C	D	F

3.2 Selecting Machine Learning Techniques

This paper, we utilize AI strategies and information digging in predicting precisely historic student grades dataset. On this historical student dataset for the tertiary institution degree, techniques of supervised learning will be utilized in deciding a prescient model that will establish the framework for the improvement of things to come of a system for the student grade prediction. Predicting students' scholastic execution is said to be one of the trending problems, furthermore, it speaks to an unbending assignment of information mining in education. Regression is one of the widely used techniques, and

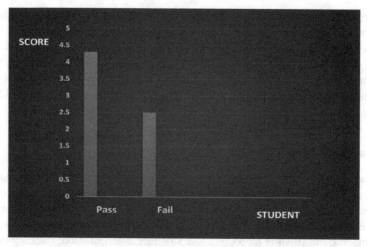

Fig. 2. Histograms of the pass and fail variable.

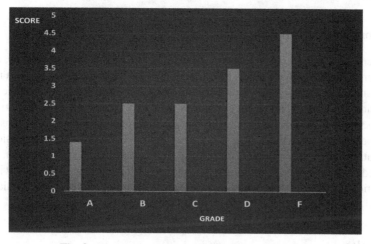

Fig. 3. Histograms of the cumulative grade variables.

it is applied to get a prescient model that can be utilized to foresee future information records. The procedure incorporates Training and testing [33]. In the preparation step, the preparation dataset is broken down using the picked regression calculation.

3.3 Experimental Process

During the test stage, before utilizing the ML technique, an investigation was done in gathering the information to rapidly distinguish students with a specific type of conduct. The assignment of information grouping specifically is applicable since it is the main stage in mining information. During this task, it has the chance of recognizing similarities with comparative qualities, which can be applied as a beginning point to investigate future forecasts. In a subsequent stage, utilizing the regression calculation against the qualities with the student's grades, with this we are expecting the measure of student who passed the subjects to be distinguished. At that point, it is an expectation endeavored with different evaluations and qualities. After recognizing the patterns utilizing various significant attributes against the G3 (final grade), the models were also tested with various machine learning techniques namely LR, KNN, SVM, and NN with this we could depict the best model. The results will be discussed in the following sections.

3.4 Data Visualization

The fundamental point of representation is displaying all the attributes of this dataset and speaking to it graphically. Imagining this information in a graphical illustration which comprises the help of attributes, just so the outcomes of the experiment are exhibited instinctively. The information perception process is portrayed as getting and investigating the information, information representation, structure determination, stacking information into the application, show the outcome, and conclusion, and lastly the procedure of representation is refined.

3.5 Computational Environment

The experiments carried out in this paper were implemented using the VScode, it is an open-source condition that propels the utilization of SL strategies. VScode is a no-pay and a standard programming condition consisting of a solid suite of instruments for information examination and factual methods. It takes a shot on multiple platforms like Windows, macOS, or Linux, and with this current highlights can be included. Tensorflow for VScode, is a library that set forward many thorough capacities for regression and classification tasks. In particular, the library makes use of linear Regression, (NN), KNN, and (SVM) packages. Although, the present implementation was not built in light of execution yet, but summarizing the patterns and the best models. The operation was evaluated on a pc with, 2.6 GHz and 8 GB RAM.

4 Results

Here the objective isn't to surmise about the prescient capacities of the model but to recognize a pattern in their final grade in regards to some attribute and compare the accuracy with other models, as discussed in the previous sections. But this is to give a simple description of the patterns and to summarize the best models. Thus, certain attributes will be selected in the recognition of patterns but the whole dataset will be used when comparing it with other models. The lists of attributes are G1, G2, study time, failures, and absences against the final grade which is G3. The figures below show the outcome of the prediction against G3.

4.1 Recognizing the Pattern in the Grades

In recognizing a pattern there must be a consideration in the extraction of certain features, it must get a matching pattern with the use of a memory reference template (comparing against each other) and then finally make a decision. The figures below represent the graphical illustration that will be used in recognizing a pattern with the student grades. Where G1, G2, and G3, are first grade, second grade, and last grade respectively. With the various attributes against the final grade, it shows that some attributes like absence from school and the time spent on studying affected the student's grades. With this the number of students who passed due to their absence and lack in study time was low. To help improve the students' performance they should spend more time studying and they should be more punctual in school to increase their success rate.

In Fig. 4 it is observed that the strength of the student's study time against their final grade is of great significance. It shows that the more time spent on studying increases their chances of getting a higher final grade. However, students with lower study time are on an average scale. If it is worth mentioning, the institution should consider balancing the study time for students for them to have a higher chance of getting a good grade.

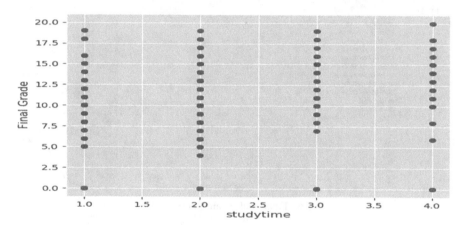

Fig. 4. Final grade against study time.

In Fig. 5 it is observed that the strength of the student's final grade against their failures is highly significant. The pattern shows that the amount of failures in the final grade is much in contrast to the number of people with less failure. However, students with an average failure rate are on an average scale. If it is worth mentioning, the institution should consider improving the academic activities when it comes to their final exams for them to have a higher chance of getting a good grade. While in Fig. 6, it shows that the number of students presents in school all the time or most time, in this case, it increases their chances of performing well in school. However, students with most absenteeism are on an average or less average failure rate. If it is worth mentioning, the institution should consider improving and adding care to the absentees in school due to one thing or an order, just for them to have a higher chance of getting a good grade.

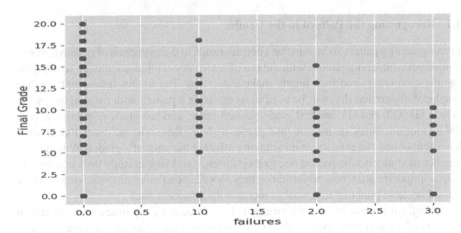

Fig. 5. Final grade against Failures.

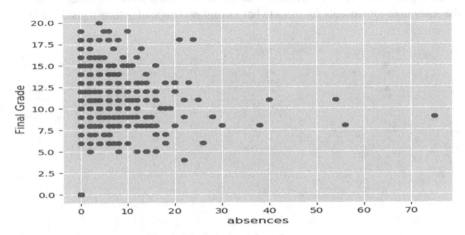

Fig. 6. Final grade against absences.

In Fig. 7 it is observed that the capability of the student's final grade against their first grade is significant. It shows that the number of students who did well in their first grade performed well in their final grade. If it is worth mentioning, the institution should encourage the students in performing better in their first and second grades for them to have a higher chance of getting a good grade in their finals as shown in Fig. 8.

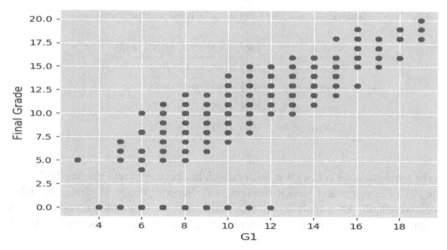

Fig. 7. Final grade against grade 1.

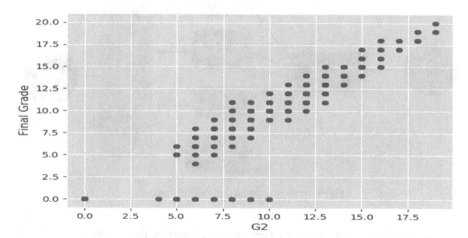

Fig. 8. Final grade against G2.

4.2 Accuracy with Other Models

The aim here is not to deduce the capability of prediction for each model, but to give a simple depiction that outlines the differences in the SL models. Thus, all attributes will be used in this implementation. In Table 5 shows the variance in each model after cross-validation.

Where:

Experiment 1: With all variables except G3.
Experiment 2: Similar to Experiment 1 yet no G2 (the second grade).
Experiment 3: Similar to Experiment 2 yet no G1 (the first grade).
Experiment 4: With all variables.

Table 5. Accuracies of various models on the experiments.

Models	LR	SVM	NN	KNN (=13)
Experiment 1	0.82	0.86	0.89	0.75
Experiment 2	0.89	0.80	0.81	0.73
Experiment 3	0.88	0.75	0.79	0.70
Experiment 4	0.86	0.77	0.81	0.72

The whole data set collected in this research has been split into training (90%) and testing (10%) subsets and Neural Network, LR, Support Vector Machine, and KNN models were built. After applying the cross-validation, the ensemble method combines four machine learning algorithms that were applied in the experiment as shown in Fig. 9.

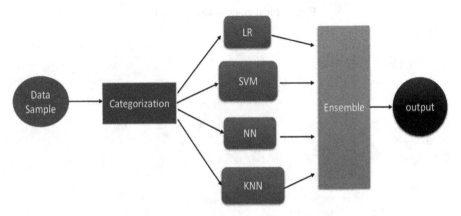

Fig. 9. 90% split prediction ensemble mode.

After models are built, they have been assembled into the final prediction system. It is observed that the data is "almost" linearly separable and good accuracy is obtained using LR. Thus, with the other models used with the given data to predict the accuracy, were still good predictions in contrast to the LR. The distinguishing attributes are still the grades. The used techniques were at that point prepared on the new preparing set acquired by consolidating approval and preparing set utilized in the previous experiment. On assessing the final execution, models were tried on the data, and assessment of the models was finalized by looking at the final results. It is demonstrated in Table 5 that KNN accuracy is low in contrast to other models. Table 5 displays the general significance of each info variable as estimated by the model. To explain the examination, just the four most pertinent models are utilized with 4 experiments. These four models present an overall impact on the whole data. Also, G2 is the feature that is more important for the experiment 1, while G1 is important for the test 2 arrangement. Additionally, the quantity of past disappointments, related to the past performance of students, is a significant factor when student scores are not accessible. In any case, there are other seen factors, for instance, school-related segment, and social factors while thinking about student performance. The K-Nearest Neighbor calculation (k-NN) is the most broadly utilized technique for classifying or regression dependent on nearest records in the element space. It is a sort of case-based learning or lethargic learning approach, where the capacity is just approximated locally and all calculation is conceded until characterization. In k-NN, an item is characterized by a dominant part vote of its neighbors, with the article being relegated to the class generally it is basic among its k closest neighbors. There is no general most ideal decision of k, it differs from information to information and is normally decided through hit and preliminary mode. However, it make limits between classes less unmistakable. We tried different values with various estimations of k including, 1, 3, 5, 7, 9, and 11. The best outcomes is k = 13 and we present them in Table 5 even if it wasn't the best model.

5   Conclusion

Education is a pivotal component in our locale. ML methods permit a high-level method for extricating information from crude information, offering a fascinating chance for areas with regards to the education system. Although, proportionate studies have made use of ML techniques in improving school resource management and the quality of education is enhanced. In this paper, an accomplishment was made in the recognition of patterns and prediction of the student evaluations of two classes by utilizing their past grades, social, segment, and other related information from the school. ML procedures objectives like, Linear Regression, NN and SVM, KNN, were tried. Additionally, explicit info determinations were investigated. The outcomes gotten uncovers that it is practical in accomplishing a high precision of forecast, given that the previous school grades are known. This affirms student achievement is exceptionally influenced by their past exhibitions. In this paper, a methodology was put forth in monitoring and foreseeing the presentation of students in the education framework. The point of the methodology was to get the best precise outcome and the best pattern to be followed for student improvement so that the learning system can be deduced for the institution. However, with the recognition of patterns, we were to determine some factors that will hinder the improvement of student's grades if taken into consideration. Also, there should be a consideration in increasing the experiments capability to more schools so the student databases can be enriched. However, this is with the expectation for the nonlinear function techniques to be of more benefit, since they are more sensitive to inputs that are not irrelevant. Also, more research is to be carried out to get more understanding of why and how some attributes affect the performance of students. This study is said to increase student performance greatly if taken into consideration.

References

1. Minaei-Bidgoli, B., Kashy, D., Kortemeyer, G. Punch, W.: Predicting student performance: an application of data mining methods with an educational web-based system. In Proceedings of of IEEE Frontiers in Education, Colorado, USA, pp. 13–18 (2003)

2. Pritchard, M., Wilson, S.: Using emotional and social factors to predict student success. J. Coll. Stud. Dev. **44**(1), 18–28 (2003)
3. Aud, S., Nachazel, T., Wilkinson-flicker, S., Dziuba, A.: The condition of education 2013. Government Printing Office (2013)
4. Callender, C., Feldman, R.: Part-time undergraduates in higher education: a literature review. Prepared for HECSU to inform Future track: part-time students. London, Birkbeck, University of London (2009)
5. Macdonald, I.: Meeting the needs of non-traditional students: challenge or opportunity for higher education. Scott. J. Adult Educ. **1**(2), 34–46 (1992)
6. Visvizi, A., Lytras, M.D., Daniela, L.: Education, innovation and the prospect of sustainable growth and development. In: The Future of Innovation and Technology in Education: Policies and Practices for Teaching and Learning Excellence; Emerald Publishing Limited: Bingley, UK, pp. 297–305 (2018)
7. Jin, J., Sun, W., Al-Turjman, F., Khan, M., Yang, X.: Activity pattern mining for healthcare. IEEE Access **8**(1), 56730–56738 (2020)
8. Ullah, Z., Al-Turjman, F., Mostarda, L., Gagliardi, R.: Applications of artificial intelligence and machine learning in smart cities. Comput. Commun. J. **154**, 313–323 (2020)
9. Al-Turjman, F., Baali, I.: Machine learning for wearable IoT-based applications: a survey. Wiley Trans. Emerg. Telecommun. Technol. (2019). https://doi.org/10.1002/ett.3635
10. Hussain, A.A., Bouachir, O., Al-Turjman, F., Aloqaily, M.: AI techniques for COVID-19. IEEE Access **8**, 128776–128795 (2020). https://doi.org/10.1109/ACCESS.2020.3007939
11. Casanova, D., Moreira, A., Costa, N.: Technology enhanced learning in higher education: results from the design of a quality evaluation framework. Proc. Soc. Behav. Sci. **29**, 893–902 (2011)
12. Daniela, L., Kalnina, D., Strods, R.: An overview on effectiveness of technology enhanced learning (TEL). Int. J. Knowl. Soc. Res. **8**, 79–91 (2017)
13. Castro, F., Vellido, A., Nebot, A., Mugica, F.: Applying data mining techniques to e-learning problems. In: Jain, L.C., Tedman, R.A., Tedman, D.K. (eds.) Evolution of Teaching and Learning Paradigms in Intelligent Environment, vol. 62, pp. 183–221. Springer, Heidelberg (2007). https://doi.org/10.1007/978-3-540-71974-8_8
14. Villegas-Ch, W., Luján-Mora, S., Buenaño-Fernandez, D., Palacios-Pacheco, X.: Big data, the next step in the evolution of educational data analysis. In: Rocha, Á., Guarda, T. (eds.) ICITS 2018. AISC, vol. 721, pp. 138–147. Springer, Cham (2018). https://doi.org/10.1007/978-3-319-73450-7_14
15. Buenaño-Fernandez, D., Villegas-CH, W., Luján-Mora, S.: The use of tools of data mining to decision making in engineering education. A systematic mapping study. Computer. Appl. Eng. Educ. **27**, 744–758 (2019)
16. Piekarski, M.L.: Student Retention - An issue, a discussion and a way forward. Brittany Cotter Cobek Softw. Ltd. **1**, 29–35 (2013)
17. Márquez-Vera, C., Cano, A., Romero, C., Noaman, A.Y.M., Fardoun, H.M., Ventura, S.: Early dropout prediction using data mining: a case study with high school students. Expert Syst. **33**, 107–124 (2016)
18. Sekeroglu, B., Dimililer, K., Tuncal, K.: Student performance prediction and classification using machine learning algorithms. Student performance prediction and classification using machine learning algorithms. In: Proceedings of the 8th International Conference on Educational and Information Technology, pp. 7–11 (2019)
19. Sekeroglu, b., dimililer, k., tuncal, k.: artificial intelligence in education: application of student performance evaluation. J. Contemp. Dilemmas Educ. Polit. Values **15**(1) (2019)
20. Dimililer, K.: Use of intelligent student mood classification system (ISMCS) to achieve high quality in education. Qual. Quant. **52**(1), 651–662 (2017). https://doi.org/10.1007/s11135-017-0644-y

21. Sin, K., Muthu, L.: Application of big data in education DATA mining and learning analytics—a literature review. ICTACT J. Soft Comput. **5**, 1035–1049 (2015)
22. Lu, O.H., Huang, A.Y., Huang, J.C., Lin, A.J., Ogata, H., Yang, S.J.: Applying learning analytics for the early prediction of students' academic performance in blended learning. Educ. Technol. Soc. **21**, 220–232 (2018)
23. Gil, D., Fernández-Alemán, J., Trujillo, J., García-Mateos, G., Luján-Mora, S., Toval, A.: The effect of Green software: a study of impact factors on the correctness of software. Sustainability **10**, 3471 (2018)
24. Hong, S.J., Weiss, S.M.: Advances in predictive models for data mining. Pattern Recognit. Lett. **22**, 55–61 (2001)
25. Brooks, C., Thompson, C.: Predictive modelling in teaching and learning. In: Lang, C., Siemens, G., Wise, A., Gasevic, D. (eds.) Handbook of Learning Analytics, pp. 61–68. Society for Learning Analytics Research (SoLAR), AnnArbor (2017)
26. Rechkoski, L., Ajanovski, V.V., Mihova, M.: Evaluation of grade prediction using model-based collaborative filtering methods. In: Proceedings of the 2018 IEEE Global Engineering Education Conference (EDUCON), Tenerife, Spain, 17–20 April 2018, pp. 1096–1103, April 2018
27. Bydžovská, H.: Are collaborative filtering methods suitable for student performance prediction? In: Proceedings of the Progress in Artificial Intelligence - 17th Portuguese Conference on Artificial Intelligence (EPIA), Coimbra, Portugal, pp. 425–430, 8–11 September 2015
28. Polyzou, A., Karypis, G.: Grade prediction with models specific to students and courses. Int. J. Data Sci. Anal. **2**, 159–171 (2016). https://doi.org/10.1007/s41060-016-0024-z
29. Thai-Nghe, N., Drumond, L., Krohn-Grimberghe, A., Schmidt-Thieme, L.: Recommender system for predicting student performance. Proc. Comput. Sci. **1**, 2811–2819 (2010)
30. Al-Turjman, F., Deebak, D.: Seamless authentication: for IoT-big data technologies in smart industrial application systems. IEEE Trans. Ind. Inf. (2020). https://doi.org/10.1109/tii.2020.2990741
31. Sedkaoui, S., Khelfaoui, M.: Understand, develop and enhance the learning process with big data. Inf. Discovery. Delivery. **47**, 2–16 (2019)
32. Dahdouh, K., Dakkak, A., Oughdir, L., Ibriz, A.: Large-scale e-learning recommender system based on Spark and Hadoop. J. Big Data **6**(1), 1–23 (2019). https://doi.org/10.1186/s40537-019-0169-4
33. Meier, Y., Xu, J., Atan, O., Van der Schaar, M.: Predicting grades. IEEE Trans. Signal Process. **64**(4), 959–972 (2016)
34. Zimmermann, J., Brodersen, K.H., Heinimann, H.R., Buhmann, J.M.: A model based approach to predicting graduate-level performance using indicators of undergraduate-level performance. JEDM-J. Educ. Data Min. **7**(3), 151–176 (2015)
35. Thai-nghe, N., Drumond, L., Horvath, T., Krohn-grimberghe, A., Nanopoulos, A., Schmidt-thieme, L.: Factorization techniques for predicting student performance. In: Educational Recommender Systems and Technologies: Practices and Challenges, pp. 129–153 (2011)
36. Thai-nghe, N., Drumond, L., Horváth, T., Nanopoulos, A., Schmidt-thieme, L.: Matrix and tensor factorization for predicting student performance. In: CSEDU (1), pp. 69–78. Citeseer (2011)
37. Knowles, J.E.: Of needles and haystacks: Building an accurate state wide dropout early warning system in wisconsin. JEDM-J. Educ. Data Min. **7**(3), 18–67 (2015)
38. Sweeney, M., Lester, J., Rangwala, H.: Next-term student grade prediction. In: 2015 IEEE International Conference on BigData (Big Data), pp. 970–975. IEEE (2015)
39. Elbadrawy, A., Polyzou, A., Ren, Z., Sweeney, M., Karypis, G., Rangwala, H.: Predicting student performance using personalized analytics. Computer **49**(4), 61–69 (2016)

RapidAuth: Fast Authentication
for Sustainable IoT

Muhammad Naveed Aman[1] , Shehzad Ashraf Chaudhry[2](✉) ,
and Fadi Al-Turjman[3,4]

[1] Department of Computer Science, National University of Singapore,
Singapore, Singapore
dcsmnam@nus.edu.sg
[2] Department of Computer Engineering, Faculty of Engineering and Architecture,
Istanbul Gelisim University, Istanbul, Turkey
sashraf@gelisim.edu.tr
[3] Artificial Intelligence Department, Near East University, Nicosia, Mersin 10, Turkey
fadi.alturjman@neu.edu.tr
[4] Research Center for AI and IoT, Near East University, Nicosia, Mersin 10, Turkey

Abstract. The exponential growth in the number of Internet of Things
(IoT) devices, the sensitive nature of data they produce, and the simple
nature of these devices makes IoT systems vulnerable to a wide range
cyber-threats. Physical attacks are one of the major concerns for IoT
device security. Security solutions for the IoT have to be accurate and
quick since many real time applications depend on the data generated
by these devices. In this article, we undertake the IoT authentication
problem by proposing a fast protocol RapidAuth, which also restricts
physical attacks. The proposed protocol uses Physical Unclonable Functions to achieve the security goals and requires the exchange of only two
messages between the server and an IoT device. The analysis of RapidAuth proves its' robustness against various types of attacks as well as
its' efficiency in terms of computation, communication, memory over-
heads and energy consumption.

Keywords: IoT security · Authentication · ProVerif · PUF

1 Introduction

The world has seen an exponential growth in the number of IoT devices. These
devices are envisioned as the enablers of smart cities, smart factories, and smart
healthcare, among others. Many IoT devices are simple and low cost devices generating huge amounts of sensitive data. Moreover, IoT devices often use wireless
interfaces and the Internet to communicate data to a server or data center,
exposing them to a wide range of cyber attacks/threats. Some of the major
security requirements for the correct operation of the IoT based systems include
authentication, secure booting, authorization, data integrity and privacy [1–5].

E. Ever and F. Al-Turjman (Eds.): FoNeS-IoT 2020, LNICST 353, pp. 82–95, 2021.
https://doi.org/10.1007/978-3-030-69431-9_7

Traditionally, security protocols/techniques for the Internet were designed with two major assumptions: (i) any device connected to the Internet is physically well protected, i.e., an adversary may try to launch an attack from a remote location by eavesdropping, tampering, and injecting packets etc. into the network but cannot physically access the device and (ii) the systems connected to the Internet have no limitation of power and memory. However, both of these assumption are no longer valid for the IoT. IoT devices may be deployed in remote location in the field where an adversary can easily gain physical access to the device. Moreover, many IoT devices are constrained in terms of energy, memory, and processing capabilities. Therefore, any security protocol designed for the IoT not only needs to be computationally efficient but must also be secure against physical and side channel attacks [6]. To address these issues, we propose the use of Physical Unclonable Functions (PUFs). PUFs are hardware security primitives that provide a challenge-response mechanism. PUFs exploit the variations in the physical factors during the manufacturing process of integrated circuits (ICs) to produce a unique response when excited with a given challenge. The inherent variability in IC manufacturing makes it practically impossible to clone or replicate a PUF, making them an attractive choice to establish a root of trust in IoT systems.

Elliptic curve cryptography (ECC) has emerged as a cryptographic technique which is not only computationally efficient but also requires shorter keys for the same level of security as compared to traditional crypto-systems [7]. The advent of TinyECC [8] has further made it an attractive choice for security protocols in the IoT. This paper uses ECC to speed up the authentication process and propose an authentication protocol which requires the exchange of only two messages between an IoT device and the server.

1.1 Contributions

In this paper, we tackle the issue of authentication in IoT systems. Following are the major contribution of this work:

1. We propose RapidAuth, a protocol for IoT that achieves mutual authentication of an IoT device and server in the minimum possible number of messages, i.e., the server needs to send and receive only one message to complete authentication.
2. The proposed protocol uses PUFs to eliminate the requirement of any stored secrets on the IoT device, making it secure against physical attacks.
3. The RapidAuth can support in forming a session key without any extra overhead.

1.2 Paper Outline

The rest of the paper is organized as follows: Sects. 2 and 3 present the related work and a brief introduction to PUFs, respectively. Section 4 presents the network model, assumptions, and notations for the system model. We present the proposed RapidAuth in Sect. 5. Sections 7 and 8 present a security and performance analysis of RapidAuth, respectively. Finally, concluding remarks are given in Sect. 9.

2   Related Work

Most of the existing techniques for authentication in IoT systems [9–11] suffer from two major problems. Firstly, they rely on complex computations and secondly, the IoT devices need to store some secrets in their memory. These properties make them inapt for IoT devices.

PUFs as the hardware security primitives are proposed in [1] to be used in IoT devices for high optimization. The existing literature on authentication for RFID and wireless sensor networks using PUFs include [12–14]. However, these techniques also rely on some initial secrets stored in the memory of communicating device; while theses secrets are vulnerable to physical attacks. Moreover, the exisitng methods [12–14] lose the efficiency due to communication extensive and time consuming challenge-response pairs (CRPs) for each device at the server making them non-scalable.

One of the most relevant protocols in literature for our work is [15], which used zero-knowledge proof of knowledge (ZKPK) to extend physical security in combination with password and PUF. Although protocol [15] does not rely on stored secrets, their technique is undermined by the user password requirement. Moreover, Sect. 8 shows that their technique is not only computationally complex but also has a higher communication overhead.

3   Preliminary Background

PUFs are building blocks of the proposed RapidAuth protocol. Therefore, this sections briefly describes the characteristic of PUFs. A PUF is a noisy function defined through the random variations settled during chip manufacturing and is embedded in a physical circuit [16–18]. A PUF takes a challenge C as the input and produces a unique output R, which is a function of C and physical structure of related circuit, i.e., $R \leftarrow PUF(C)$.

The physical basis of a PUF resists the production of its' physical clone [19]. This property makes them appealing in the field of security to safeguard against invasive or side-channel attacks. PUFs have the following desirable properties [20]:

- Straightforward and easy to construct and evaluate.
- Output is tantamount to a random function.
- The same challenge always produces the same response with high probability. However, the same challenge produces a response differ with high probability with a different PUF.

4   System Models

Following subsections briefly define the network model along with some assumptions made for the environment and the notation guide in Table 1 for the symbols employed in the paper:

4.1   Network Model

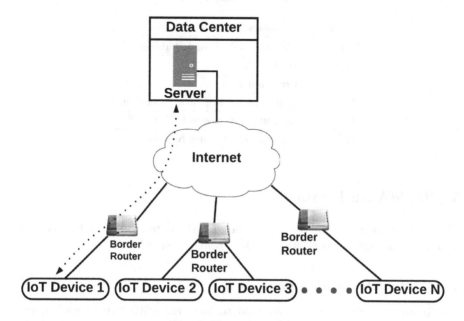

Fig. 1. Network model

The network model is shown in Fig. 1, where the IoT devices are connected to data center through borer router and by the using public internet.

4.2   Assumptions

The following assumptions are made regarding the network model and proposed protocol:

a. Each IoT device has an embedded PUF.
b. The IoT device and the PUF is considered a system-on-chip. A tempering attempt to PUF will render the PUF useless [15].
c. There is a secure channel between microcontroller and PUF within an IoT device and all communication between the both mentioned entities is through the secure channel [22].

d. The data center/server is considered to have unlimited resources and is trusted; whereas, IoT devices have limited energy, memory, and processing capabilities.
e. The adversary is assumed to have capabilities of eavesdropping the communication, injecting new packets and replaying old ones. The adversary can also initiate session or impersonate other users.

Table 1. Notation guide

Notations	Meanings
ID_j	Identity (ID) of the IoT device
$H(X)$	Hash of X
$\|$	Concatenation
C^i	Challenge message in i^{th} iteration
R^i	Output/Response of PUF for C^i
$\{M\}_K$	Encrypting M using K as key

5   RapidAuth Protocol

This section illustrates the proposed RapidAuth protocol designed specifically to provide mutual authentication for IoT systems using PUFs.

5.1   Mutual Authentication

For RapidAuth, the server is assumed to have the CRP pair of each device prior to authentication, added manually or electronically for each IoT device from the manufacturer provided list. Moreover, RapidAuth makes use of elliptic curve cryptography (ECC) and keeping in consideration an elliptic curve C, finite and prime field $\mathbb{F}_q$, where $q = p^n$, an elliptic curve point $G \in C$ an embedding function $m \mapsto E_m$, are publicly available [23]. RapidAuth consists of the following steps:

1. The server generates a nonce N_1 and an integer a randomly and then computes $z_1 = aG$. The server then reads the corresponding CRP (C^i, R^i) for ID_A and sends the ECC challenge z_1, the PUF challenge C^i, and $\{M_1, N_1\}_{R^i}$ along with the respective MAC to the device ID_A.
2. As shown in Fig. 2, the IoT device carries out the following operations after receiving message 1:
   i) Uses its PUF and the challenge C^i to obtain the PUF response R^i.
   ii) Uses R^i to obtain N_1 and verifies the received MAC. If the verification fails, the authentication request is terminated.

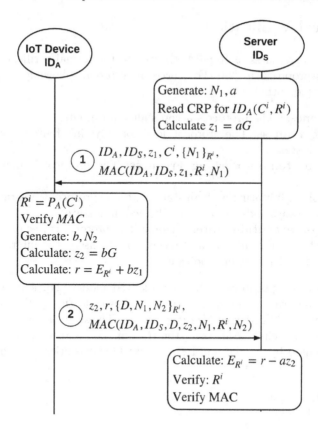

Fig. 2. Authentication phase

iii) Generates b and N_2 randomly.

iv) Calculates $z_2 = bG$ and $r = E_{R^i} + bz_1$, where E_{R^i} is the response of embedding function to R^i.

v) Sends z_2, r, $\{D, N_1, N_2\}_{R^i}$ and the respective MAC in message 2 to the server, as shown in Fig. 2. Note that D is used to represent any data the IoT device ID_A may wish to send to the server.

At the conclusion of the protocol, the server has successfully authenticated the IoT device ID_A and has received data D.

5.2   Session Key Formation

To construct a session key, both the device ID_A and the server can use the secret nonces N_1 and N_2. For example, they may use $H(N_1) \oplus H(N_2)$ as the secret key for the current session. Note that if an adversary somehow succeeds in obtaining the secret key, the system may remain uncompromised, as adversary remains unable to compute R^i as well as the valid data.

6 Protocol Verification

To prove the correctness of RapidAuth, we use the formal verification method for protocols proposed in [24]. For correctness proof, following properties are proved for RapidAuth:

1. **Completeness:** The protocols accepts all valid inputs.
2. **Deadlock freeness:** The protocol does not stays indefinitely and there are no deadlock states.
3. **Livelock or tempo-blocking Freeness:** The protocol is free of infinite loops.
4. **Termination:** Initiating with an start state, the protocol transitions on valid inputs and always ends up in a well-defined final state.
5. **Free of non-executable interactions:** The protocol is free of any interaction except the transmission and reception. Precisely, the interaction paths are followed under normal conditions.

For verification purposes under the adopted model [24], a directed graph for each communicating entity is created as shown in Fig. 3, where g_S and g_A represent server and the device ID_A respectively. The state of a protocol machine is represented by a circle. Moreover, the transmission and reception of message m are represented by -m and +m respectively. One execution of RapidAuth for g_A and g_S is shown below:

- g_A: $[0]$ $+1[1]$ $-2[0]$
- g_S: $[0]$ $-1[1]$ $+2[0]$

The bracket numbers show the state in Fig. 3. The in-sequence events for g_A (ID_A) initiates from state 0, and after receiving message 1 goes to state 1. Now in state 1, g_A (ID_A) sends message 2 and enters in state 0 again. Similar is the in-sequence interpretation of server states against the corresponding events. For both entities, state 0 is initial as well as final state.

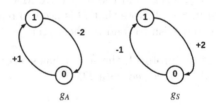

Fig. 3. Directed graph/FSM for RapidAuth

For reachablitiy analysis, we adopted the methods proposed in [24,25]. Here, the system states are represented by a matrix and the state matrix for RapidAuth can be given by:

$$\begin{bmatrix} Server & server \rightarrow A \\ STATE & CHANNEL \\ \\ A \rightarrow server & A \\ CHANNEL & STATE \end{bmatrix}. \tag{1}$$

The elements in the matrix represent the message by the corresponding entity or current state of the finite state machine (FSM) of the same and at initiation, every entity is in its' initial state i.e. state 0 as shown in Fig. 3. Now if server sends message 1 to ID_A, the FSM of the server transitions into state 1. Following is representative state matrix:

$$c\begin{bmatrix} S_1 & 1 \\ E & S_0 \end{bmatrix}. \tag{2}$$

The S_1 at row 1 ($R1$), column 1($C1$) in state representative matrix (2) shows that server state is 1, while 1 at $\{R1, C2\}$ shows that server has sent message 1 to the device (ID_A). Likewise, E at $\{R2, C1\}$ represents that ID_A has not transmitted any message and is currently in state 0 represented by S_0.

The results of the reachability analysis of RapidAuth are shown in Fig. 4, where SSi represents overall system states; whereas, subsystems subsequent states are shown through S_i notations. Furthermore, the sending and receiving of message i by X (server or device) causes a state change, which s represented on corresponding directed arcs as X^{-i} (X^{+i}).

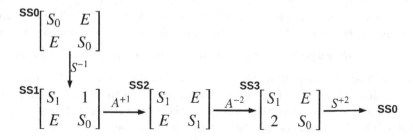

Fig. 4. Reachability analysis for RapidAuth

Figure 4 shows that RapidAuth accepts all valid inputs thereby inferring the completeness property. A potential deadlock state occurs if all channels are empty instead of start or final state. Figure 4 shows that RapidAuth is free of any potential deadlock state, indicating deadlock freeness. Similarly, we observe that RapidAuth does not contain any potential deadlock state and always terminates in state $SS0$, implying deadlock freeness and termination. Moreover, Fig. 4 shows that RapidAuth is free of infinite loops and always transitions on realizable inputs, inferring livelock freeness, and absence of non-executable interactions. Thus, this shows that RapidAuth can be considered correct.

7 Security Analysis

The Mao & Boyd logic [26] is used to provide a formal security analysis of RapidAuth. The readers are referred to [26] for further details of the methodology [26]. For proof purposes, the device ID_A and server ID_S are represented by A and S, respectively. Note that we want to formally prove the authentication goals using the Mao & Boyd logic, i.e, authentication of S to A and A to S [27].

As first step, the idealized version of RapidAuth messages using Mao & Boyd logic is as follow:

1. $S \rightarrow A : S, A, z_1, \{N_1\}_{R^i}$.
2. $A \rightarrow S : z_2 | r\mathbf{R}N_1 | N_2, \{D, N_1\mathbf{R}N_2\}_{R^i}$.

The set of initial assumptions for the RapidAuth is as follows:

1. $A \models A \overset{R^i}{\leftrightarrow} S$ and $S \models A \overset{R^i}{\leftrightarrow} S$: A can generate R^i by giving the correct challenge C^i to its PUF. Similarly,S maintains the database of CRPs for all devices.
2. $A \overset{R^i}{\triangleleft} N_1$: Message 1 in the idealized protocol.
3. $S \overset{R^i}{\triangleleft} N_2$: Message 2 in the idealized protocol.

To prove the authentication properties we can use the set of inference rules given in [26]. The authentication proof is given in Fig. 5a; where, realization of the transmission of N_1 by S verifies the authentication of S to A To prove this, the statement we intend to prove is written in the bottom i.e., $A \models S \overset{R^i}{\hspace{-0.3em}\sim} N_1$ which represents the claim that "A believes S sent N_1 using R^i". The next rule that is applied is the authentication [26]. This rule states that S sent N_1 if it can be proven that R^i is a good secret key between A and S, i.e., $A \models A \overset{R^i}{\leftrightarrow} S$ and that A has obtained N_1 using R^i as the decryption key, i.e., $A \overset{R^i}{\triangleleft} N_1$. The circles in Fig. 5a indicate that both of these statement are part of the initial assumptions. Thus, this establishes the authentication of the server to the IoT device ID_A. Similarly, Fig. 5b shows the tableau for the proof of the authentication of IoT device ID_A to the server.

7.1 Elliptic Curve Cryptography Security

RapidAuth uses ECC for mutual authentication between the IoT device and the server. The proposed scheme can be compromised by an attacker if he/she can extract a or b from the ECC parameters i.e., z_1, z_2, and r. Thus, the attacker has to solve the discrete logarithm problem (DLP) based on elliptic curve denoted as ECDLP:

Definition 7.1. *Let $\mathcal{C}$ be an elliptic curve defined over $\mathbb{F}_q$ with P_1, $P_2 \in \mathcal{C}$ (EC points), then the ECDLP problem is to find an integer r such that $P_2 = rP_1$.*

$$\frac{A \models A \overset{R^i}{\leftrightarrow} S \wedge A \overset{R^i}{\vartriangleleft} N_1}{A \models S \overset{R^i}{|\sim} N_1}$$

(a) **A** believes **S** sent N_1 using R^i as the encryption key" (S to A proof)

$$\frac{A \models A \overset{R^i}{\leftrightarrow} S \wedge S \overset{R^i}{\vartriangleleft} N_2}{S \models A \overset{R^i}{|\sim} N_2}$$

(b) **S** believes **A** sent N_2 using R^i as the encryption key" (A to S proof)

Fig. 5. Authentication proofs

The ECDLP problem is believed to be harder than the general DLP. Therefore, the attacker needs to solve an intractable puzzle where-as the IoT device only requires simple arithmetic operations (e.g.. addition/subtraction). Apart from computational efficiency, the key lengths for ECC are much shorter than contemporary crypto-systems for the same level of security. Moreover, shorter keys can in turn also reduce the consumption of crucial resources such as power and bandwidth.

7.2 Cloning and Physical Attacks

RapidAuth uses PUFs to safeguard against cloning attacks. It has been shown that every PUF outputs a unique value and it is a hard problem to clone a PUF [18]. As IoT devices may be deployed at locations that are easily accessible to an adversary, it is desirable that these devices do not reveal any secrets even if an adversary has physical access to them. Most of the existing PUF based authentication protocols discussed in Sect. 2 require the IoT device to store some private key and/or other secrets, which makes them vulnerable to physical attacks. However, RapidAuth does not store any secrets in the IoT device. Moreover, as the PUF and the device's microcontroller are assumed to be a SOC, therefore, an adversary cannot listen to the communication between the PUF and the chip [21]. This shows that physical attacks are rendered useless in RapidAuth.

8 Performance Analysis

This section presents a comparative analysis of the performance of RapidAuth and the existing relevant protocol proposed by Frikken et al. [15], keeping into consideration the metrics consisting of computation, communication costs and verification delays.

8.1   Computational Complexity

The computational complexity as illustrated in Table 2, consists of the basic operations and their frequency involved in completion of authentication process; the basic operations include: hash (N_H), MAC (N_{MAC}), encryption/decryption (N_{ENC}), modular exponentiation (N_{exp}), modular multiplication ($N_\times$), point addition (N_{ECC_+}) and point multiplication ($N_{ECC_\times}$). For proposed scheme, these values can be directly obtained from Fig. 2 by analyzing the basic operation involved and their number of occurrences.

Table 2. Computational complexity

Scheme	IoT device	Server
RapidAuth	$1N_{MAC} + 1N_{ENC} + 1N_{ECC_+} + 1N_{ECC_\times}$	$1N_{MAC} + 1N_{ENC} + 1N_{ECC_\times}$
[15]	$2N_H + 2N_{exp} + N_\times + 2N_{MAC}$	$1N_H + 3N_{exp} + 1N_{MAC}$

The universal hashing based MAC (UMACS) [28] with $O(n)$ as worst case running time for input size n [29,30], is kept in consideration for comparison purposes. For block ciphers, the time complexity is also $O(n)$; whereas, for m bit field size the complexities of ECC addition and multiplication are $O(m^k)$ and $O(m^{k+1})$, respectively, where $k = 1.585$ by following the results presented in [32]. Therefore, time complexity of RapidAuth for both ID_A and S can be shown as $O(n + m^{k+1})$. We assume MACs based on universal hashing (UMACS) [28] with $O(n)$ as that have a worst case time complexity of $O(n)$ [29,30] for a message size n; while the complexity of the protocol presented in [15] can be given by $O(n + M(l)k)$ for both entities, as [15] used modular exponentiation; where, k represents exponent and l represent the key size (bit operands) [31]. Note that the key size for [15] is at least 5 orders of magnitude larger than the field size of ECC used in RapidAuth [7]. This shows that the computation complexity of RapidAuth is significantly lower than [15].

Table 3. Parameter lengths

Parameter	Size (bits)
ID	8 [33]
N_1, N_2	48 [34]
C, R	128 [35]
MAC	128 [28]

8.2   Communication Overhead

To compute the communication overhead incurred in proposed and related scheme [15], we consider the parameter sizes as shown in Table 3. Referring Table 3, for encryption/decryption, the block cipher (e.g.. CLEFIA) with length 128-bits is considered [35]. UMAC has also same 128-bit length [28]. Therefore, the length of message 1 is 60-byte (480-bits) and size of message 2 is 68-byte (544-bits). Message 1 is longer and has byte length less than a single transmission unit with length 128-bytes in 6LowPAN [36]. Therefore, RapidAuth takes acquires single transmission unit for each message (message 1 and 2); whereas, the protocol in [15] completes the process in 3 transmission units. His shows that RapidAuth has higher communication efficiency due to transmission of less messages.

8.3   Verification Delay

As evident from the previous discussion, RapidAuth is not only offers computational efficiency but also has a lower communication overhead. Moreover, unlike most authentication protocols which require the exchange of at-least three messages, RapidAuth requires only two messages to complete authentication. Note that a PUF has extremely high throughput with a negligible delay [13]. Thus, this shows that RapidAuth can significantly reduce the delay of authentication and is fast enough to be used in real time applications with strict timing delay requirements.

9   Conclusions

In this paper, we presented a novel protocol RapidAuth to extend authentication between a server and an IoT device. RapidAuth uses ECC to complete mutual authentication by the exchange of only two messages between the server and a device. Moreover, RapidAuth employs PUFs as hardware security primitives and does not store any secret parameter in device memory to restrict physical attacks. RapidAuth can also be used for authenticated key exchange for establishing session keys. We showed that RapidAuth is not only robust against various types of attacks including physical attacks but is also efficient enough for simple and low cost IoT devices.

References

1. Aman, M.N., Chua, K.C., Sikdar, B.: Physically secure mutual authentication for IoT. In: Proceedings of IEEE Conference on Dependable and Secure Computing, Taipei, pp. 310–317 (2017). https://doi.org/10.1109/DESEC.2017.8073853
2. Aman, M.N., et al.: HAtt: hybrid remote attestation for the internet of things with high availability. IEEE Internet Things J. **7**(8), 7220–7233 (2020). https://doi.org/10.1109/JIOT.2020.2983655

3. Kamal, M., Tariq, M.: Light-weight security and blockchain based provenance for advanced metering infrastructure. IEEE Access **7**, 87345–87356 (2019). https://doi.org/10.1109/ACCESS.2019.2925787

4. Chaudhry, S.A., Yahya, K., Al-Turjman, F., Yang, M.: A secure and reliable device access control scheme for IoT based sensor cloud systems. IEEE Access **8**, 139244–139254 (2020). https://doi.org/10.1109/ACCESS.2020.3012121

5. Chaudhry, S.A., Shon, T., Al-Turjman, F., Alsharif, M.H.: Correcting design flaws: an improved and cloud assisted key agreement scheme in cyber physical systems. Comput. Commun. **153**, 527–537 (2020). https://doi.org/10.1016/j.comcom.2020.02.025

6. Aman, M.N., Sikdar, B.: ATT-auth: a hybrid protocol for industrial IoT attestation with authentication. IEEE Internet Things J. **5**(6), 5119–5131 (2018). https://doi.org/10.1109/JIOT.2018.2866623

7. Kerry, C.F.: Digital signature standard (DSS). National Institute of Standards and Technology (2013)

8. Liu, A., Ning, P.: TinyECC: a configurable library for elliptic curve cryptography in wireless sensor networks. In: Proceedings of IPSN, SPOTS Track, pp. 245–256, April 2008)

9. Shivraj, V., et al.: One time password authentication scheme based on elliptic curves for Internet of Things (IoT). In: Proceedings of NSITNSW, Riyadh, KSA, pp. 1–6, February 2015

10. Porambage, P., et al.: Two-phase authentication protocol for wireless sensor networks in distributed IoT applications. In: Proceedings of IEEE WCNC, Istanbul, Turkey, pp. 2728–2733, April 2014

11. Kim, Y., et al.: DAoT: dynamic and energy-aware authentication for smart home appliances in internet of things. In: Proceedings of IEEE ICCE, Las Vegas, NV, pp. 196–197, January 2015

12. Suh, G.E., Devadas, S.: Physical unclonable functions for device authentication and secret key generation. In: Proceedings of IEEE/ACM DAC, San Diego, CA, pp. 9–14, June 2007

13. Cotese, P., et al.: Bernardo, efficient and practical authentication of PUF-based rfid tags in supply chains. In: Proceedings of IEEE RFIDTA, Guangzhou, China, pp. 182–188, June 2010

14. Lee, Y.S., et al.: Mutual authentication in wireless body sensor networks (WBSN) based on physical unclonable function (PUF). In: Proceedings of IEEE IWCMC, Sardinia, Italy, pp. 1314–1318, July 2013

15. Frikken, K.B., Blanton, M., Atallah, M.J.: Robust authentication using physically unclonable functions. In: Samarati, P., Yung, M., Martinelli, F., Ardagna, C.A. (eds.) ISC 2009. LNCS, vol. 5735, pp. 262–277. Springer, Heidelberg (2009). https://doi.org/10.1007/978-3-642-04474-8_22

16. Aman, M.N., Sikdar, B., Chua, K.C., Ali, A.: Low power data integrity in IoT systems. IEEE Internet Things J. **5**(4), 3102–3113 (2018). https://doi.org/10.1109/JIOT.2018.2833206

17. Kamal, M., Tariq, S.: Light-weight security and data provenance for multi-hop internet of things. IEEE Access **6**, 34439–34448 (2018). https://doi.org/10.1109/ACCESS.2018.2850821

18. Aman, M.N., Basheer, M.H., Sikdar, B.: Two-factor authentication for IoT with location information. IEEE Internet Things J. **6**(2), 3335–3351 (2019). https://doi.org/10.1109/JIOT.2018.2882610

19. Bohm, C., Hofer, M.: Physical Unclonable Functions in Theory and Practice. Springer, Heidelberg (2012). https://doi.org/10.1007/978-1-4614-5040-5

20. Aman, M.N., Basheer, M.H., Sikdar, B.: Data provenance for IoT with light weight authentication and privacy preservation. IEEE Internet Things J. **6**(6), 10441–10457 (2019). https://doi.org/10.1109/JIOT.2019.2939286
21. Guilley, S., Pacalet, R.: SoCs security: a war against side-channels. Ann. Telecommun. **59**(7), 998–1009 (2004)
22. Aman, M.N., Basheer, M.H., Sikdar, B.: A lightweight protocol for secure data provenance in the internet of things using wireless fingerprints. IEEE Syst. J. https://doi.org/10.1109/JSYST.2020.3000269
23. Hankerson, D., et al.: Guide to Elliptic Curve Cryptography, 1st edn. Springer, Heidelberg (2010)
24. Sidhu, D.P.: Authentication protocols for computer networks: I. Comput. Netw. ISDN Syst. **11**, 287–310 (1986)
25. Varadharajan, V.: Verification of network security protocols. Comput. Secur. **8**(8), 693–708 (1989)
26. Mao, W., Boyd, C.: Towards formal analysis of security protocols. In: Proceedings of Computer Security Foundations Workshop VI, pp. 147–158 (1993)
27. Aman, M.N., Chua, K.C., Sikdar, B.: Mutual authentication in IoT systems using physical unclonable functions. IEEE Internet Things J. **4**(5), 1327–1340 (2017). https://doi.org/10.1109/JIOT.2017.2703088
28. Krovetz, T.: UMAC: message authentication code using universal hashing. IETF RFC 4418, March 2006
29. Babka, M.: Properties of universal hashing. Charles University in Prague, Master thesis (2010)
30. Mansour, Y., et al.: The computational complexity of universal hashing. Theoret. Comput. Sci. **107**(1), 121–133 (1993)
31. Kivinen, T., Kojo, M.: More modular exponential (MODP) Diffie-Hellman groups for internet key exchange (IKE). IETF RFC 3526, May 2003
32. Karatsuba, A.: The complexity of computations. In: Proceedings of the Steklov Institute of Mathematics, vol. 211, pp. 169–183 (1995)
33. Kim, P.: IoT specific IPv6 stateless address autoconfiguration with modified EUI-64. IETF Internet-Draft, July 2015
34. Whiting, D., et al.: Counter with CBC-MAC (CCM). IETF RFC 3610, September 2003
35. Katagi, M., Moriai, S.: The 128-bit blockcipher CLEFIA. IETF RFC 6114, March 2011
36. Montenegro, G., et al.: Transmission of IPv6 packets over IEEE 802.15.4 networks. IETF RFC 4944, September 2007

Analysis of Machine Learning Techniques for Lightweight DDoS Attack Detection on IoT Networks

Eric McCullough[(✉)], Razib Iqbal, and Ajay Katangur

Missouri State University, Springfield, MO 65897, USA
eric96@live.missouristate.edu, {riqbal,
ajaykatangur}@missourisate.edu

Abstract. As botnet style distributed denial of service (DDoS) attacks continue to proliferate the Internet of Things (IoT) landscape, researchers have struggled to provide a definitive way of addressing concerns related to the IoT's security. In this paper, we work from the axiom that DDoS attacks are easiest to detect at the target of the attack but are best mitigated closer to the attacker by implementing four machine learning models that detect botnet-infected DDoS attackers on their access network. These models operate on network packet counts, which can easily be gathered by an access router, and run in real-time or near real-time, even on a low power device, namely a Raspberry Pi. We introduce a novel method for visualizing network activity as graphical heatmaps and use convolutional neural network (CNN) models designed for embedded devices and mobile platforms to classify network traffic as benign or malicious. We compare this approach using a support vector machine (SVM) and a long short-term memory recurrent neural network (LSTM). Based on our results, we conclude that the use of lightweight CNNs to analyze network traffic through graphical heatmaps provides highly accurate botnet-based DDoS attack detection for IoT access networks, with an average accuracy of 99.8%, despite our training dataset being between $73\times-2170\times$ smaller than those seen in related works, and runtimes ranging from 334 ms to 2 s on a Raspberry Pi.

Keywords: Convolutional neural networks · Deep learning · Distributed denial of service attacks · IoT security · LSTM · Support vector machines

1 Introduction

Internet of Things Devices (IoTDs) are often characterized by their limited computational resources. For the first time in the relatively short history of the field, security experts are having to work toward securing devices less powerful than their predecessors, all while these connected IoTDs are causing network sizes to grow immensely. As a consequence, modern security practices and procedures as used in the modern Internet cannot be applied here. In an effort to address these mounting concerns, researchers are faced with

© ICST Institute for Computer Sciences, Social Informatics and Telecommunications Engineering 2021
Published by Springer Nature Switzerland AG 2021. All Rights Reserved
E. Ever and F. Al-Turjman (Eds.): FoNeS-IoT 2020, LNICST 353, pp. 96–110, 2021.
https://doi.org/10.1007/978-3-030-69431-9_8

the task of providing an acceptable level of security to the IoT that is dependable and suited to its unique technological landscape.

As the authors of [1] highlight, many researchers have turned to deep learning as a method of achieving IoT security. Deep learning's state-of-the-art results across machine learning domains and excellence at processing large quantities of data with little feature engineering make it a promising candidate for network security applications, as they provide a low cost to the access router in terms of gathering and computing metrics for a model to operate on. However, the use of deep learning is not without its shortcomings. The authors in [2] explain that IoTDs are often too power constrained to effectively carry out deep learning on their own but the latency introduced by offloading the work to a cloud-based server is unacceptable in many time-sensitive applications.

To address these concerns, in this paper, we present an DDoS attack detection system which gathers ingressing and egressing packet counts for each host on the network, so that a standard access router will not be overly burdened by data collection, from an IoT access network and presents it to lightweight machine learning models for analysis. The novelty of our proposed approach is in representing network traffic in a given window of time as a graphical heatmap and utilizing lightweight CNNs to label the heatmap as representing normal or malicious traffic. We compare the performance of lightweight CNNs using graphical heatmaps with SVMs and LSTMs in terms of accuracy and processing time on a Raspberry Pi.

The rest of the paper is organized as follows: previous approaches for attack detection in IoT using deep learning techniques as well as architectures for deploying scalable and decentralized attack detection systems are explored in Sect. 2. Our novel approach of producing visual representations of network traffic in a given period of time and utilizing lightweight CNN image classifiers to detect malicious activity on IoT networks presented in Sect. 3 along with our implementation details. In Sect. 4, we present our experimental results. Finally, in Sect. 5 we explore directions for future work and present our concluding remarks.

2 Related Works

Diro and Chilamkurti presented a deep learning approach to IoT security in [3]. They posited that deep learning would be effective in safeguarding against the large number of derivative zero-day attacks seen in the IoT which are merely small variations of previously encountered attacks. Additionally, the authors proposed a method of bringing their detection model closer to the ground by distributing it across multiple fog layer nodes. This would ensure that internet latency would not render their system ineffective while sidestepping the difficulties of deploying their system directly to IoTDs. To test their approach, Diro and Chilamkurti used 1-to-n encoding to transform instances from the NSL-KDD dataset into input to their deep neural network. The authors then trained and tested their network, achieving results in excess of 99% accuracy. Diro and Chilamkurti's work stands out from their peers in terms of their detailed analysis of their method's detection performance outside of accuracy alone. The authors also provided their network's detection rates, false alarm rates, precision, recall, and F1 score, all of which provide valuable information for comparing their approach to others. Their work is also notable in that they keep their detection mechanism close to the network edge; however, the work presented by Diro and Chilamkurti lacks design decisions around targeting deployment on edge devices and does not show that their approach would remain effective in such environments.

McDermott, Majdani, and Petrovski explored the application of using deep learning to detecting botnet-style DDoS attacks, such as Mirai, where DDoS attacks are launched from compromised IoT devices in [4]. They deployed Mirai against a testbed of IoTDs and used the resulting data to develop a method of transforming captured packets from a string to a neural network input vector using word embedding. The authors then leveraged a bidirectional long short-term memory recurrent neural network to achieve highly accurate results in identifying traffic from botnet infected IoTDs. McDermott, Majdani, and Petrovski compared their bi-directional LSTM to a traditional LSTM and found that it achieved slightly higher accuracy; however, the authors only provided their performance metrics in terms of accuracy alone, so we are unsure how their approach compares to other works in terms of metrics such as false alarm rate and precision. Similar to Diro and Chilamkurti, McDermott, Majdani, and Petrovski's work does not show that their proposed solution would remain viable on edge devices.

Similarly, Median et al. took on the challenge of securing against botnet style attacks in [5]. Unlike [3] and [4], the authors utilized an unsupervised approach by training autoencoders on normal traffic data that could serve as anomaly detectors. In their approach, each IoTD would have a deep autoencoder responsible for differentiating between normal and suspicious traffic. In experimental tests, this approach also achieved a high degree of accuracy. It achieved a very promising detection rate of 100%, a low average false alarm rate of 0.007, and a low detection time of 174 ms with a standard deviation of 212 ms. Unfortunately, this solution requires training a different model for each host on a network, making it infeasible for real world deployment.

In contrast to the previous works, Bhardwaj, Miranda, and Gavrilovska sought to use edge computing to detect and mitigate DDoS attacks in [6]. Their work was largely based on the principle that detection is most effective when deployed close to the victim's access link whereas mitigation is best carried out close to the attack source. In the case of botnet style IoT DDoS attacks, deploying the detection and mitigation scheme to the network edge accomplishes both of these goals simultaneously. The authors forewent deep learning methods in favor of lighter weight approaches due to the resource constraints present in edge level devices and achieved a very low detection latency. However, they were unable to provide data on the detection accuracy of their approach, so we cannot be certain how their work compares to others in that regard.

A similar idea was explored by Bhunia and Gurusamy in [7], who leveraged the emerging concept of software defined networking to achieve attack detection and mitigation. Utilizing the power provided by the control plane, the authors were able to apply more powerful techniques than in [6], specifically a support vector machine, while still remaining close to the network edge for the purposes of attack detection and mitigation. The most compelling aspect of Bhunia and Gurusamy's work is that they utilized an SVM as opposed to more cutting-edge machine learning approaches. SVM's are far less computationally complex than deep learning models, meaning that they would provide detection at a much lower overhead than deep learning approaches. If SVMs can perform the task of network traffic classification with acceptable accuracy, they could prove to be the idea learning model for this domain; however, emerging deep learning techniques may render the increased efficiency of SVMs irrelevant.

Several researchers have attempted to reduce the computational cost of deep learning and make them deployable to mobile platforms and embedded systems. The results of their efforts are known as lightweight models. Two in particular have risen to prominence for their effectiveness on low power devices are SqueezeNet [8] and MobileNet [9].

SqueezeNet, introduced by Iandola et al. in [8], sought to design a compressed AlexNet style convolutional neural network suitable for embedded systems and FPGAs. The outcome of their effort was a CNN that used $50\times$ fewer parameters and took up $510\times$ less memory than AlexNet without sacrificing accuracy.

MobileNet, as seen in [9], is a family of deep learning models designed with mobile platforms, such as cellphones, in mind. It leverages novel deep learning features to achieve $200\times$ less computations with $10\times$ fewer parameters than YOLOv2.

Motivated by the advancements seen in SqueezeNet and MobileNet, we utilize these models to analyze network traffic through a novel method presented in Sect. 3. In doing so, we hope to achieve the high degree of accuracy seen by other deep learning approaches without sacrificing runtime efficiency. We utilize SVMs as seen in Bhunia and Gurusamy's work to compare our approach with an extremely efficient learning model. Motivated by McDermott, Majdani, and Petrovski, we also compare our approach with an LSTM; however, in order to prioritize computational efficiency, we utilize a single-directional LSTM as opposed to a bi-direction LSTM, which only achieved slightly better results in their work. Finally, inspired by Diro and Chilamkurti's excellent analysis of their model's performance, we will utilize their accuracy metrics when comparing these four models.

3 Proposed Approach and Implementation

Bringing the aforementioned concepts together, we hypothesize that a system can be created to accurately detect DDoS attacks against an IoT network that can operate on the network edges. As illustrated in Fig. 1, it consists of two main components: a data aggregation module and a machine learning network traffic classification module. The data aggregation module counts the number of packets sent and received by each host on the network across a predefined interval of time. The network traffic classification module labels aggregated network traffic as either normal traffic or attack traffic and transmits this information back to the access router so that steps toward mitigating any ongoing attacks could be taken.

Both of the lightweight CNN models we use were originally designed as image classifiers and therefore expect an input matrix representing a 255×255 image with 3 color channels. We introduce the new concept of representing traffic on the network in a period of time as a graphical heatmap, as seen in Figs. 2 and 3. Each row of the graph represents the amount of traffic as measured in packets sent and received by a device on the network in the window of time. The first column represents the volume of packets received by the device and the second column represents the volume of packets the device sent. Darker colors represent lower amounts of traffic, with black representing a device

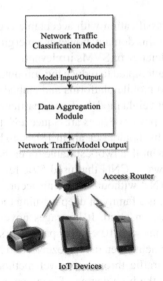

Fig. 1. Proposed system design.

which sent or received nearly no traffic over the network in the time frame, and purple and blue representing gradually increasing amounts of traffic respectively. Brighter colors represent higher amounts of traffic with red, orange, and white representing increasing amounts of traffic. Extraneous visual information that would not be useful to the models, namely the y-axis labels, was then removed.

Fig. 2. An example heatmap used to train the CNN models.

In order to ascertain the effectiveness of our proposed system, we selected a dataset to simulate real-time traffic. Our selected dataset is the Bot IoT dataset created by Koroniotis et al. [10]. It contains network flow CSVs of a simulated IoT network. The authors of the dataset gathered network flow statistics from their simulated network under several types of botnet-style attacks, which can be categorized into roughly three categories: data theft, probing attacks, and denial of service attacks [10]. The denial of service attacks category includes single-source DoS and DDoS attacks taking place over UDP, TCP, and HTTP. Seeing as Botnet based denial of service attacks are usually distributed and rarely single origin, we focused on the DDoS attack examples. According to Wang,

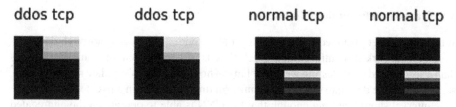

Fig. 3. An example image training batch used to train the CNN models.

Mohaisen, Chang, and Chen's extensive analysis of botnet-based DDoS attacks, the overwhelming majority are carried out with the HTTP, TCP, and UDP communication protocols, therefore we elected to use all DDoS subclasses available in the dataset for training and comparison [11].

To simulate this system, we implement a pipeline from dataset to model that formats the data such that it represents traffic from a small interval of time on an IoT network and creates an input appropriate for a given machine learning model. This data pipeline is illustrated in Fig. 4. First, the data is split into discrete time intervals by a Data Transformation Module. Then, a Dataset Factory formats that data into input appropriate for each model under consideration and splits it into a training, testing, and, where applicable, cross-validation dataset. We describe each component of this simulation in the following subsections.

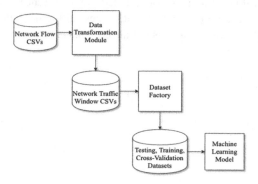

Fig. 4. Testbed data pipeline

3.1 Data Transformation Module

While the dataset provided by Koroniotis et al. provides useful and thorough data, it is stored as network flow information. Each flow is of variable length, some lasting less than a second and some lasting well over half an hour. In order to simulate real-time data, we separated the data into discrete and uniform time intervals. In a live deployment, the time interval should be long enough that the CNN is able to operate on the aggregated data, but short enough as to minimize the delay from the beginning of an attack to its detection. According to the Botnet characteristic analysis in [11], botnet-based DDoS attacks usually last between 6–7 min, 20–40 min, or 2–3 h. To allow for early detection even on the low end of these distributions, we use an interval of 20 s.

To extract the number of packets sent and received by each device in a frame of time, we first select all flows matching a specific target class, for example DDoS TCP traffic, and sort them by the flows' start time. We use the earliest start time available in the list of flows and use it as the beginning time for each frame. We then iterate over each flow and determine if its start and end times are contained within the current frame. If this is true, we add the flow's source address and the total number of source to destination and destination to source packets to the current frame. If the flow begins in the current window, but extends past the end of the current frame, we calculate the total percentage of the flow which occurs in the current frame and add that percentage of the packet counts the current frame and create a new flow with a start time corresponding with the ending time of the current frame, the original flow's ending time, and packet counts equal to the original flow's minus the ones added to the current frame. Once a flow is encountered with a start time past the current frames ending time, the current frame is considered complete and a new frame is initialized. This is expressed in pseudo code in Algorithm 1.

Algorithm 1: Transforming network flows into traffic frames of uniform length

```
Input: Array of flows sorted by start time
current_frame = []
frame_start = flows[0].start_time
frame.end = frame_start + frame_length
for each flow in flows do
  if startsAndEndsInFrame(flow) then
    current_frame.append(flow)
  if startsInFrameEndsAfter(flow) then
    percent_in_frame = findOverlap(flow, frame_start,
      frame_end)
    // Packets sent in current frame
    src_pckts_in = flow.src_pkts * percent_in_frame
    dst_pckts_in = flow.dst_pkts * percent_in_frame
    // Packets sent after current frame
    src_pckts_out = flow.src_pkts * (1-percent_in_frame)
    dst_pckts_out = flow.dst_pkts * (1-percent_in_frame)
    // Make flow containing data outside current frame
    newFlow = newFlow(flow.addr, src_pckts_out,
      dst_pckts_out)
    flows.insert(newFlow)
    flow.src_pckts = flow.src_pckts_in
    flow.dst_pckts = flow.dst_pckts_in
    current_frame.append(flow)
  else
    write(current_frame)
    current_frame = []
    frame_start = frame_end
    frame_end += frame_length
  end if
end for
```

3.2 Dataset Factory

The dataset factory is responsible for taking the network flows generated by the data transformation module and creating datasets compatible with our various machine learning models. To provide the lightweight CNNs the visual data they were designed for, heatmaps as described in Sect. 3 are produced for each network frame. For both the LSTM and SVM, each frame is translated into a one-dimensional array of the sent and received packet counts for each host. This array is of length $2n$, where n is the number of hosts on the network.

We split our data into four distinct datasets: a UDP traffic dataset, a TCP traffic dataset, a TCP and HTTP traffic dataset, and a dataset where all traffic regardless of protocol is separated into two classes (normal vs DDoS). The reasoning behind these datasets is that each protocol exhibits different patterns and characteristics, therefore maintaining and utilizing multiple models for different protocols may be worth the associated cost if it leads to a more accurate detection mechanism. However, if a single general-purpose model is sufficient for detection, the increased efficiency would be ideal. While HTTP is carried over the TCP protocol, the authors of [10] kept them as distinct classes in the BoT IoT dataset. We chose to preserve this distinction in our traffic frame datasets, although they would likely appear identical to a network router, which does not have awareness of application level protocols. Nevertheless, using one dataset of only Koroniotis et al.'s TCP data and comparing it to datasets with their HTTP data included allows us to observe if there are any notable effects on the accuracy of our machine learning algorithms based on this factor.

For the SVMs, each dataset is split in half with 50% of the data being used for testing and training respectively. Similarly, the LSTM and lightweight CNN models also used 50% of their available data for testing; however, only 30% was used for training, leaving 20% of the data to be used as a cross-validation set. To eliminate class bias in the deep learning models, the training set was down sampled to provide roughly even representation between classes. The size and distribution of the testing datasets are given in Table 1. Because the SVM datasets were split evenly, the training dataset sizes were equal to the testing dataset size ±1 sample per class. Table 2 shows the size and distribution of the down sampled training datasets for the deep learning models. There are far fewer training samples for the normal traffic class here due to the dataset being down sampled to provide even representation of each class.

Table 1. Testing datasets description

Dataset	Normal	DDoS
UDP	2037	62
TCP	2030	57
TCP + HTTP	2030	89
All traffic	4067	150

Table 2. LSTM and CNN training dataset description.

Dataset	Normal	DDoS
UDP	36	36
TCP	34	34
TCP + HTTP	53	53
All traffic	89	89

Note that even our largest training set for the deep learning models, the all traffic dataset, only consists of 178 samples. This is over 2,170× smaller than the smallest testing dataset utilized by McDermott, Majdani, and Petrovski in [4], 707× smaller than the dataset utilized by Diro and Chilamkurti in [3], and 73× smaller than the smallest dataset utilized by Meidan et al. in [5].

4 Results

4.1 Model Performance Analysis

Of the sources we discussed in our literature review, Diro and Chilamkurti provided the most detailed analysis of their model's performance; therefore, we utilize their metrics in measuring our networks accuracy. Accuracy is used to measure the overall number of correctly labelled inputs in the testing dataset. Detection ratio (DR) measures the ratio of attack examples correctly labelled (this is particularly useful when the representation of classes in the testing dataset is unbalanced). False alarm rate (FAR) gives a measure of how many examples of benign traffic were labelled as attack traffic. Precision measures how many of the samples labelled as attack traffic are actual attack traffic. Recall measures how often attack traffic was correctly labelled. Finally, because an ideal traffic classifier will balance precision and recall, the F1 score is used to measure how well the network balanced these two metrics.

Given the following values:

- **True Positive (TP):** the number of training examples correctly labelled as attack traffic
- **True Negative (TN):** the number of training examples correctly labelled as benign traffic
- **False Positive (FP):** the number of training examples incorrectly labelled as attack traffic
- **False Negative (FN):** the number of training examples incorrectly labelled as normal traffic

the accuracy metrics listed in the above paragraph can be calculated as follows:

$$Accuracy = \frac{(TP + TN)}{(TP + TN + FP + FN)} \tag{1}$$

$$DR = \frac{TP}{(TP + FN)} \tag{2}$$

$$FAR = \frac{FP}{(TN + FP)} \tag{3}$$

$$Precision = \frac{TP}{(TP + FP)} \tag{4}$$

$$Recall = \frac{TP}{(TP + FN)} \tag{5}$$

$$F1Score = \frac{2TP}{(2TP + FP + FN)} \tag{6}$$

4.2 Accuracy

The results for model accuracy, detection rate, and false alarm rate calculated for each dataset are given in Table 3. Table 4 gives the results for precision, recall, and F1 scores. Table 5 takes the average accuracy, detection rate, false alarm rate, and F1 scores for each model across all datasets to allow for comparison between each model.

Table 3. Accuracy (Acc), detection rate (DR), and false alarm rate (FAR) for each classifier

Model	Dataset	Acc (%)	DR (%)	FAR (%)
SVM	All traffic	99.5	94.0	0.3
	TCP	99.9	98.2	0.0
	TCP + HTTP	99.9	97.8	0.0
	UDP	99.7	90.3	0.0
SqueezeNet	All traffic	99.8	98.7	0.2
	TCP	99.8	98.2	0.1
	TCP + HTTP	97.8	98.9	0.1
	UDP	99.7	100.0	0.3
MobileNet	All traffic	99.8	100.0	0.2
	TCP	99.8	100.0	0.1
	TCP + HTTP	99.9	100.0	0.1
	UDP	99.7	100.0	0.3
LSTM	All traffic	99.7	97.4	0.2
	TCP	99.9	100.0	0.1
	TCP + HTTP	99.8	98.9	0.1
	UDP	99.9	96.8	0.0

Table 4. Precision, recall, and F1 Scores for each classifier

Model	Dataset	Precision (%)	Recall (%)	F1 Score (%)
SVM	All traffic	91.0	94.0	92.5
	TCP	100.0	98.2	99.1
	TCP + HTTP	100.0	97.8	98.9
	UDP	100.0	90.3	94.9
SqueezeNet	All traffic	95.5	98.7	97.1
	TCP	94.9	98.2	96.6
	TCP + HTTP	97.8	98.9	98.3
	UDP	91.2	100.0	95.4
MobileNet	All traffic	95.0	100.0	97.4
	TCP	96.6	100.0	98.3
	TCP + HTTP	97.8	100.0	98.9
	UDP	89.9	100.0	94.7
LSTM	All traffic	94.8	97.4	96.1
	TCP	96.6	100.0	98.3
	TCP + HTTP	96.7	98.9	97.8
	UDP	98.4	96.8	97.6

Table 5. Average accuracy, detection rate (DR), false alarm rate (FAR), and F1 score for each model

Metric	SVM	SqueezeNet	MobileNet	LSTM
Acc (%)	99.75	99.28	99.80	99.83
DR (%)	95.08	98.95	100.0	98.28
FAR (%)	0.08	0.18	0.18	0.1
F1 Score (%)	96.35	96.85	97.33	97.45

From the above tables, we can see that the SVM performed the worst out of all compared models in terms of detection rate and F1 score. MobileNet outperformed SqueezeNet in every metric except for false accuracy rate, where it got the same score. The LSTM demonstrates slightly better performance in Accuracy, false alarm rate, and F1 score, but it did not achieve MobileNet's perfect detection rate, indicating that MobileNet is the better choice for this task.

4.3 Runtime Performance

To ascertain the performance of our models when running on a resource constrained system, we ran our models on a Raspberry Pi 4 with 4 gigabytes of RAM and 1.5 gigahertz processor. Table 6 gives the average time to label a traffic frame as normal or malicious taken over 4,219 frames.

The SVM had the fastest processing time of all compared models; however, both SqueezeNet and the LSTM achieved acceptable performance. While MobileNet had the longest runtime, slightly over 2 s, we observe that according to Wang, Mohaisen, Chang, and Chen's work that the majority of botnet-based DDoS attacks take place over one of these three time intervals: 6–7 min, 20–40 min, and 2–3 h [11]. Even on the scale of the smallest interval, 2 s is an insignificant length of time, especially when considering the detection mechanism is constrained to a Raspberry Pi's processing power. Therefore, we conclude that MobileNet remains a strong candidate for botnet-based DDoS attack detection on edge hardware.

Table 6. Model performance on raspberry pi.

Model	Average runtime (seconds)	standard deviation
SVM	0.0003	5.919×10^{-5}
SqueezeNet	0.334	0.053
MobileNet	2.043	0.149
LSTM	0.001	1.011×10^{-4}

5 Conclusion and Future Work

In this paper we presented a system for detecting botnet DDoS attacks originating on an IoT access network. We introduced a novel method of visualizing network traffic as graphical heatmaps and using lightweight CNN models to classify them as representing normal or malicious traffic. The results of our experiments are very promising. Based on the results presented in Sect. 4, we draw the following conclusions:

- Our novel method of utilizing lightweight CNN's trained to classify visual representations of network traffic windows presented in Sect. 3 proved to be highly accurate. MobileNet achieved an average accuracy of 99.8%, exceeding Diro and Chilamkurti's result of 99.2% accuracy in [3], and McDermott, Majdani, and Petrovski's average accuracy of 96.1% in detecting botnet-based DDoS attacks [4].
- Our approach is network based and does not require training a different classifier for each host on the network as seen in Meidan et al.'s work in [5]. This means that our proposed solution has far better scalability for increasing network sizes.
- Our accuracy was achieved on a comparatively tiny dataset, between $73\times$–$2170\times$ smaller than those seen in [3, 4], and [5].

- Our slowest classifier exhibited an average processing time of 2.043 s, while every other model performed in a fraction of a second when run on a Raspberry Pi, showing that these classifiers could operate on access networks without specialized hardware.

For future work, we observed that there are several shortcomings of using a dataset to ascertain the effectiveness of our system. First, the emulated IoT network used to gather the dataset we utilized has the botnet attackers and the attack target on the same network. We understand from the botnet analysis provided in [11] that botnet attackers are usually located far away from their target geospatially to avoid detection. Secondly, in our current work, it is possible for a network frame labelled as a DDoS instance to very closely resemble normal traffic. This is because the overlap between the frame and the DDoS flows in the data transformation module can be very small. If a 20 s frame only has a few milliseconds worth of DDoS traffic, this would be flagged by our analysis model as a false negative, when in reality it only represents a delayed detection. Finally, while SqueezeNet demonstrated far lower processing latency than MobileNet, it failed to match MobileNet in terms of accuracy. Considering the extremely small size of our dataset, it is reasonable to speculate that using an emulated IoT network to gather an expanded training dataset may allow us to train a SqueezeNet classifier with accuracy comparable to MobileNet while retaining its faster runtime. To address these issues, we are now actively working toward the development of an emulated IoT network testbed.

References

1. Al-Garadi, M.A., Mohamed, A., Al-Ali, A., Du, X., Guizani, M.: A survey of machine and deep learning methods for Internet of Things (IoT) security (2018). https://arxiv.org/abs/1807.11023
2. Tang, J., Sun, D., Liu, S., Gaudiot, J.-L.: Enabling deep learning on IoT devices. Computer **50**(10), 92–96 (2017)
3. Diro, A.A., Chilamkurti, N.: Distributed attack detection scheme using deep learning approach for Internet of Things. Future Gener. Comput. Syst. **82**, 761–768 (2018)
4. McDermott, C.D., Majdani, F., Petrovski, A.V.: Botnet detection in the Internet of Things using deep learning approaches. In: 2018 International Joint Conference on Neural Networks (IJCNN), pp. 1–8 (2018)
5. Meidan, Y., et al.: N-BaIoT—network-based detection of IoT Botnet attacks using deep autoencoders. In: IEEE Pervasive Computing, vol. 17, no. 3, pp. 12–22, July–September 2018
6. Bhardwaj, K., Miranda, J.C., Gavrilovska, A.: Towards IoT-DDoS prevention using edge computing. In: Proceedings USENIX Workshop Hot Topics Edge Computing (2018)
7. Bhunia, S.S., Gurusamy, M.: Dynamic·attack detection and mitigation in IoT using SDN. In: 27th International Telecommunication Networks and Applications Conference (ITNAC), pp. 1–6. IEEE (2017)
8. Iandola, F.N., Han, S., Moskewicz, M.W., Ashraf, K., Dally, W.J., Keutzer, K.: Squeezenet: alexnet-level accuracy with 50x fewer parameters and, 0.5mb model size. arXiv:1602.07360, 2016
9. Howard, A.G., et al.: MobileNets: efficient convolutional nueral networks for mobile vision applications. https://arxiv.org/abs/1704.04861, 2017

10. Koroniotis, N., Moustafa, N., Sitnikova, E., Turnbull, B.: Towards the development of realistic botnet dataset in the internet of things for network forensic analytics: bot-IoT dataset. arXiv preprint arXiv:1811.00701, 2018
11. Wang, A., Chang, W., Chen, S., Mohaisen, A.: Delving into internet DDoS attacks by botnets: characterization and analysis. IEEE/ACM Trans. Netw. **26**(6), 2843–2855 (2018)

Light Communication for Controlling Industrial Robots

Fadi Al-Turjman[1,2], Diletta Cacciagrano[3], Leonardo Mostarda[3(✉)],
Mattia Paccamiccio[3], and Zaib Ullah[3]

[1] Artificial Intelligence Department, Near East University, Nicosia, Mersin 10, Turkey
[2] Research Center for AI and IoT, Near East University, Nicosia, Mersin 10, Turkey
`fadi.alturjman@neu.edu.tr`
[3] Computer Science Division, University of Camerino, 62032 Camerino, Italy
{`diletta.cacciagrano,leonardo.mostarda,`
`mattia.paccamiccio,zaibullah.zaibullah`}`@unicam.it`

Abstract. Optical Wireless Communication (OWC) is regarded as an auspicious communication approach that can outperform the existing wireless technology. It utilizes LED lights, whose subtle variation in radiant intensity generate a binary data stream. This is perceived by a photodiode, that converts it to electric signals for further interpretation. This article aims at exploring the use of this emerging technology in order to control wirelessly industrial robots, overcoming the need for wires, especially in environments where radio waves are not working due to environmental factors or not allowed for safety reasons. We performed experiments to ensure the suitability and efficiency of OWC based technology for the aforementioned scope and "in vitro" tests in various Line-of-Sight (LoS) and Non-Line-of-Sight (NLoS) configurations to observe the system throughput and reliability. The technology performance in the "clear LoS" and in the presence of a transparent barrier, were also analyzed.

Keywords: Visible light communication · Optical Wireless Communication · Industrial Robots · Performance

1 Introduction

Autonomous robots are a crucial component of Industry 4.0 [1]. They can be used in order to improve the speed and accuracy of operations, especially in warehousing and manufacturing environments. Robots can work alongside with humans for added efficiency while reducing the employee injury risk in dangerous environments. To date most of the commercially available robots are supported by wired consoles that are used to move the robot during its programming stage while in production its motion is automated. The necessary features that a robot console should have are joint movements, dead-man button, and emergency stop. The dead-man button is a switch that is activated or deactivated if the human

© ICST Institute for Computer Sciences, Social Informatics and Telecommunications Engineering 2021
Published by Springer Nature Switzerland AG 2021. All Rights Reserved
E. Ever and F. Al-Turjman (Eds.): FoNeS-IoT 2020, LNICST 353, pp. 111–128, 2021.
https://doi.org/10.1007/978-3-030-69431-9_9

operator becomes unable, such as through death, loss of consciousness, or being bodily removed from control. The robot is allowed to move until such button is pressed, once it is released the robot is prevented to move, both by stopping the motions and by preventing new motions to start. The emergency stop button is a mushroom-headed red button that, when pressed, will immediately stop the robot. This is typically implemented in a purely hardware fashion in order to have a high reliability. The emergency stop uses a communication line that is separated from the robot manoeuvring communication line. This is done to totally exclude software logic that could impact on the reliability and real-timeness of this critical feature. Although wired consoles can ensure real-time and reliable communication they reduce the operator degree of movement hence efficiency. This is way various wireless console by using Radio Frequency (RF) based solutions have been attempted (e.g., WiFi and Bluetooth). The problem of these solutions is that they fail to operate in many real industrial factories. This can be consequence of harsh signal propagation conditions together with interference with coexisting radio technologies that operate in the same frequency. This may lead to poor network performance or even failures [2]. The contribution of this paper is the application of the OWC technology for wireless manoeuvring of robots in industrial environment.

1.1   Optical Wireless Communication at Glance

OWC is a communication standard that operates in the electromagnetic spectrum of light, which is 1 mm to 10 nm wavelength. A photodiode acts as a receiver while a light source performs as a data transmitter [3,4]. OWC can enhance the data rate capacity of wireless networks, enables energy-efficient communication, and materializes data communication in susceptible environments. OWC is certain to replace the older radio waves based technology due to the highly congested radio spectrum, at least in very localized environments such as supermarkets, offices and industries. Currently various research challenges such as modulation schemes, throughput and advanced networking are being investigated to achieve the highest data rates for next-generation communication [5]. Many OWC-based applications have been developed, including toys, air conditioners, TV remotes controllers, human sensing, vehicle-to-vehicle communication, underwater communication and bar code readers. In the near future, unmanned aerial vehicles (UAVs) will play a significant role in commercial activities and are expected to make use of OWC technologies besides radio frequency technologies for stable, secure and high bandwidth communications [6,7]. The academia and research industry have established the IEEE 802.11bb task group to modify the existing MAC and physical layer according to OWC [8].

2   Paper Contribution

The contribution of this paper is the application of the OWC technology for wireless manoeuvring of robots in industrial environment. To this ending we need to address the following basic questions: (i) would OWC have satisfactory performance in terms of latency, reliability and throughput when compared to wired and RF-based wireless communication?; (ii) will these non functional requirements be satisfied in case of a moving operator?; (iii) how can we implement the dead-man button and emergency stop channel with the highest possible reliability?. In order to answer these questions we performed cautious 'in vitro' experiments to test the latency, reliability and throughput of a prototype OWC system. After successful completion of the 'in vitro' settings we replicated the experiments in real case study scenarios for moving robots inside various farms. Experiments were performed in various LoS and NLoS configurations to observe the system throughput and reliability. The technology performance in the "clear LoS" and in the presence of a transparent barrier, were also analyzed. We also analyzed the use of a pointing system for the link to be kept always in optimal conditions and proposed an additional communication channel for a reliable emergency stop. Our experiments show that OWC based communication can be used for wireless manoeuvring of robots.

This article can be summarised as follows: Sect. 3 presents a review of the most recent and relevant literature, Sect. 4 presents our experimental setup, Sect. 5 provides a detailed analysis of the experimental results and Sect. 6 concludes the article and offers future research directions.

3   Literature Review

In this section we report various case studies where OWC technology has been tested.

OWC Based Vehicle Collision Avoiding System. Intelligent transportation system and vehicles safety are one of primary concerns of smart city projects [9–11]. The researchers in academia and industry are working to develop advanced systems that could drastically minimize the rate of accidents [12–14]. In order to achieve the preceding goal, OWC has been proposed as a possible solution because of its properties. First of all it has a huge and unregulated spectrum, high transmission capacity, and mature enough LED technology. Many solutions have been proposed, such as microwave radar systems and short range radio systems, but all of these architectures suffer from frequency competition and weather conditions changing. These studies focus on the rear-end collision scene, that is the most common type of accident.

In [15], the authors have proposed a OWC based prototype to enhance the safety and efficiency of intelligent transport systems (ITS). In the proposed methodology, light emitted from the brake lamps of a vehicle can be used to transmit messages to the following vehicle so that necessary safety measures can be taken in time. The experimental results show that the prior prototype can identify hard brakes over a distance of 20 m and can offer an alert warning to following vehicles driving slower than 80 km/h. The authors in [16] have also proposed a OWC based rear-collision avoidance system. The efficiency of the proposed technique has been verified by implementing different case studies.

In [17], the authors developed a OWC-based V2V communication prototype. Various techniques like frequency shift keying (FSK), phase shift keying, and amplitude shift keying were implemented. Different measuring parameters e.g., received optical power, bit error rate (Ber), and received signal voltage were assessed to characterize V2V communication. The results reveals that 3.5 Mb/s and 500 Kb/s data rates were achieved over the distances of 0.5 and 15 m respectively. The experimental results validated the efficiency of OWC-based proposed architecture and its importance in V2V communication.

OWC and Underwater Robots. Nowadays, OWC is emerging as a method to provide high data rates and low latency for underwater wireless communication [18]. The OWC-based systems outperform radio wireless in terms of reach and bandwidth with the LoS as a prerequisite. The proposed solution to this problem is to implement a feedback control to direct the light emitters and detectors to each other.

The system is motivated by the need for wireless communication systems in the robotic inspection of nuclear reactors, which are permanently underwater. An approach based on OWC has been pursued due to the significant range and bandwidth advantages of the technology in this specific environment.

There is an urgent need for a more thorough investigation of underwater structures as an added safety measure. The need for a pointing system is crucial as the optical components are inherently directional and require a continuous LoS to maintain a data link.

The authors in [19] mainly focus on the use of light as a localization medium via an unusual general strategy, where the light source is integrated into a full inertial measurement unit for estimation of orientation and position. In this way, the optical communication system is in a dual-use configuration. The light signal is both interpreted using a circuit to attain a data signal and analyzed using different sensors and techniques to gain an estimate of the orientation and position of the vehicle.

OWC Technology Based Robots in Pipelines. In the near future, robots are expected to be employed in pipelines with protracted distances and complicated networks. These robots need to be highly efficient in terms of wireless communication but the presence of EM interference, Faraday cage effects and low energy efficiency can undermine their performance in said environment. In [20], the authors proposed to employ a wheeled robot equipped with a OWC-based transmitter and receiver to assess their efficacy inside a pipeline. The attained experimental results are satisfactory as the proposed system is capable to establish a good communication link and provide illumination inside the pipe.

OWC for Enhanced Control of Autonomous Delivery Robots. The existing robot systems are mainly focused on robot functionality and position accuracy with fewer concerns about their safety. Regarding robot safety, OWC shows promising potential. The authors in [21], developed a robot having an enhanced navigation control system using a joint of navigation sensors and OWC-based technology using in-building installed LEDs. The proposed robot system has been tested in a real hospital and shown satisfactory experimental results.

Fig. 1. The access point.

Fig. 2. The TX driver.

4 Experimental Setup

In this section we explain all details that are related to our experiments. We provide hardware, software and strategies chosen together with the motivations that led to such choices.

Our experiments were performed by using the development kit manufactured by pureLiFi. It consists of two USB Li-Fi dongles (see Fig. 3), two Li-Fi ready LED lamps and two access points (see Fig. 1). The access point (in which is implemented an infrared receiver) is wired to the lamp via the TX driver (see Fig. 2) and to the rest of the wired network. It acts as a signal modulator and is responsible for generating the signal the lamp will reproduce.

The dongle is wired to the computer via USB and it has implemented an infrared transmitter and a visible light photodiode so that it can transmit and receive data.

Fig. 3. The USB dongle.

The data link layer of the pureLiFi system is compliant with the 802.11 protocol (CSMA/CA with RTS/CTS and ACK) while its physical layer uses light has the medium of data communication.

4.1   Reference System Architecture

Figure 4 and 5 show the setup we used for our 'in vitro' experiments. Communication was performed by assuming that a host computer 2 (this simulates the console) exchanges data with a host computer 1 (this simulates the robot's continuous numeric control (CNC)). The continuous numeric control provides instructions on where and if to move the robot's joints. The console is connected with the OWC access point while the CNC is connected with a local router. Router and access point are connected by means of a local Ethernet cable. We used this setting in order to emulate the robot controlling scenario.

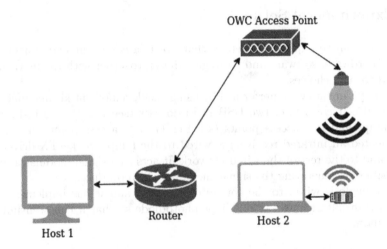

Fig. 4. The proposed architecture for test setup.

In the 'in vitro' experiments the wired network was isolated from the traffic, i.e., only the traffic sent via OWC was observable and we made sure that no light interference was present. This was not the same in the industrial experiments where interference was possible.

4.2   Performance Measures

Our aim is to estimate reliability in terms of Packet Error Rate (PER), throughput and Latency. These were evaluated by performing various experiments (e.g., LoS and NLoS).

Fig. 5. The "in vitro" environment.   **Fig. 6.** The "real life" environment.

Packet Error Rate (PER) Estimation. We are interested in evaluating the PER that is related to the link between the console and the OWC access point. This can give an estimate on the quality of the light channel under various conditions. There are various methods for performing PER tests for wireless networks [22]. On way is to compare the raw data bits that are received by the OWC access point with the ones that are sent by the consoles. This can allow us to measure the Bit Error Rate (BER) that can be used in order to estimate the PER. This is calculated by assuming a uniformly distributed error which can lead to gross overestimation of PER. Another way to estimate the PER is to count the number of CRC mismatches at the OWC access point. With the 32-bit CRC used by the 802.11 standard the probability of undetected erroneous packets is very small (i.e., 2.3E−10). Both methods (BER and CRC) require a specific vendor software to get data from the MAC layer. When this is not available, packets with an unreliable protocol (such as UDP) can be transmitted. The PER can be obtained by counting the number of missing packets at the router side since any packets with errors is dropped. We use this technique in order to estimate the quality of the connection between the OWC access point and the console [1] since no specific vendor software to get OWC MAC layer data was available.

For each time slot T_i (all time slots have equal duration) we have calculated the average packet error rate PER_{T_i} according to the following formula:

$$PER_{T_i} = \frac{F_{T_i}^A - F_{T_i}^R}{F_{T_i}^A}$$

where $F_{T_i}^R$ is the number of frames that were received at the router during transmission between the console and the router via OWC; $F_{T_i}^A$ is the total

---

[1] This measure gives a good indication of the OWC to console connection. In fact, the wired connection between router and OWC has a constant and very low PER.

number of frames that were sent; $F_{T_i}^A - F_{T_i}^R$ is the number of frame that were not received.

The average error rate PER was calculated according to the following formula:

$$PER = \frac{\sum_{i=0}^{N} PER_{T_i}}{N}$$

where N is the total number of time slots.

The confidence interval of the experiment was calculated in the following manner:

$$PER \pm Z \frac{s}{\sqrt{N}}$$

where s is the standard deviation and Z is the confidence interval (0.95 in our case) and $Z \frac{s}{\sqrt{N}}$ the margin of error. In all graphs we always plot the average in blue and we always plot the statistics endpoints $\overline{PER} - Z \frac{s}{\sqrt{N}}$ and $\overline{PER} + Z \frac{s}{\sqrt{N}}$ in red and yellow, respectively. For instance, Fig. 7 shows in blue the average PER, in red the lower endpoint and in blue the upper one.

For each experiment, we have collected several days of data exchange. More precisely, for each day all packets exchanged during 4.5 h of communication between console and OWC have been collected. These have been divided into chunks of 10 min. For each chunk we calculated PER_{T_i}. These have been averaged together in order to obtain the PER of an experiment.

We have implemented a client UDP program that sends packets to a server program. Sent and received packets have been counted at the client and server side, respectively. We have double checked the packet counting by using the Wireshark packet analyser.

Throughput. Throughput is the number of messages that are successfully delivered per unit of time. This is consequence of the available bandwidth, quality of links (error rate) and hardware limitations. Throughput is measured from the arrival of the first bit from console at the router. This is done in order to decouple the concept of throughput from the concept of latency. We use a TCP throughput based estimation where for each time slot T_i the console sends to the router packets as fast as the hardware will allow. We calculated the throughout R_i for the time slot T_i by using the following formula:

$$R_i = \frac{B_i}{T_i}$$

where B_i is the total amount of byte that were sent during the time slot T_i. For each experiments we collected thousands of time slots T_i which were used to calculate the following average throughput rate R:

$$R = \frac{\sum_{i=0}^{N} R_i}{N}$$

where N is the total amount of time slots and R_i is the throughout of the time slot T_i. The confidence interval of the experiment was calculated by using the following formula:

$$R \pm Z \frac{s}{\sqrt{N}}$$

where s is the standard deviation and Z is the confidence interval (0.95 in our case) and $Z \frac{s}{\sqrt{N}}$ the margin of error. Like for the PER, in all graphs we always plot the average in blue and we always plot the statistics endpoints $\overline{R} - Z \frac{s}{\sqrt{N}}$ and $\overline{R} + Z \frac{s}{\sqrt{N}}$ in red and yellow, respectively.

We have implemented a client TCP program that sends packets to a server program. The client runs on the console while the server at the router. The time to receive the packets have been taken at the client side. We have double checked the throughput results obtained by using the Wireshark packet analyser and the iPerf 3 tool. This is a widely used command-line tool written in C for network performance measurement. We did not use iPerf only since it might use other protocols such as TELNET or serial to output the intermediary results at each interval which might introduce undesired overhead. This may negatively impact the throughput results.

Latency. We use the round-trip time (RTT) in order to estimate the time it takes for an acknowledgement to be received by the console. More precisely, we measure the time it takes for 512 bytes to be sent by the console to the router and the related acknowledgement to be received back. We have chosen 512 byte since it is a sufficient amount of data for controlling the movement of the robots.

For each slot S_i we have estimated the average RTT_i by applying the following formula:

$$RTT_i = \sum_{j=0}^{j=N_i} T(P_j)$$

where $T(P_j)$ is the round-trip time for the packet P_j and N_i the number of packet sent for the slot S_i (this has been set to a thousand). We have also calculated the $peaks_i$. This counts the number of packet whose RTT exceeds the time of 30 ms for the slot S_i. Exceeding this time is considered no safe when controlling the arm of a robot.

For each experiment we have calculated the average RTT by using the following formula:

$$RTT = \frac{\sum_{j=0}^{j=N} RTT_i}{N}$$

where N is the number of slots which have been set to a thousand. The total percentage of peaks was calculated according to the following formula:

$$peaks = \frac{\sum_{j=0}^{j=N} peaks_i}{\sum_{j=0}^{j=N} N_i}$$

where $\sum_{j=0}^{j=N} N_i$ is the total amount of packets sent for all slots.

The confidence interval of the experiment was calculated in the following manner:

$$\overline{RTT} \pm Z \frac{s}{\sqrt{N}}$$

where s is the standard deviation and Z is the confidence interval (0.95 in our case) and $Z \frac{s}{\sqrt{N}}$ the margin of error. Like for the PER, in all graphs we always plot the average in blue and we always plot the statistics endpoints $\overline{RTT} - Z \frac{s}{\sqrt{N}}$ and $\overline{RTT} + Z \frac{s}{\sqrt{N}}$ in red and yellow, respectively.

We have implemented a client TCP program that sends packets to a server program. The client runs on the console while the server at the router. The time to receive the ack on the client side has been recorded every time. We have double checked the throughput results obtained by using the Wireshark packet analyser and the TCP-latency tool. This is a command-line tool implemented in Python that is born from the need of running network diagnosis tasks on serverless infrastructure (many providers do not include ICMP support).

5 Experiments and Test Results

In this section, we describe all experiments that we have performed and we discuss their results.

5.1 Throughput and per Tests

We performed various experiments in order to observe the variation in throughput, PER and Latency by changing the following settings: (i) LoS and NLoS; (ii) the vertical position of the lamp from 0.5 m to 5 m while keeping the dongle stationary under the lamp (horizontal position 0 m); (iii) changing the horizontal position of the dongle from 0 m to 2 m while keeping the vertical position of the lamp at 2.5 m and 5 m from the ground. In line-of-sight the coupled transmitters and receivers directly "face" each other while in NLoS the signal is not carried by the light beam directly but by its reflection.

"In Vitro" Tests. Figures 7 and 8 show the results for LoS tests where the dongle position varies vertically between 0.5 and 2.5 m. This scenario is shown is Fig. 9. As expected, the speed and error rate have opposite behaviour. From the results, it is evident that as the distance increases, the throughput decreases. At the test's poles, the speed dropped by approximately one-third of the peak value and the error rate is doubled.

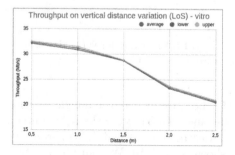

Fig. 7. Throughput for vertical distance variation, LoS. (Color figure online)

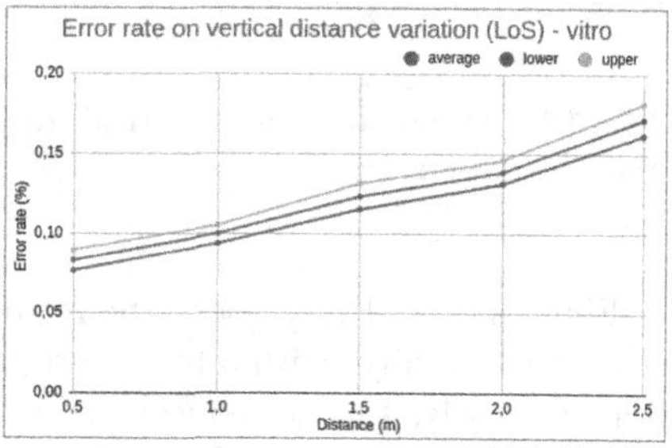

Fig. 8. Error rate for vertical distance variation, LoS.

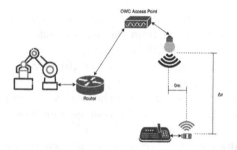

Fig. 9. Vertical 'in vitro' scenario with LoS.

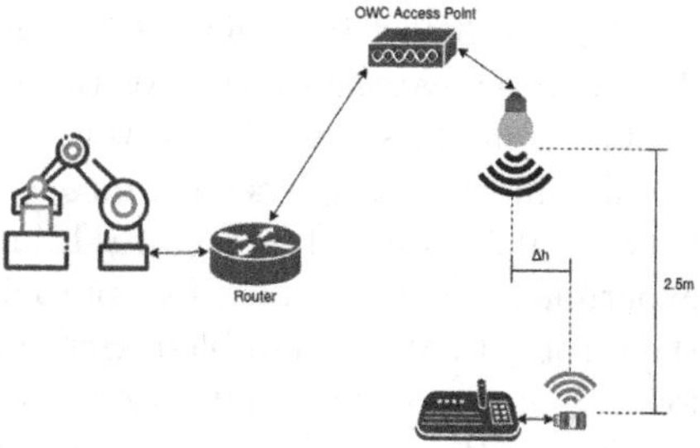

Fig. 10. Horizontal 'in vitro' scenario with LoS.

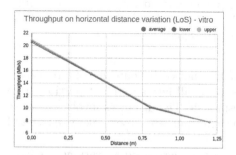
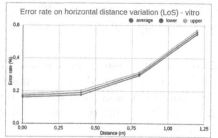

Fig. 11. Throughput for horizontal distance variation, LoS.

Fig. 12. Error rate for horizontal distance variation, LoS.

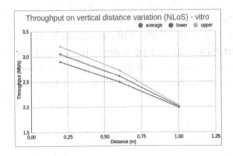

Fig. 13. Throughput for vertical distance variation, NLoS.

Fig. 14. Error rate for vertical distance variation, NLoS.

Figures 11 and 12 present the results for LoS tests where the dongle position varies horizontally (with a fixed vertical distance of 2.5 m from the light source). More precisely, the horizontal distance varies between 0 and 1.25 m from the centre of the cone light. This setting is shown in Fig. 10. We can observe that the speed and error rate have diverging responses. At the extreme values of the test, speed dropped by around three times from the peak performances and the error rate gets tripled.

Figures 13 and 14 depict the results for NLoS tests where the position of the dongle varies vertically (the distance is considered from the surface reflecting light). Figure 15 shows this setting. We can see that the console is faced toward a reflecting surface. The distance from this surface (Δv in Fig. 15) is varied between 0.25 m and 1 m. Figures 13 and 14 show that at the polar values of the experiment, speed reduces by approximately one third from the peak value and the error rate almost doubled. Here the values in terms of throughput are much lower than the LoS configuration and the error rate is also higher.

Figures 16 and 17 portray the results for the NLoS experiments where the position of the dongle changes horizontally (the vertical distance is constant and is 0.2 m, the nearest possible to the reflected light source so that the reflection of the infrared light can reach the access point). Considering the extreme values of the attained results (Figs. 16 and 17), the speed becomes almost half of the peak value and the error rate exceeds the threefold.

Experiments Inside the Farms. The first noticeable outcome of farm experiments was that the NLoS experiments inside all farms were not possible since communication links simply failed to establish. The distances involved were to large (see Fig. 6) thus the reflection of the light source was too weak to be received at the OWC access point.

The experiments inside the farms were only performed by varying the horizontal distance from the center of the light cone. The operator's console would be around 1.5 m from the ground in the best case while the lamp was about 5 m from the console. This was the height of all the warehouse ceiling where the experiments were performed. Two types of experiments were conducted, in

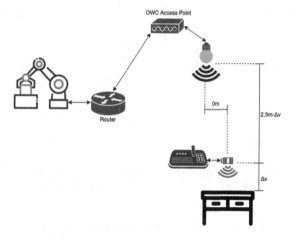

Fig. 15. Vertical 'in vitro' scenario with NLoS.

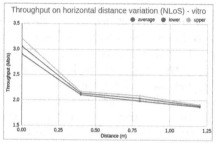

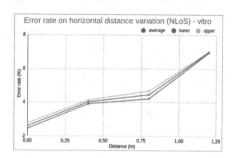

Fig. 16. Throughput for horizontal distance variation, NLoS.

Fig. 17. Error rate for horizontal distance variation, NLoS.

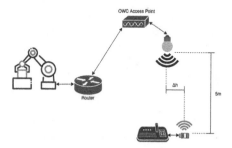

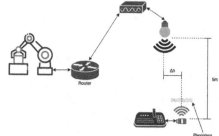

Fig. 18. Experiments inside the industry with LoS.

Fig. 19. Experiments inside the industry with a transparent obstacle in the middle

one case the console and the lamp were in LoS without any obstacle in between (see Fig. 18). In the second case a transparent barrier during between the OWC communication and the console was placed (see Fig. 19). This was done in order

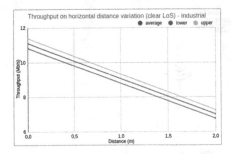

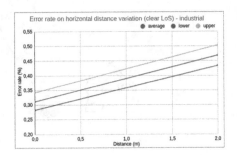

Fig. 20. Throughput for horizontal distance variation in LoS test.

Fig. 21. Error rate for horizontal distance variation in LoS test.

to simulate a plexiglass material that could separate the operator and the robot. The addition of the transparent barrier definitely affected the packet error rate and the throughput but real time (i.e., response time) within certain time limit can be still ensured.

Figure 20 and 21 show the throughput and the packet error rate when the dongle position varies horizontally from 0 to 2 m and no obstacle is used. It is worth noticing that the throughput almost halved when compared to the 'in vitro' experiments of Figs. 11. This is because the height of the lamp doubled (from 2.5 m to 5 m). It is also worth noticing that the packet error rate increased approximately by 50% when compared to the 'in vitro' experiments of Fig. 17.

Figures 22 and 23 show the throughput and the packet error rate in the presence of transparent plexiglass barrier between the console and the lamp. The position of the dongle varies horizontally from 0 to 2 m. The throughput drops by about 25% and the error rate increase of 20%. This is consequence of the plexiglass introduction.

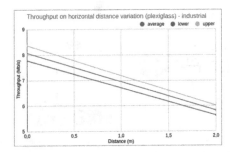

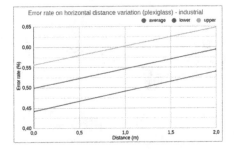

Fig. 22. Throughput for horizontal distance variation in LoS case test when plexiglass acts as communication obstacle.

Fig. 23. Error rate for horizontal distance variation in LoS case experiment when plexiglass is inserted as communication barrier.

5.2   Latency Tests

Table 1. RTTs test "in vitro".

Scenario	Average (ms)	Lower (ms)	Upper (ms)	Peaks
LoS 1	7,7124	7,7038	7,721	$897\ 10^{-7}$
LoS 2	7,7516	7,4248	7,7608	$901\ 10^{-7}$
NLoS 3	7,7582	7,7461	7,7703	$900\ 10^{-7}$

"In Vitro" Tests. We have tested the latency our 'in vitro' scenarios by using the following three scenarios: (Los 1) the height of the lamp is 2.5 m while the horizontal distance Δh is 0 m (see Fig. 9); (Los 2) the height of the lamp is 2.5 m while the horizontal distance Δh is 1.2 m (see Fig. 9); (NLos 1) the height of the lamp is 2.5 m while the horizontal distance is 0 m (see Fig. 15), the console has no line of sight with the OWC lamp and faces a surface at distance $\Delta h = 0.25$. The latency results of these scenarios are shown in Table 1. We can see that for all scenarios the response time is always very low. This is consequence on the very small amount of data that is sent for each packet (512 byte) and its periodicity (every 100 ms). We can also notice that in all scenarios that we have considered there is always a good throughput and a low PER (see Sect. 5.1 for details). It is worth noting that the percentage of packets that exceeds the 30 ms (that is the peaks) is extremely low in all scenarios.

Table 2. RTT tests in real-life environment.

Scenario	Average (ms)	Lower (ms)	Upper (ms)	Peaks
LoS 1	7,7337	7,7194	7,7479	$908\ 10^{-7}$
LoS 2	7,7762	7,7619	7,7904	$907\ 10^{-7}$

Real-Life Environment Test. We have tested the latency also for our industrial case study by using the following two scenarios: (Los 1) the height of the lamp is 5 m while the horizontal distance Δh is 2 m (see Fig. 17); (Los 2) the height of the lamp is 5 m while the horizontal distance Δh is 2; a plexiglass between console and lamp is added (see Fig. 19). The latency results of these scenarios are shown in Table 2. We can see that in all scenarios the response time is always very low and the results obtained are equal to the 'in vitro' scenario.

5.3   Discussion

Our research questions were positively answered. The Light technology has satisfactory performance in terms of latency, reliability and throughput when compared to wired and RF-based wireless communication inside factories. While our experiments show that was possible to manoeuvre robots by using OWC, they also showed that WiFi could not be used because of various forms of interference. This lead to poor reliability and throughput.

Thanks to the high reliability of the light channel the dead-man button could be implemented. We recall that this is a switch that is activated or deactivated if the human operator becomes unable, such as through death, loss of consciousness, or being bodily removed from control. The robot is allowed to move until such button is pressed, once it is released the robot is prevented to move. The man dead button was impossible to implement over WiFi.

6   Conclusion and Future Work

We conducted various experiments to observe the suitability and efficiency of OWC based technology for anthropomorphic robots control in industrial environments. The tests have shown overall satisfying results. In the "in vitro" tests, where the hardware was in the working range specified by the manufacturer, throughput and reliability tests have always shown acceptable results in LoS configuration. The real-life environment based tests presented satisfactory results in the assumed configurations. From the performance comparison between the "clear LoS" and the plexiglass tests, it's evident that a transparent obstacle is not that much of high concern for the technology, but it is highly preferable to have a clear LoS. As for the real-timeness tests are concerned, they have shown very good results as the latency peaks are very few and the average latency is very low, hence making OWC a very good candidate for this kind of application.

We achieved all the proposed objectives, though for this kind of application there is the need for a specific implementation in order to make it usable when bigger distances are in play.

6.1   Future Developments

In future research work, we aim to take measurements regarding light intensity using available hardware, so that can be sized a new hypothetical system which can be developed for simulation purposes. After the simulation phase, will be conducted an estimate of the hardware needed to build a prototype. Then will be built a prototype that implements the additional safety channel and a pointing system analogous to the one described in Sect. 3. Regarding the safety channel its communications will be processed separately from the motion's in order to respect industrial standards regarding safety and for the system to be as robust as possible, as this is the most critical feature in this application. We are also planning to implement a pointing system. This is deemed as necessary in order to offer the operator the highest degree of movement while maintaining the optical link's quality as close as possible to the best conditions.

Acknowledgment. We thank the start-up Misco Valley for supporting all the experiments and providing the experimental hardware.

References

1. Lu, Y.: Industry 4.0: a survey on technologies, applications and open research issues. J. Ind. Inf. Integr. **6**, 1–10 (2017). https://doi.org/10.1016/j.jii.2017.04.005
2. Wetzker, U., Splitt, I., Zimmerling, M., Boano, C.A., Romer, K.: Troubleshooting wireless coexistence problems in the industrial internet of things. In: 2016 IEEE International Conference on Computational Science and Engineering (CSE) and IEEE International Conference on Embedded and Ubiquitous Computing (EUC) and 15th International Symposium on Distributed Computing and Applications for Business Engineering (DCABES). IEEE (2016). https://doi.org/10.1109/cse-euc-dcabes.2016.167
3. Martinek, R., Danys, L., Jaros, R.: Visible light communication system based on software defined radio: performance study of intelligent transportation and indoor applications. Electronics **8**(4), 433 (2019)
4. Biton, C., Arnon, S.: Improved multiple access resource allocation in visible light communication systems. Opt. Commun. **424**, 98–102 (2018)
5. Shao, S., et al.: Design and analysis of a visible-light-communication enhanced WiFi system. J. Opt. Commun. Netw. **7**(10), 960–973 (2015)
6. Soner, B., Ergen, S.C.: A Low-SWaP, low-cost transceiver for physically secure UAV communication with visible light. In: Avdaković, S., Mujčić, A., Mujezinović, A., Uzunović, T., Volić, I. (eds.) IAT 2019. LNNS, vol. 83, pp. 355–364. Springer, Cham (2020). https://doi.org/10.1007/978-3-030-24986-1_28
7. Ullah, Z., Al-Turjman, F., Mostarda, L.: Cognition in UAV-aided 5G and beyond communications: a survey. IEEE Trans. Cogn. Commun. Netw. **6**, 872–891 (2020)
8. Galisteo, A., Juara, D., Giustiniano, D.: Research in visible light communication systems with OpenVLC1.3. In: 2019 IEEE 5th World Forum on Internet of Things (WF-IoT), pp. 539–544. IEEE (2019)
9. Ullah, Z., Al-Turjman, F., Mostarda, L., Gagliardi, R.: Applications of artificial intelligence and machine learning in smart cities. Comput. Commun. **154**, 313–323 (2020)
10. Al-Turjman, F., Lemayian, J.P., Alturjman, S., Mostarda, L.: Enhanced deployment strategy for the 5G drone-BS using artificial intelligence. IEEE Access **7**, 75999–76008 (2019)
11. Al-Turjman, F., Mostarda, L., Ever, E., Darwish, A., Khalil, N.S.: Network experience scheduling and routing approach for big data transmission in the internet of things. IEEE Access **7**, 14501–14512 (2019)
12. Masini, B.M., Bazzi, A., Zanella, A.: A survey on the roadmap to mandate on board connectivity and enable V2V-based vehicular sensor networks. Sensors **18**(7), 2207 (2018)
13. Goto, Y., et al.: A new automotive VLC system using optical communication image sensor. IEEE Photon. J. **8**(3), 1–17 (2016)

14. Raza, N., Jabbar, S., Han, J., Han, K.: Social vehicle-to-everything (V2X) communication model for intelligent transportation systems based on 5G scenario. In: Proceedings of the 2nd International Conference on Future Networks and Distributed Systems, pp. 1–8 (2018)
15. Siddiqi, K., Raza, A., Muhammad, S.S.: Visible light communication for V2V intelligent transport system. In: 2016 International Conference on Broadband Communications for Next Generation Networks and Multimedia Applications (CoBCom), pp. 1–4. IEEE (2016)
16. Bao, Y., Wang, Y., Yu, J., Shen, J.: A visible light communication based vehicle collision avoiding system. In: 2016 15th International Conference on Optical Communications and Networks (ICOCN), pp. 1–3. IEEE (2016)
17. Dahri, F.A., Mangrio, H.B., Baqai, A., Umrani, F.A.: Experimental evaluation of intelligent transport system with VLC vehicle-to-vehicle communication. Wirel. Pers. Commun. **106**(4), 1885–1896 (2018). https://doi.org/10.1007/s11277-018-5727-0
18. Zhou, Y., et al.: Common-anode LED on a Si substrate for beyond 15 Gbit/s underwater visible light communication. Photon. Res. **7**(9), 1019–1029 (2019)
19. Rust, I.C., Asada, H.H.: A dual-use visible light approach to integrated communication and localization of underwater robots with application to non-destructive nuclear reactor inspection. In: 2012 IEEE International Conference on Robotics and Automation, pp. 2445–2450. IEEE (2012)
20. Zhao, W., et al.: A preliminary experimental study on control technology of pipeline robots based on visible light communication. In: 2019 IEEE/SICE International Symposium on System Integration (SII), pp. 22–27. IEEE (2019)
21. Murai, R., et al.: A novel visible light communication system for enhanced control of autonomous delivery robots in a hospital. In: 2012 IEEE/SICE International Symposium on System Integration (SII), pp. 510–516. IEEE (2012)
22. Khalili, R., Salamatian, K.: A new analytic approach to evaluation of packet error rate in wireless networks. In: 3rd Annual Communication Networks and Services Research Conference (CNSR 2005), pp. 333–338 (2005)

Classification of IoT Device Communication Through Machine Learning Techniques

Sheraz Ahmad[1], K. N. R. Surya Vara Prasad[2], Zaib Ullah[1(✉)],
Leonardo Mostarda[1], and Fadi Al-Turjman[3,4]

[1] Computer Science Division, University of Camerino, 62032 Camerino, Italy
zaibullah.zaibullah@unicam.it
[2] Department of Electrical and Computer Engineering,
University of British Columbia, Columbia, Canada
[3] Artificial Intelligence Department, Near East University, Nicosia, Mersin 10, Turkey
[4] Research Center for AI and IoT, Near East University, Nicosia, Mersin 10, Turkey

Abstract. The Internet of Things (IoT) also called the Internet of Everything is a system of smart interconnected devices. The smart devices are uniquely identifiable over the network and perform autonomous data communication over the network with or without human-to-computer interaction. These devices have a high level of diversity, heterogeneity, and operates with various computational capabilities. It is highly necessary to develop a framework that allows to classify the devices into different categories from effective management, security, and privacy perspectives. Various solutions such as network traffic analysis, network protocols analysis, etc. have been developed to solve the problem of device classification. The signal of a device is an important feature that could be utilized to classify various network devices. We propose a framework to identify network devices based on their signal analysis. We have developed a training data set, by collecting signals from various Wi-Fi and Bluetooth devices in a specific geographic area. A machine learning-based model is proposed for the prediction of network device classification (e.g., a Wi-Fi or Bluetooth device) with 100% accuracy. Furthermore, clustering techniques are applied to the acquired signals to predict the total number of active Wi-Fi devices in a given region.

Keywords: Machine learning · Bluetooth and Wi-Fi classification · IoT · Clustering technique

1 Introduction

The term IoT was first introduced by Kevin Ashton in 1999 and with time it became an integral part of our daily life [1,2]. IoT is a system of smart interconnected devices that are uniquely recognizable over the network and are capable

E. Ever and F. Al-Turjman (Eds.): FoNeS-IoT 2020, LNICST 353, pp. 129–143, 2021.
https://doi.org/10.1007/978-3-030-69431-9_10

of autonomous data communication. The IoT has various applications in different areas such as smart agriculture, smart homes, autonomous transportation, telemedicine and healthcare, supply chain management, logistics, automobile, telecommunication, industry, security and surveillance, industry, and Wireless sensor networks, etc. [1,3,5].

According to literature by the end of the year 2020, there will be around 50 billion internet- connected devices [4]. These devices will have different levels of homogeneity and heterogeneity. The IoT is a potential field for academia to explore device classification, device connectivity, intercommunication, and network configuration in IoT scenarios.

The growing number of IoT devices introduces several challenges to keep track of network activities. The research community is working on how to automatically classify devices of the IoT in groups to better manage them for security and privacy, services and functionalities enhancements [7,8]. Different technologies provide wireless connectivity for IoT devices and the technologies implement various standards in terms of frequency bands, communication protocols, and coverage areas [6,9]. There are two types of wireless communication technologies i.e., short-range and long-range [10]. The short-range communicate within a small coverage area of a minimum 1 m to a maximum of 100 m^2. Some of the renowned short-range technologies are Wi-Fi, Bluetooth, ZigBee, and 6LoW-PAN. The long-range wireless communication technologies cover an area of 10 to 100 km, and it includes cellular technologies mainly the 3rd Generation Partnership Project (3GPP), Global System for Mobile Communications (GSM), Long Term Evolution (LTE), 2G to 5G, etc. [10,20]. A detailed description of Short-Range and Long-Range communication technologies is shown in Fig. 1. The Fig. 1

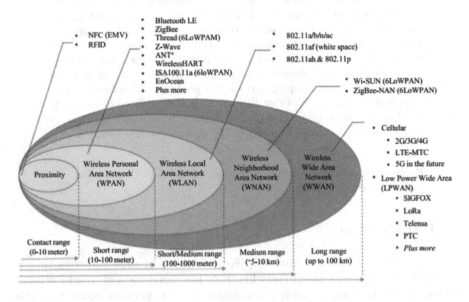

Fig. 1. Wireless connectivity technologies for IoT [20]

describes its coverage area, standards, and the underline sub-technologies. Bluetooth operates on the Industrial, Scientific, and Medical (ISM) frequency band that starts 2.402 GHz and ends at 2.480 GHz. Bluetooth sends data in a short-range of max 100 m with a data rate of 1Mb/s to 3Mb/s. Similarly, a typical Wi-Fi system supports a speed of up to 54 Mb/s and a coverage range of 100 m [9].

Machine learning (ML) is a sub-field of computer science and artificial intelligence (AI). The ML allows the system to self-learn from the given data without being explicitly programmed to make some intelligent decisions, classifications, or predictions by itself. The ML and Data mining is often considered the same terms because of the significant overlap of the techniques.

ML learns from the training data and makes some predictions based on the known patterns while data mining focuses on extracting the unknown patterns in the data. ML uses some of the data mining techniques in unsupervised learning, and data preprocessing and data mining also make use of ML techniques. ML techniques are usually reliable for making classification or predictions from the given data or dealing with real-world scenarios. These techniques can describe and autonomously detect a linear and nonlinear relationship between the dependent and independent variables, called patterns, and the primary source for predictions.

To better manage the network, we need to classify these devices to handle them accordingly. The research community proposed several mechanisms for classifying devices in the IoT network. A signal is a potential feature for device classification as each device uses some standard to connect to the network. In short, we can classify devices by analyzing their signals.

This article aims to develop a framework by using ML techniques that automatically recognize a device, whether it is a Wi-Fi or Bluetooth device by analyzing its signal. We have a data set that has been created by collecting Wi-Fi and Bluetooth devices signals from a geographical area. We train a ML model with the existing data set and use it to recognize any newly provided signal either from Wi-Fi or Bluetooth devices. Furthermore, there are hundreds of signals belonging to several Wi-Fi devices in a given area. We aim to employ an unsupervised clustering algorithm to calculates the total number of Wi-Fi devices in the given area. The article layout (shown in Fig. 2) is organized as that Sect. 1 presents a generalized introduction of the IoT, ML techniques, technologies, and their limitation. Section 2 describes a brief literature review of Wi-Fi and Bluetooth devices, and ML techniques that are best suited to solve the problem. Section 3 provides a detailed discussion regarding the model and attained experimental results, and Sect. 4 concludes the article.

2   Literature Review

In this section, we provide a brief literature review of Bluetooth, Wi-Fi technologies, and ML techniques.

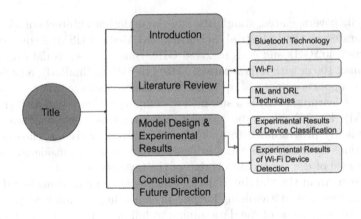

Fig. 2. This figure shows the article layout.

2.1 Bluetooth Technology

The idea of Bluetooth was originally introduced by Ericsson Mobile Communications back in 1994 in Lund (Sweden). When Ericsson started studying to replace traditional wired connection in short-range communication between laptop, Phone, and PDAs [11,14]. Bluetooth was initially standardized by IEEE 802.15.1 but now it is maintained by Bluetooth SIG (Special Interest Group). The SIG was formed in 1998 by a group of tech giants, namely Ericsson, IBM, Nokia, Toshiba, and Intel. Bluetooth operates on the Industrial, ISM frequency band that starts 2.402 GHz and ends at 2.480 GHz. Bluetooth devices need a point-to-point connection for communication. To initiate a connection between two different Bluetooth devices one will act as a Master and the other will act as a Slave. Master initiates the connection first and slave accept to join, this single hope network is known as piconet [15].

According to [16] there will be over 10 billion Bluetooth devices in the market by the year 2018. With such an increase the Bluetooth (SIG) started working on other short-range wireless communications technologies, such as IoT and machine to machine (M2M) wireless communication. To enable Bluetooth for battery-powered IoT and M2M applications Bluetooth should reduce its energy consumption. Therefor the Bluetooth SIG introduced Bluetooth Low Energy (BLE) in 2010 as Bluetooth 4.0 which was specifically designed for low power wearable devices for example actuators, and sensors [17,18] etc.

2.2 WiFi

Wi-Fi stands for "Wireless Fidelity" that indicates if a device has Wi-Fi it can be connected to the wireless local area network. An advantage of WLAN is the replacement of traditional wiring. A device in the coverage area of a Wi-Fi can be connected to the internet via a wireless connection. Wi-Fi is a wireless local area networking (WLAN) technology that allows portable mobile devices e.g. smartphones, laptops, printers, tablets, cameras, and many other devices, to wirelessly connect to the internet. A typical Wi-Fi network consists of three parts, a smartphone or computer, a wireless access point (AP), and a wired connection between the access point and broadband provider [19]. To build a WLAN, a device called router is required to receive and transmit wireless signals. A router receives the internet from an internet service provider (ISP) and transmits it wirelessly to the nearby devices. Wi-Fi belongs to the family of IEEE 802.11 wireless networks standard. IEEE 802.11 operates on radio wave and uses 2.4 GHz, ISM band. It can also operates 5 GHz which is mainly used in enterprises. A typical Wi-Fi system supports a speed of up to 54 Mb/s and a coverage range of 100 m [9]. In 1997, IEEE 802.11 was recognized as the first version of the standard for WLAN. That specified the license-free ISM 2.4 GHz frequency band with a speed of 1 to 2 Mb/s. IEEE 802.11 is not a single standard but it is a family of multiple versions. The IEEE 802.11a is a standard of WLAN that works on orthogonal frequency division multiplexing (OFDM). It has 52 channels to support a data rate of up to 54 Mb/s. IEEE 802.11b is the standard of WLAN that uses direct sequence spread spectrum (DSSS) and achieves a maximum speed of 11 Mb/s with the utilization 2.4 GHz band. To achieve a high data rate 2.4 GHz band a new 802.11 g was developed in 2000 which uses OFDM. The new OFDM achieves a required data rate for multimedia applications [19] and high data speed internet.

2.3 ML and DRL Techniques

ML is based on data processing where some statistical methods are applied to the given data to train a model. This trained model then applies the same statistics on the new data and compares the obtained results with the previous one. The process of training a model evolves in several steps including data collection, data preparation, model selection, model training, and evaluation of the model. The ML operational procedure has been shown in the Fig. 3.

Fig. 3. Work flow or necessary steps of ML process [20].

ML techniques can be classified into three extensive categories, supervised ML, unsupervised ML, and reinforcement learning as shown in Fig. 4 [12,13]. Supervised learning is based on the prediction of a dependent variable (class, label, or target). A function also called features, attributes, or inputs are used as independent variables. While in unsupervised learning the model learns by itself. There are no specified dependent variables hence the model has to focus on catching some patterns in all the variables in the data. Similarly, reinforcement learning is useful when there is no available data as input, the model has to generate it from some real-time scenario.

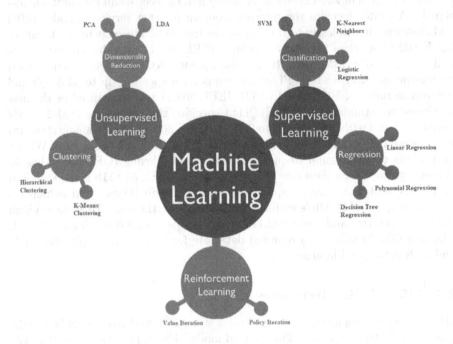

Fig. 4. Classification of ML techniques.

Supervised Learning. The term supervised learning is quite self-explanatory and is the most widely used ML technique. In this type of ML technique, the model is trained by supervised examples. In supervised learning, the model is provided with the two sets of data, namely training and test data set. With the training set the model will be trained and with the test set the model's prediction performance will be checked. Training set consists of input variables that are paired with the corresponding correct output variables. During the learning phase, the model will try to detect some patterns in the data that correlate inputs with the corresponding output variables [21]. Now in the test phase, the model will be provided with the input variables but with no corresponding output variables. So the ML model will try to detect some patterns in the newly provided data. The attained patterns are compared with the one it calculated during the training phase. By matching these patterns the model will be able to predict the class for the newly provided data in a classification problem or will be able to predict a value for a regression problem. Supervised learning is further divided into two subclasses known as classification and regression. Classification is used to predict a category while regression is used to predict some continuous values. There is a wide variety of algorithms that comes under the umbrella of classification. These algorithms usually belongs to one of the four working principles. For example, K-NN is instance-based, Bayesian and Support Vector Machine (SVM) are statistical calculation based, deep learning and ANN are perception based, Random forest and decision trees are logic-based [22]. Similarly, regression is a supervised ML technique, used for the prediction of real value. It is a statistical method that detects a relationship between dependent and independent variables. Prediction algorithms predict the value of the dependent variable for a given value of the independent variable. There exist several regression models that are based on the type of relationship between the dependent and independent variables. Some of the most common are linear regression, nonlinear regression and, polynomial regression, etc.

Unsupervised Learning. Unsupervised learning also known as Learning without a teacher [23], is a ML technique that deals with the unlabeled data. In unsupervised learning, an agent learns by itself through finding some hidden patterns in the data. In unsupervised learning, the model is unaware of the labels for the training data, so there is no way to calculate its accuracy. Therefore accuracy is not a measure that we analyze with unsupervised learning. In unsupervised learning the model is provided with a set of unlabeled data. The model is going to perform complex mathematics to find some patterns from the data and will extract some useful features from it. Unsupervised learning is further divided into Clustering and Dimensionality Reduction. Clustering is an unsupervised learning technique that is used for statistical data analysis to group the given data based on the similarities and dissimilarities. There are several clustering techniques, such as Hierarchical Clustering and K-Means clustering. In this article, we have used K-Means clustering in our model implementation. Similarly, the dimensionality reduction is the process of mapping high dimensional data into a low dimensional data that best represents the original data patterns. Some real-world data for example images, voice, MRI scans, and digital signals are usually high dimensional data. To adequately process such a high dimensional data for analysis is not an easy task. Thus we need to reduce the dimension of the data for effective processing and to maintain the original data features [25,26]. There exist several algorithms for dimensionality reduction e.g., Principle Component Analysis (PCA), etc.

Reinforcement Learning. Reinforcement Learning (RL) is one of the ML techniques that is based on trial and error [24]. In Reinforcement Learning, we have a decision maker called Agent that interacts with the environment that is placed in. These interactions occur sequentially over time. At each time step the agent will get some representation of the environment state. Agent acts and the environment is then transitioned to some new state while the agent gets a reward in response to the action it performed. So to summarize the reinforcement learning contains, Environment, Agent, State, Actions, and Rewards.

3 Model Design and Experimental Results

In this section we explain the results that have been obtained during the implementation of the SVM and K-Nearest Neighbors (KNN) algorithms. First, we will describe the system specifications in order to run the framework on local machine. Secondly we will briefly explain the performance metrics, used to evaluate and interpret the classifier results. Furthermore, we will explain the obtained results for classification and for detecting the total number of active Wi-Fi devices in a given area.

System Specification. To run the framework, our local machine has the following specifications. OS Name: Microsoft Windows 10, Processor Intel(R) Core(TM) i5-7200U CPU 2.50 GHz, 2 Core(s), 4 Logical Processor, Installed Physical Memory (RAM) 8.00 GB, Physical Memory 160 GB (SSD), with the above-mentioned system specifications each algorithm takes approximately 2 to 3 s to run.

Performance Metrics. To evaluate and interpret performance results of the ML model for device classification we have used the following four metrics.

Confusion Matrix. A confusion matrix is used in the field of ML to describe the classification performance of a model for a set of labeled data.

Sensitivity. Sensitivity is correctly identified class for the given object by the classifier. It also called true positive, and shows how good the classifier is to detect the correct class for a given event. Sensitivity is calculated as,

$$Sensitivity = \frac{TP}{TP + FN}$$

Where TP stands for True Positive, TN for True Negative, FP for False Positive, and FN for False Negative.

Specificity. Specificity also called true negative, which indicate how good the classifier is to identify a device true nature e.g., if a signal does not belongs to a Wi-Fi device, it should supposed to be true. Specificity can be calculated as,

$$Specificity = \frac{TN}{TN + FP}$$

Accuracy. Accuracy is the accurately identified result either it is positive or negative i.e., Accuracy is the combination of sensitivity and specificity and can be defined as,

$$ACC = \frac{TP + TN}{TP + TN + FP + FN}$$

3.1 Experimental Results of Device Classification

In this subsection, we discuss the classification results of our classifiers. For classification, we used two different algorithms SVM and KNN, for performance metrics we have use confusion matrix, sensitivity, specificity, and accuracy.

SVM. In this problem, we intend to classify devices in IoT networks. In our framework, we have targeted signals and focused to recognize a device based on its signal either it is Wi-Fi or Bluetooth device. It is a binary classification problem for which SVM is the best-suited approach. The results are as follow.

Confusion Matrix. We have trained the model with the training set, consists 80% of the original dataset. Further, we test the classifier with the test set which is 20% of the original data set. The preceding data set consists of a total 677 observation (signals), of whom 176 are Wi-Fi devices and 501 are Bluetooth devices as shown in Fig. 5. The classifier did not made any mistake by recognizing a Wi-Fi device as a Bluetooth device and vice versa.

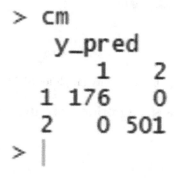

Fig. 5. Confusion matrix for SVM.

Sensitivity. Sensitivity for the device classification by using the SVM algorithm is shown in Fig. 6. According to the confusion matrix there is no FP and FN values thus the classification result is 100% accurate.

Specificity. Specificity for the device classification by using the SVM algorithm is shown in Fig. 7 as according to the confusion matrix there are no FP values thus the classification result is 100% accurate.

Accuracy. If we calculate the overall accuracy of the SVM classifier from the given confusion matrix. According to the formula used for accuracy we attained 100% accuracy because there are no FP and FN values. Which indicates that the classifier 100% accurately classified Wi-Fi and Bluetooth devices for newly provided signals as shown in Fig. 8. If we combine Sensitivity, Specificity, and Accuracy in one graph it will look like Fig. 10.

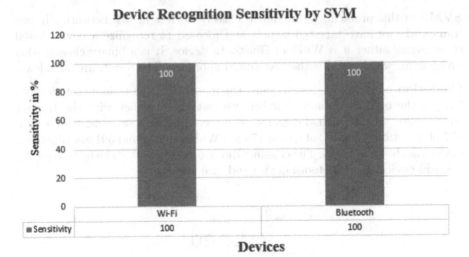

Fig. 6. Sensitivity graph for SVM.

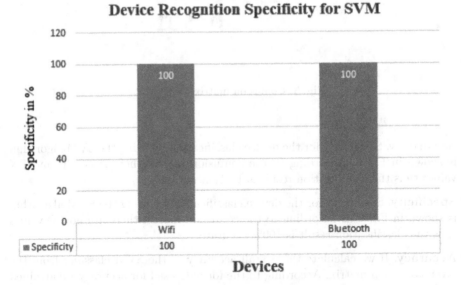

Fig. 7. Specificity graph for SVM.

KNN. Device classification specifically recognizing two types of devices (Wi-Fi and Bluetooth) is a binary problem therefor we first used the SVM algorithm. By applying SVM we got 100% accuracy. To double-check the obtained results we have applied K-NN that is a multiclass classification algorithm and attained the following results.

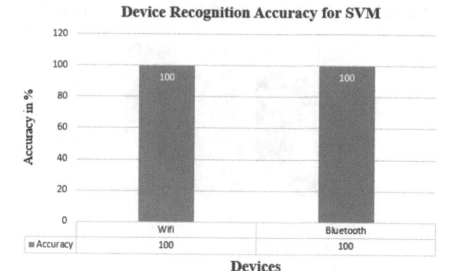

Fig. 8. Accuracy graph for SVM.

```
> cm
     y_pred
        1    2
  1  220    0
  2    0  626
>
```

Fig. 9. Confusion matrix for K-NN.

Confusion Matrix. For applying the K-NN algorithm we have also changed the split ratio of 20:80 to 25:75. That means 25% of the original data set goes to test set and 75% to the training set and obtained the results shown in Fig. 9. The test set consists of a total of 846 observation (signals). Where 220 of them represents Wi-Fi devices and 626 Bluetooth devices. 0, 0 in the matrix represents that none of the Wi-Fi devices is recognized as Bluetooth device and vice versa.

Sensitivity, Specificity, and Accuracy. By applying k value as 3 we got the same results as of SVM. Figure 10 shows the overall results for the sensitivity, specificity, and accuracy of the K-NN algorithm. Getting 100% accuracy is not astonishing because if we look at the signal parameters. We have one of them

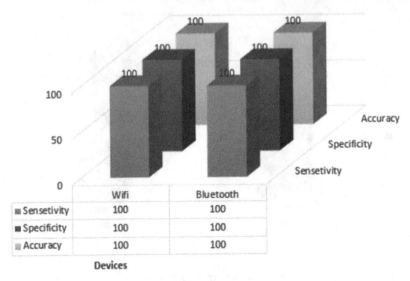

Fig. 10. K-NN sensitivity, specificity and accuracy.

called Bandwidth in Mhz that is very different for each of the devices which contributes very well in pattern formation.

3.2   Experimental Results of Wi-Fi Device Detection

In our framework, we applied a ML algorithm that identifies the total number of Wi-Fi devices in a given area. In this subsection, we discusses the obtained experimental results for the prior problem. To identifying the total number of Wi-Fi devices in a given area we utilized the K-Means Clustering algorithm.

K-Means Clustering. To apply K-means clustering algorithm we need to predefined the total number of clusters for the algorithm. Elbow method which is based on "within cluster sum of square (WCSS)", is used to calculate the appropriate number of clusters. In Fig. 11 there are 15 clusters and each cluster independently represents an individual Wi-Fi device. Consequently it shows that there are 15 different Wi-Fi devices in the given region.

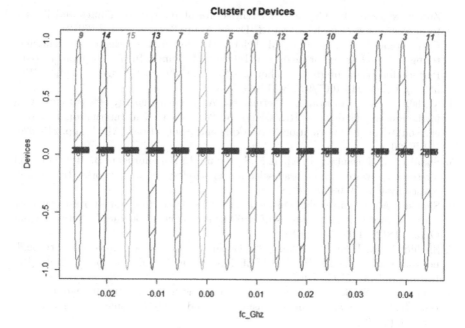

Fig. 11. Total number of Wi-Fi devices.

4   Conclusion

We have developed a framework using R language that classifies a device in an IoT network by its signal analysis. To the best of our knowledge, this is the first time a signal has been utilized for device classification. We developed a data set that consists of signals, collected from Wi-Fi and Bluetooth devices. Then we applied supervised ML techniques to build a classifier. First, we trained the model with the existing data set and then utilized it for the prediction of the type of a new devices. We utilized SVM and KNN to split the data into two sets with a ratio of 20:80. Where 80% of data has been used as a training data. While 20% has been utilized as a test data to verify the classifier accuracy. In both cases, we attained a 100% accuracy in device recognition. Similarly, we successfully utilized the K-Means Clustering technique to find out the number of active Wi-Fi devices in a given region. For future work, we plan to identify devices precise locations in the network, by embedding localization techniques in our framework. We also plan to identify a Wi-Fi version and a Bluetooth device type (classic or BLE) by utilizing data rate and bandwidth of the given signal.

References

1. Chen, S., Hui, X., Liu, D., Bo, H., Wang, H.: A vision of IoT: applications, challenges, and opportunities with china perspective. IEEE Internet Things J. **1**(4), 349–359 (2014)

2. Zhang, M., Sun, F., Cheng, X.: Architecture of Internet of Things and its key technology integration based-on RFID, vol. 1, pp. 294–297. IEEE (2012)
3. Cacciagrano, D., Culmone, R., Micheletti, M., Mostarda, L.: Energy-efficient clustering for wireless sensor devices in Internet of Things. In: Al-Turjman, F. (ed.) Performability in Internet of Things. EICC, pp. 59–80. Springer, Cham (2019). https://doi.org/10.1007/978-3-319-93557-7_5
4. Micheletti, M., Mostarda, L., Piermarteri, A.: Rotating energy efficient clustering for heterogeneous devices (REECHD). In: 2018 IEEE 32nd International Conference on Advanced Information Networking and Applications (AINA), pp. 213–220. IEEE (2018)
5. Shankar, A., Jaisankar, N., Khan, M.S., Patan, R., Balamurugan, B.: Hybrid model for security-aware cluster head selection in wireless sensor networks. IET Wirel. Sensor Syst. 9(2), 68–76 (2018)
6. Shankar, A., Jaisankar, N.: Optimal cluster head selection framework to support energy aware routing protocols of wireless sensor network. Int. J. Netw. Virtual Organ. 18(2), 144–165 (2018)
7. Shahid, M.R., Blanc, G., Zhang, Z., Debar, H.: IoT devices recognition through network traffic analysis. In: 2018 IEEE International Conference on Big Data (Big Data), pp. 5187–5192. IEEE (2018)
8. Ammar, N., Noirie, L., Tixeuil, S.: Autonomous IoT device identification prototype. In: 2019 Network Traffic Measurement and Analysis Conference (TMA), pp. 195–196 (2019)
9. Gil, R.: Wireless connectivity for the Internet of Things. Europe, 433:868MHz (2014)
10. Ding, J., Nemati, M., Ranaweera, C., Choi, J.: IoT connectivity technologies and applications: a survey. arXiv preprint arXiv:2002.12646 (2020)
11. Ferro, E., Potorti, F.: Bluetooth and Wi-Fi wireless protocols: a survey and a comparison. IEEE Wirel. Commun. 12(1), 12–26 (2005)
12. Ullah, Z., Al-Turjman, F., Mostarda, L., Gagliardi, R.: Applications of artificial intelligence and machine learning in smart cities. J. Comput. Commun. 154, 313–323 (2020)
13. Ullah, Z., Al-Turjman, F., Mostarda, L.: Cognition in UAV-Aided 5G and beyond communications: a survey. IEEE Trans. Cognit. Commun. Netw. 6(3), 872–891 (2020)
14. Golmie, N., Van Dyck, R., Soltanian, A., Tonnerre, A., Rebala, O.: Interference evaluation of bluetooth and IEEE 802.11 b systems. Wireless Netw. 9(3), 201–211 (2003). https://doi.org/10.1023/A:1022821110023
15. Petrioli, C., Basagni, S., Chlamtac, M.: Configuring bluestars: multihop scatternet formation for bluetooth networks. IEEE Trans. Comput. 52(6), 779–790 (2003)
16. Chang, K.-H.: Bluetooth: a viable solution for IoT? [industry perspectives]. IEEE Wirel. Commun. 21(6), 6–7 (2014)
17. Seyed Mahdi Darroudi and Carles Gomez: Bluetooth low energy mesh networks: A survey. Sensors 17(7), 1467 (2017)
18. Mikhaylov, K., Plevritakis, N., Tervonen, J.: Performance analysis and comparison of bluetooth low energy with IEEE 802.15. 4 and simpliciti. J. Sensor Actuator Netw. 2(3), 589–613 (2013)
19. Ullah, I.: A study and analysis of public WiFi (2012)
20. Mahmoud, M.S., Mohamad, A.A.: A study of efficient power consumption wireless communication techniques/modules for Internet of Things (IoT) applications (2016)

21. Learned-Miller, E.G.: Introduction to supervised learning. I: Department of Computer Science, University of Massachusetts (2014)
22. Kumar, D.P., Amgoth, T., Annavarapu, C.S.R.: Machine learning algorithms for wireless sensor networks: a survey. Inf. Fusion **49**, 1–25 (2019)
23. Hastie, T., Tibshirani, R., Friedman, J.: Unsupervised learning. In: The Elements of Statistical Learning, pp. 485–585. Springer (2009). https://doi.org/10.1007/b94608_14
24. Kaelbling L.P., Littman M.L., Moore A.W.: An introduction to reinforcement learning. In: The Biology and Technology of Intelligent Autonomous Agents, pp. 90–127. Springer (1995). https://doi.org/10.1007/978-3-642-79629-6_5
25. Hadsell, R., Chopra, S., LeCun, Y.: Dimensionality reduction by learning an invariant mapping. In 2006 IEEE Computer Society Conference on Computer Vision and Pattern Recognition (CVPR 2006), vol. 2, pp. 1735–1742. IEEE (2006)
26. Van Der Maaten, L., Postma, E., Van den Herik, J.: Dimensionality reduction: a comparative. J. Mach. Learn. Res. **10**(66–71), 13 (2009)

Share: A Design Pattern for Dynamic Composition of IoT Services

Rosario Culmone[1], Diletta Cacciagrano[1], Fadi Al-Turjman[2,3],
and Leonardo Mostarda[1(✉)]

[1] Computer Science Division, University of Camerino, 62032 Camerino, Italy
{rosario.culmone,diletta.cacciagrano,leonardo.mostarda}@unicam.it
[2] Artificial Intelligence Department, Near East University, Nicosia, Mersin 10, Turkey
[3] Research Center for AI and IoT, Near East University, Nicosia, Mersin 10, Turkey
fadi.alturjman@neu.edu.tr

Abstract. The Internet-of-Things (IoT) is one of the modern technological revolutions that enables communication amongst a plethora of
different devices. To date 30 billion devices are connected to the internet
more than 75 billion devices are foreseen to be connected worldwide by
2025, a five fold increase in ten years. Devices can have different brands
and developers and can be designed to function on a proprietary ecosystem, with separate applications, gateways and tools to support them.
This fragmentation can be disastrous in certain industries, such as the
medical ones, and limit integration between different systems. In this
paper, we envision a solution to overcome this interaction problems. We
propose *Share* a novel programming standard through a design pattern.
This allows on the fly service composition of resource constrained IoT
devices. To this ending, IoT devices exchange integration codes which
specify the data format and the interaction protocol. The design by contract scheme (DCS) is used to make sure that the matching services
verify the constraints dictated by the composition. Unlike other on the
fly approaches, *Share* can run on very small and resource constrained
devices. *Share* has been implemented by using LUA programming language and has been validated on the ESP30 embedded device.

Keywords: Design pattern · IoT device integration · IoT
programming

1 Introduction

The Internet-of-Things (IoT) is composed of interconnected computing
machines, mobile devices, sensors and actuators with unique identifiers that have
the capability of sending data over a network without the need of human interaction. To date 30 billion devices [1] are connected to the internet more than
75 billion devices are foreseen to be connected worldwide by 2025, a five fold
increase in ten years. About 20% of these devices are short range sensors or are

E. Ever and F. Al-Turjman (Eds.): FoNeS-IoT 2020, LNICST 353, pp. 144–156, 2021.
https://doi.org/10.1007/978-3-030-69431-9_11

used for home automation [2]. These are usually installed as consequence of new user needs and new equipment without any pre-arranged installation plan. Short range devices such as watches, glasses, and any wearable devices vary according to the user needs. Devices can have different brands and developers and can be designed to function on a proprietary ecosystem, with separate applications, gateways and tools to support them. This fragmentation can be disastrous in certain industries, such as the medical ones and limit integration between different systems. More precisely, the implementation of services that integrate different devices can be very complicated or even impossible when proprietary or closed application level protocols are employed. Standardisation in this sector has been proved to be very difficult since there is a wide variety of services. They can range from smart home services to domestic appliance management and health care services [3,4]. These services can include heterogeneous IoT devices [5], such as drones, appliances, wearable devices, connected cars, that have different peculiarities and have limited capabilities in terms of memory, CPU and energy.

To date service integration of IoT services has been faced by using different approaches. Various IoT cloud players [6] offer centralised solutions where data are centrally collected and users can define centralised applications in order to define integrated services. Centralised solutions may not scale, this is why current trend is to move the service computation as close as possible to the edge [7,8]. This enables in-network computation, peer-to-peer service provisioning, can improve reliability and allow interaction when no connection to the centralised cloud is available [9]. Middlewares have been widely adopted for integration purposes [10–12]. They often require an *a priori* methodological approach where client and server agree on the format and semantic of each service before the composition takes place. In contrast, an approach that offers dynamic composition should be used [13]. On the fly IoT service composition is a widely studied problem [14,15]. Frameworks like OSGi, SM4ALL [13] and WSDL [16–18] offer a valid solution for service compositions. Their major drawback is the impossibility of running on small memory and CPU embedded IoT devices in order to enable a decentralised and peer-to-peer service integration.

In this paper we propose *Share*, a novel programming standard through a design pattern. This allows on the fly service composition of resource constrained IoT devices (in terms of memory and CPU). To this ending, IoT devices exchange integration codes which specify the data format and the interaction protocol. This overcomes the limits of data-oriented standards and allow the dynamic composition of services on the fly. *Share* allows the finding of services (for composition purposes) by using a matching language. The design by contract scheme (DCS) [19] is used to make sure that the matching services verify the constraints dictated by the composition. The novelty introduced by *Share* is twofold: to run on very small and resource constrained devices; and to allows peer-to-peer on the fly service composition without the addition of any centralised entity. *Share* has been formally defined, and has been implemented by using the LUA programming language. This implementation has been tested on ESP32 embedded devices.

The rest of the article is organised as follows: Sect. 2 introduces the related work; Sect. 3 introduces the *Share* design pattern in details; Sect. 3.1 describes the structure of the design pattern while Sect. 3.2 its behavioural part; Sect. 4 discusses the pros and cons of using *Share*; finally, Sect. 5 concludes the article and outlines future work.

2   Related Work

Device integration for service implementation has been faced by using a plethora of different approaches. In [20] the W3C community proposes the use of the IoT-Lite ontology. This is a lightweight ontology that describes Internet of Things (IoT) resources, entities and services. It allows the description and use of IoT platforms without consuming excessive processing time when querying the ontology. IoT-Lite can be used with a quantity taxonomy, such as qu-taxo, which allows the discovery and interoperability of IoT resources in heterogeneous platforms by using a common vocabulary. Various IoT cloud players try to solve the integration problem [6] by offering tools for collecting data and for developing applications. In this case integration is obtained in a centralised way. Although this approach solves the integration problem it does not scale, computation should be moved to the edge [7,8] in order to favour in-network computation and peer-to-peer service provisioning. This could improve reliability and allow interaction when no connection to the centralised cloud is available [9]. In [21] the Representational State Transfer (REST) approach is used. This uses HTTP methods, devices are addressed by using Universal Resource Indicators (URI) and data is exchanged through standard XML. Although this approach solves the peer-to-peer integration problems, it requires the installation of web based components which may be infeasible when limited memory IoT devices are considered.

On the fly IoT service composition is a widely studied problem. In [14,15] the authors propose a middleware for home area network (HAN). They synthesise new services without user intervention by using third-party "service providers" (SPs). This solution requires the use of a third party device whereas a peer-to-peer solution without the connection to a third party device could indeed enable opportunistic on the fly mobile composition. A different approach is based on asynchronous and synchronous primitive communications [10–12,22]. Synchronous based solutions such as RPC [10] and asynchronous ones such as pub/-sub [11,22] requires an *a priori* methodological approach where client and server agree on the format and semantic of each service before the interaction takes place. In contrast, our approach offers dynamic composition of services by providing modularity. Unlike well known dynamic service composition approaches [13] that cannot run on constrained devices, *Share* is suitable to run on small IoT embedded systems and allows peer-to-peer communications.

Data oriented integration approaches such as WSDL [16–18] are complicated because they need an amount of computational resources that are not available in many IoT devices. They requires validators [23] in order to check service compatibility. Validators can be complex and may not run on embedded devices since they have limited computation and memory resources. In addition, complex constraints on service integration cannot be verified in WSDL since checkers that are based on first order logic [24–26] are needed. The design by contract scheme (DCS) [19] seems to be a reasonable approach in order to verify that the constraints during a service call are satisfied. DCS requires that software designers define formal, precise and verifiable interface specifications for software components, which extend the ordinary definition of abstract data types with preconditions, postconditions and invariants. These specifications are referred to as *contracts*. The verification that the specifications of the callee are compatible with the one of the caller can be done by using Satisfiability Modulo Theories. There are different tools such as Boogie [27] and Z3 [28] that allows the constraint verification to be performed. These approaches can be prone to the state explosion problems. For a more efficient and real time verification, a solution that is widely adopted is the *a posteriori* constraint verification. More precisely, the service invocation is performed without any previous verification. If the failure is in the invocation phase, it means that the caller's preconditions do not satisfy those of the called party. If the failure is in the verification of the caller's post conditions, it means that the value produced by the called party does not meet the caller's post conditions. *Share* uses this approach.

The OSGi [29] specification describes a modular system and a service platform for Java that implements a complete and dynamic component model. Applications or components, takes the form of bundles and can be remotely installed, stopped, started, updated, and uninstalled without requiring a reboot. The OSGi specifications have evolved beyond the original focus of service gateways, and are now used in applications ranging from mobile phones to automobiles, industrial automation, building automation, PDAs, grid computing, entertainment, fleet management and application servers. This approach seems to be inapplicable for small sensors devices which may not have enough computational power to run a JVM and any other OSGi service. For instance an ESP32 microcontroller [30] which costs few dollars cannot run an OSGi framework. *Share* can be executed directly on the IoT device node. We have successfully run *Share* on a ESP32 micro controller [31] by using LUA code. Devices were able to communicate successfully in a peer-to-peer fashion without the need of any extra components.

In [32] the authors present various approaches for IoT service composition. They focus on the "Docker Compose" orchestration which can run on constrained devices. In [33] the authors present CHOREO which allows the definition of a logically centralised orchestration of pervasive services. CHOREO generates a peer-to-peer choreography implementation from the logically centralised orchestration. The limitation of [32] and [33] is the need of agreement on the format and semantic of each service before the interaction takes place. *Share* overcomes this limitation by allowing on the fly service composition.

3 Design Pattern

3.1 Class Diagram

Figure 1 shows the class diagram of the *Share* pattern. This is composed of the following three classes: (i) *Share*; (ii) *Service*; and (iii) *Feature*.

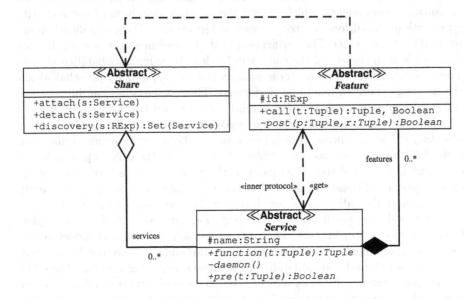

Fig. 1. Class diagram

The class *Share* implements a space where *Service* objects can be stored. The public methods *attach(s : Service)* can be used to add a *Service* s to a *Share* object while the method *detach(s : Service)* allows the removal of the *Service* s. Finally the *discovery(s : RExep) : Set(Service)* method can be used in order to search all *Service* objects that match the regular expression *s*. A set *Set(Service)* of all services that match the regular expression *RExep* are returned to the caller. For instance a Service *double hypotenuse(double a, double b)* can be defined in order to find the length of the hypotenuse of a right triangle by using the two edges *a* and *b*. This can be added by using the method *attach*. We use the string "1.4.3.6" in order to identify the *hypotenuse* service. The service *hypotenuse* can be searched by using a regular expression *RExep* = "1.4.3.6" when the *discovery* service is used.

The *Service* class defines a service. This includes a service name which is refereed to as the attribute *name* in Fig. 1. This is a unique identifier such as a MIB (Management Information Base) of the SNMP protocol which can be used as an unique object identifier (OID) of the function performed by the service [34,35]. We have used the MIB "1.4.3.6" for the *hypotenuse* service example. A *Service* class defines a *pre* predicate. This is a method that takes as an input a *Tuple t* and returns a boolean value. The tuple *t* can include the list of parameters that are taken as an input by the service. The predicate should returns *true* when the tuple *t* verifies the preconditions required to run the service *false* otherwise. In our *double hypotenuse(double a, double b)* example the tuple *t* is composed by the two double numbers *a* and *b* and a precondition *boolean pre([a, b])* could be used to check that the two edges are positive numbers. A *Service* class needs also to specify a *Tuple function(t Tuple)* and a *daemon()*. The *function* is a connector that is sent to the client requesting the service and is used in order to interact with the *daemon*. This implements the service behaviour. More precisely, *function(t Tuple)* is a client stub that serialises the service parameters *t* into a format that can be understood by the related *daemon()* method. The method *function* opens a connection and send data to the *daemon*, it may also wait for the reply (if any). We emphasise that the serialisation and deserialisation that are performed by *function* and *daemon* are not necessary when client and server are written by using the same language and run on the same hardware architecture. This situation leads to very efficient data transfer when complex or large quantities of data must be transferred. When *function* and *daemon* are written by using the same language the use of verification tools for consistency and correctness of the data are simplified.

The class *Feature* provides a primitive service that is a basic building block of the share pattern. More precisely, the *daemon()* of a *Service* class can compose one or more *Features* in order to implement its behaviour. The *Features* regular expression *id : RExp* describes the functionality that is implemented by the feature. This will be used when calling a *Share* object in order to find the feature that is needed. Effectively, a Feature defines a service that has been already defined and added to a *Service* repository. A *call* can return the output *Tuple, Boolean. Tuple* is the output of the *call* functionality while *Boolean* is true when the call execution terminates without error, *false* otherwise. This can be consequence of a connection problem, a service not found error or other types of errors that are defined inside the *call* implementation.

A *Features* class defines a *post* predicate. This is a method that takes as an input a *Tuple t* and returns a boolean value. The predicate should returns *true* when the *t* verifies the postconditions after running *call*, *false* otherwise. In our *double hypotenuse(double a, double b)* example the *Feature* could implement the square root and the value must have the desired precision. In this case the call would take the tuple $[a^2 + b^2]$ and return the square root value. This could be used to calculate the hypotenuse value. Effectively, the class *Service* integrate the service call *sqrt* in order to provide the new service *hypotenuse*.

Listing 1.1 shows various Object Constraint Language (OCL) rules. These apply to the class diagram of Fig. 1. The first context rule specifies that the attach method of the class *Share* adds the service *s* into the *services* association. The second context rule specifies that the detach method of the class *Share* removes the service *s* from the *services* association. The third context rule specifies that the discovery method of the class *Share* returns all services whose name matches with RExp *s*. The last rule specifies that the association *services* is a set thus it does not contain duplicated services.

Listing 1.1. OCL rules for Share

```
contex Share::attach(s:Service)
  pre:  services->excludes(s)
  post: services->includes(s)

contex Share::detach(s:Service)
  pre:  services->includes(s)
  post: services->excludes(s)

contex Share::discovery(s:String):Set(Service)
  post: result = Set(services->select(name.matches(s)))

contex Share
  inv: services->asSet()
```

Listing 1.2 shows the OCL rules for ensuring consistency amongst the operations that are necessary for the call operation. Its result is specified by means of the sequence *found*. This is defined by applying on all services found with *discovery* the operation *pre*, *function* and *post* by using the tuple of the function *call*. The rule defines the correct relation between the parameters of *pre*, *function* and *post* operations. Finally, the result of the *call* operation is the first result of the *found* sequence or the couple: boolean, tuple where the *true* value specifies the successful execution of the *call* invocation (i.e., a service has been found).

Listing 1.2. OCL rules for Feature

```
contex Feature::call(t:Tuple):Boolean, Tuple
  def: found : Sequence(Service) =
    select(s : Share.discovery(id) |
      let s.pre(k:Tuple):Boolean, self.post(v,q):Boolean, s.function(w):r in
        t.isOclType() = k.isOclType() and
        t.isOclType() = v.isOclType() and
        r.isOclType() = q.isOclType() and
        s.pre(t) and self.post(t,s.function(t)))
  post: if found->notEmpty()
        then result = {true, found->first().function(t)}
        else result = {false, Sequence{}} endif
```

Listing 1.3 and 1.4 sketches a *Share hypotenuse* implementation by using the *LUA* language. Listing 1.3 shows the declaration of our *hypotenuse Service* class which takes the following parameters:

- the unique identifier of the *Service* (i.e., its MIB);
- a LUA function, i.e., the *Service function* implementation of the client stub;
- a LUA function that implements the *deamon*. This declares the following parts: (i) a *feature* with *RExp* "1.4.5.2.*"; (ii) a post condition that specifies the precision of the *square root*; and (iii) the reception of the parameters and the call of the *square root*;
- the *pre* condition on the *hypotenuse* service specifying that the edges need to be positive numbers

Listing 1.3 ends by registering the newly created service to a *Share* object by using the *attach* method.

Listing 1.4 declares *sqrt Service*. This takes as an input the following parameters:

- the unique identifier of the *Service* (i.e., its MIB);
- a LUA function, i.e., the *Service function* implementation of the client stub for connection to this service;
- a LUA function that implements the *deamon*. This includes the server stub in order to receive the parameters, perform the square root and return the result;
- the *pre* condition on the *square* root service, requiring a positive number;

Listing 1.3 ends by registering the newly created service to a *Share* object by using the *attach* method.

Listing 1.3. Service on device A

```
hypotenuse = Service.new("1.4.3.6", -- declaration of hypotenuse service
   function(a,b) -- function
   --[[ send a and b to daemon e receive result value ]]
   end,
   function() -- daemon
     local sqrt = Feature.new(
       "1.4.5.2.*", --RExp
       function(a,b) return math.abs(a-b^2)<0.000001 end -- post
     end)
   --receive parameters from function on variable x and y using inner protocol
   local r,ok = sqrt.call(x^2+y^2)
   --send result value r to function using inner protocol
   end,
   function(a,b) return a > 0 and b > 0 end -- pre
)
deviceA = Share.new(myIp)
deviceA.attach(hypotenuse)
```

Listing 1.4. Service on device B

```
sqrt = Service.new("1.4.5.2.1", -- declaration of sqrt service
   function() --[[ the call function use dofile for run this code and
                   the ip provide from discovery ]]
   "return function(a, ip)
      local host, port = ip, 7777
      tcp:connect(host, port);
      tcp:send(a);
      while true do
        local result, status = tcp:receive()
        if status == "closed" then break end
      return result
      end
   end",
   function()
     local server = socket.bind("*",7777)
     while true do
       local client = server:accept()
       local i, err = client:receive()
       if not err then
         client:send(math.sqrt(i))
         break
       end
     end
   end,
   function(a) return a > 0 -- pre
)
deviceB = Share.new(Myip)
deviceB.attach(sqrt)
```

3.2   Sequence Diagram

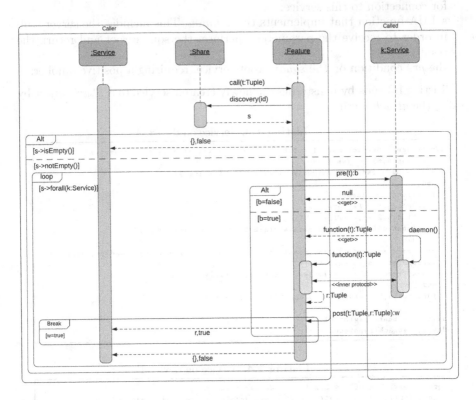

Fig. 2. The call service

Figure 2 shows a sequence diagram. This shows all the object interactions, arranged in time sequence, that take place during a *Service* call (e.g., *hypotenuse*). This calls the *call* method of the *Feature* object which tries to discover a *service* that matches the *id* : *RExp Feature* on a *Service* objects (this is done by using the *discover*(*id*) message). This returns a set *s* of *Services* objects that match the *id* : *RExp*. When *s* is empty (no service is found) an error is returned otherwise the set of all *Service* objects is explored. This is done by means of the *loop* sequence of Fig. 2. For each Service the precondition *pre*(*t*) : *b* is called. When this returns false the next service is analysed otherwise a suitable service implementation *s* is found. The object *Feature* uses the *function* stub to call the *demon* of the service *s* which executes the functionality and returns the result *r* : *Tuple, w* : *boolean*. When *w* is *true* the execution is successful and the *Service* call ends otherwise the next service is analysed.

4 Discussion

Share has been implemented as an open source software and can be executed in memory and CPU constrained devices. We have used *Share* to implement a domotic application by using the Whitecat ESP32 N2. This implementation is available at the following link:

https://francescocoppola.me/share/_build/html/index.html.

All the distributed devices (sensors and actuators) use the same hardware (i.e., the ESP32 microcontroller) and are programmed by using the same language (i.e., LUA). As a consequence of this, client server communication does not require an data format conversion only the serialisation operation has been implemented in order to send data. Devices communicate by using a broad cast protocol (i.e., in a peer to peer fashion) by using ZigBee. When new devices are added we show that service composition (with existing devices) can be easily done by using the share pattern. To the best of our knowledge no dynamic service composition approach can run on memory and CPU constrained devices. *Share* requires few kilobyte to be run.

Share allows the interaction with black box components (e.g, closed code with no source code available). In fact, the function for device integration (i.e., the *function*() code) is sent to other devices while the code implementing the functionality (i.e., the *daemon*) remain on the proprietary device as a black box component. Few Siemens devices were integrated thanks to this feature.

5 Conclusion and Future Works

In this paper we have introduced *Share* a design pattern for on the fly service composition. Unlike other on the fly approaches, *Share* can run on very small and resource constrained devices. *Share* allows service composition by using three main classes that are *Share*, *Feature* and *Service*. The *Share* class is a memory that can be used in order to store *Service* objects. These can implement composition of various *Features* which are services that have been already composed and added to a *Share* object. *Features* can be searched on the fly by means of a matching language. The design by contract scheme (DCS) is used to make sure that the matching services verify the constraints dictated by the composition. *Share* has been implemented by using the LUA programming language and has been validated on the ESP30 embedded device.

As future work we plan to investigate the security of the *Share* design pattern. *Authentication, access control* and *confidentiality* should be provided when composing a service (i.e., performing a discovery and calling the service). Security mechanisms in order to implement availability and non repudiation should be also investigated as well. The implementation of various security mechanisms on very small and resource constrained devices is still matter of research.

We also plan to solve the loop that can be generated when service composition takes place. More precisely, a service can call other services that can call recursively previously called services. This can lead to an infinite execution.

Loops can be solved by enriching the functionality of *Feature::call()* with the service list *Service::name* that are used. This must be propogated through the *Feature::call*. When a loop is discovered the service call fails.

Acknowledgment. We thank the students Francesco Coppola and Stefano Pernicola, computer science department, University of Camerino. They have implemented the *Share* pattern in LUA. The implementation is freely available at the following link: https://francescocoppola.me/share/_build/html/index.html.

Francesco also implemented the porting of LUARtos over the M5Stack platform and implemented a dashboard for smartphone. This can be used in order to monitor the functioning of domotic devices.

References

1. Atzori, L., Iera, A., Morabito, G.: The internet of things: a survey. Comput. Netw. **54**(15), 2787–2805 (2010). https://doi.org/10.1016/j.comnet.2010.05.010
2. E. M. Report, Internet of things forecast (2019). https://www.ericsson.com/en/mobility-report/internet-of-things-forecast
3. Ullah, Z., Al-Turjman, F., Mostarda, L., Gagliardi, R.: Applications of artificial intelligence and machine learning in smart cities. Comput. Commun. **154**, pp. 313–323 (2020). https://doi.org/10.1016/j.comcom.2020.02.069
4. Al-Turjman, F., Zahmatkesh, H., Mostarda, L.: Quantifying uncertainty in internet of medical things and big-data services using intelligence and deep learning. IEEE Access **7**, 115749–115759 (2019). https://doi.org/10.1109/ACCESS.2019.2931637
5. Al-Turjman, F., Abujubbeh, M., Malekloo, A., Mostarda, L.: UAVs assessment in software-defined IoT networks: an overview. Comput. Commun. **150**, 519–536 (2020). https://doi.org/10.1016/j.comcom.2019.12.004
6. Pflanzner, T., Kertesz, A.: A survey of IoT cloud providers. In: 39th International Convention on Information and Communication Technology. Electronics and Microelectronics (MIPRO), pp. 730–735 (2016). https://doi.org/10.1109/MIPRO.2016.7522237
7. Shi, W., Cao, J., Zhang, Q., Li, Y., Xu, L.: Edge computing: vision and challenges. IEEE Internet of Things J. **3**(5), 637–646 (2016). https://doi.org/10.1109/JIOT.2016.2579198
8. Bonomi, F., Milito, R., Zhu, J., Addepalli, S.: Fog computing and its role in the internet of things. In: Proceedings of the First Edition of the MCC Workshop on Mobile Cloud Computing, MCC 2012, pp. 13–16. ACM, New York (2012). https://doi.org/10.1145/2342509.2342513. http://doi.acm.org/10.1145/2342509.2342513
9. Cheng, B., Wang, M., Zhao, S., Zhai, Z., Zhu, D., Chen, J.: Situation-aware dynamic service coordination in an IoT environment. IEEE/ACM Trans. Netw. **25**(4), 2082–2095 (2017). https://doi.org/10.1109/TNET.2017.2705239
10. Bloomer, J.: Power Programming with RPC. O'Reilly & Associates Inc., Sebastopol (1992)
11. Eugster, P.T., Felber, P.A., Guerraoui, R., Kermarrec, A.-M.: The many faces of publish/subscribe. ACM Comput. Surv. **35**(2) (2003). 114–131. https://doi.org/10.1145/857076.857078. http://doi.acm.org/10.1145/857076.857078
12. Russello, G., Mostarda, L., Dulay, N.: A policy-based publish/subscribe middleware for sense-and-react applications. J. Syst. Softw. **84**(4), 638–654 (2011). https://doi.org/10.1016/j.jss.2010.10.023

13. Baldoni, R., et al.: An Embedded Middleware Platform for Pervasive and Immersive Environments for-all, University of Groningen, Johann Bernoulli Institute for Mathematics and Computer Science (2009). https://www.rug.nl/informatica/onderzoek/bernoulli

14. Pourreza, H., Graham, P.: On the fly service composition for local interaction environments. In: Fourth Annual IEEE International Conference on Pervasive Computing and Communications Workshops (PERCOMW 2006), pp. 6 pp.-399 (2006). https://doi.org/10.1109/PERCOMW.2006.104

15. Zhao, Q., Huang, G., Huang, J., Liu, X., Mei, H.: A web-based mashup environment for on-the-fly service composition. In: IEEE International Symposium on Service-Oriented System Engineering, pp. 32–37 (2008). https://doi.org/10.1109/SOSE.2008.9

16. Booth, D., Liu, C.K.: Web services description language (WSDL) version 2.0 part 0: Primer (2007). http://www.w3.org/TR/wsdl20-primer

17. Chinnici, R., Moreau, J.-J., Ryman, A., Weerawarana, S.: Web services description language (WSDL) version 2.0 part 1: Core language (2007). http://www.w3.org/TR/wsdl20

18. Chinnici, R., Haas, H., Lewis, A.A., Moreau, J.-J., Orchard, D., Weerawarana, S.: Web services description language (WSDL) version 2.0 part 2: Adjuncts (2007). http://www.w3.org/TR/wsdl20-adjuncts

19. Meyer, B.: Object-Oriented Software Construction, 2nd edn. Prentice-Hall Inc., Upper Saddle River (1997)

20. Bermudez-Edo, M., Elsaleh, T., Barnaghi, P., Taylor, K.: Iot-lite ontology (2015). http://www.w3.org/Submission/2015/SUBM-iot-lite-20151126

21. Castellani, A.P., Gheda, M., Bui, N., Rossi, M., Zorzi, M.: Web services for the internet of things through CoAP and EXI. In: IEEE International Conference on Communications Workshops (ICC), pp. 1–6 (2011). https://doi.org/10.1109/iccw.2011.5963563

22. Dulay, N., Micheletti, M., Mostarda, L., Piermarteri, A.: PICO-MP: de-centralised macro-programming for wireless sensor and actuator networks. In: 2018 IEEE 32nd International Conference on Advanced Information Networking and Applications (AINA), pp. 289–296 (2018)

23. Marchetti, E., Bartolini, C., Bertolino, A., Polini, A.: WS-TAXI: a WSDL-based testing tool for web services. In: 2009 International Conference on Software Testing Verification and Validation(ICST), pp. 326–335 (2009). https://doi.org/10.1109/ICST.2009.28. http://doi.ieeecomputersociety.org/10.1109/ICST.2009.28

24. Cacciagrano, D., Corradini, F., Culmone, R., Vito, L.: Dynamic constraint-based invocation of web services. In: Bravetti, M., Núñez, M., Zavattaro, G. (eds.) WS-FM 2006. LNCS, vol. 4184, pp. 138–147. Springer, Heidelberg (2006). https://doi.org/10.1007/11841197_9

25. Cacciagrano, D., Corradini, F., Culmone, R., Tesei, L., Vito, L.: A model-prover for constrained dynamic conversations. In: The Tenth International Conference on Information Integration and Web-based Applications Services, iiWAS 2008, Linz, Austria, 24–26 November 2008, pp. 630–633 (2008). https://doi.org/10.1145/1497308.1497428

26. Cacciagrano, D., Corradini, F., Culmone, R., Vito, L.: Constraint-based dynamic conversations. In: The Fifth International Conference on Networking and Services, ICNS 2009, Valencia, Spain, 20–25 April 2009, pp. 7–12 (2009). https://doi.org/10.1109/ICNS.2009.55

27. Barnett, M., Leino, R.: Weakest-precondition of unstructured programs. In: The 6th ACM SIGPLAN-SIGSOFT Workshop on Program Analysis for Software Tools and Engineering, PASTE 2005, pp. 82–87. ACM Press, New York (2005)
28. de Moura, L., Bjørner, N.: Z3: an efficient SMT solver. In: Ramakrishnan, C.R., Rehof, J. (eds.) TACAS 2008. LNCS, vol. 4963, pp. 337–340. Springer, Heidelberg (2008). https://doi.org/10.1007/978-3-540-78800-3_24
29. Tavares, A.L., Valente, M.T.: A gentle introduction to OSGi. ACM SIGSOFT Softw. Eng. Notes **33**(5), 1–5 (2008). https://doi.org/10.1145/1402521.1402526
30. Espressif, Esp32 soc (2019). https://www.espressif.com/
31. Whitecat, Whitecat esp32 n1 board (2019). https://whitecatboard.org/lorawan-deployment-in-cornella/
32. Qanbari, S., et al.: IoT design patterns: computational constructs to design, build and engineer edge applications. In: IEEE First International Conference on Internet-of-Things Design and Implementation (IoTDI), pp. 277–282 (2016)
33. Mostarda, L., Marinovic, S., Dulay, N.: Distributed orchestration of pervasive services. In: 2010 24th IEEE International Conference on Advanced Information Networking and Applications, pp. 166–173 (2010)
34. Hui-Ping, H., Shi-De, X., Xiang-Yin, M.: Applying SNMP technology to manage the sensors in internet of things. Open Cybern. System. J. **9**, 1019–1024 (2015)
35. iana.org. Structure of management information (SMI) numbers (MIB module registrations) (2020). https://www.iana.org/assignments/smi-numbers/smi-numbers.xhtml

A Framework of Developing Health Care Application Systems Using 6LoWPAN Based Wireless Sensor Networks

Zhongwei Zhang[1]([✉]), Jianxiong Wang[2], and Xiaohua Hu[3]

[1] School of Sciences, University of Southern Queensland, West Street,
Toowoomba 4350, Australia
`Zhongwei.Zhang@usq.edu.au`
[2] School of Health and Wellbeing, University of Southern Queensland, West Street,
Toowoomba 4350, Australia
`Jianxiong.Wang@usq.edu.au`
[3] School of Mathematics and Statistics, Hainan Normal University,
No. 99 Longkun South Road, Haikou 571158, Hainan, China
`1241957415@qq.com`

Abstract. There were an increasing number of innovative applications of Wireless Sensor Networks (WSNs) in health care domain. It has never been such clearer to appreciate the advantages and benefits of applying the WSNs to improve the quality of health care in a wide variety of areas. Thanks to the sensing and communications technology of today, it has also reached a point where these WSNs applications can be readily implemented and deployed to function although there are some limits and hinderance from the viewpoint of security concerns.

In this paper, we provide a protocol stack applicable to the WSNs for health care systems, and to outline a framework to implement the WSNs in two different health care settings. Following the proposed framework, we have simulated a WSNs based health care application for the settings of hospitals and/or nursing homes for the performance study.

Keywords: Health care · Wireless Sensor Networks (WSNs) ·
6LoWPAN · Network Simulator (NS-3) · IEEE 802.15.4 (ZigBee)

1 Introduction

With the COVID-19 pandemic infecting millions of people around the world at the moment, the health care industry is experiencing an unprecedented shortage of health care workers; the health care practitioners and providers are under enormous pressure to hold up the much-needed services for the millions of virus infected victims.

In the last couple of decades, the wireless sensor networks (WSNs) have been used in many areas including industrial and home automation, health care [10], agriculture [9] and environment [5], and military. There are many research into

© ICST Institute for Computer Sciences, Social Informatics and Telecommunications Engineering 2021
Published by Springer Nature Switzerland AG 2021. All Rights Reserved
E. Ever and F. Al-Turjman (Eds.): FoNeS-IoT 2020, LNICST 353, pp. 157–168, 2021.
https://doi.org/10.1007/978-3-030-69431-9_12

how to apply the WSNs technology to mitigate these pressures from health care service providers. In addition to that, the exploitation of WSNs technology can not only complement the human health care service providers, but also improve the quality of health care at a reduced cost. With the advances in sensing technology and communication technology, the application of WSNs makes possible for the health care service to be more affordable for public.

In general, wireless sensor networks (WSNs) comprise a number of autonomous, low-power, spatially distributed, wireless sensor nodes. A WSNs based health care system is just one type of WSNs application, primarily devised for the health care environment such as hospitals and nursing homes, etc. The potential benefits of WSNs based health care systems are enormous, yet to be fully exploited and unleashed, there are many challenges facing us while applying the WSNs applications in reality. The tangible benefits include: location flexibility, all time availability, quick adaptability and low-cost in communications. Here the flexibility refer to the WSN system collects and communicates data wirelessly with minimal input from the patient. The availability allows the physiological data to be monitored continuously. The adaptability makes possible to change the mission of the application of the WSNs as the medical needs changes. The last benefit is that using the WSNs in health care provides a low-cost communication infrastructure.

Among these many challenges, the major one is the data acquisition and communications within sensor nodes. Since the sensor nodes have a limited energy supply, the protocol responsible for data transmitting among the sensing and routing devices must be very stingy and efficient. Apart from the data communication protocol, the security protocol and security mechanism in the WSNs applications is even more complex and challenging. On the top of these security concerns that are general to all type of WSNs applications, there are more issues that are specific to the WSNs for health care, where the sensitive medical data of the individual are dealt with. Privacy is another major concern of patients and the greatest barrier to the deployment of WSNs applications. Deployment of the WSNs application for health care impose constraints on end-to-end reliability, which measures how well the system performs in the presence of disturbances. The integration of multiple sensing devices could cause a problem when operating at different frequencies.

This paper is structured as follows. In Sect. 2, an introduction to the WSNs technology is used in the development of health care system is given. Also in Sect. 2, a review of challenges of applying the WSNs in health care is delineated. In the following Sect. 3, the protocol stack for the sensor nodes is proposed, which is similar to the traditional computer network nodes such as hosts and/or routers. The implementation of the WSNs for heath care will be given in Sect. 4, it is based on a list of communications standards which has currently been used in the Low-Power and Lossy Networks using IPv6, in particular on the WSNs. In Sect. 5, three configurations of the WSNs applications for two different health care setting are described. In the final Sect. 6, we briefly summarize the progress of the current work and also the direction of future work has been presented.

2   Challenges of the WSNs for Health Care

Health care systems have evolved from the medical database to the web-based networks, to the social networks, to the ubiquitous computing, and even to the cloud computing. The scope of Health care services have been expending from the traditional hospital care to the at-home health care, to the tele-medicine, etc.

2.1   Health Care Services

We delineate these services as follows:

1. Health monitoring: This service is to monitor a patient in the clinical setting or at home regardless of the patient's or care-giver's location. Monitoring system is often necessary to constantly monitor a patient's vital signs such as blood pressure, heart rate, body temperature, and EGCG.
2. Body health monitoring: This service is to continuously monitor physiological data during the patient's stay at the hospitals or home. It can be useful for emergency cases. It can also help people by providing health care services such as memory enhancement, medical data access, cancer detection, asthma detection, and monitoring blood glucose.
3. At-home health care: This care is related to aging population. At-home health care provides affordable care to the elderly while they live independently.
4. Tele-medicine: This foresight service allows clinical work to be performed remotely. It refers to the provision of health care services and education over a distance.

2.2   Wireless Technology in Health Care and Medical Services

It is not new that the mobile ad-hoc networks (MANETs) have been widely used by doctors for health care and medical services. There are many structural resemblances between the Wireless Sensor Networks and the traditional ad-hoc networks. But the traditional ad-hoc networks have less or virtually no constrains on resources than the WSNs put on. These innate constraints of the WSNs, have rendered many technologies and protocols which worked well on the ad-hoc networks, no longer feasible for WSNs. For instance, particularly in networking or routing protocol in the network layer of the TCP/IP stack, where the Ad Hoc On-Demand Distance Vector (AODV) protocol have been proven to be efficient for the ad-hoc networks; but the ADOV is not of any good for the WSNs. In [6], a performance study show that the AODV require much higher memory in each node of the WSNs to maintain the routing state for each active used paths, which is a serious limitation for the WSNs.

Hence to ameliorate this problem, some novel and more efficient algorithms have to be developed specifically for the packets routing on the WSNs [3]. Research and development of routing algorithms in the WSNs were initially driven by defense applications; the primary design goal of a routing algorithm operating in the context of the WSNs is to minimize power consumption and thereby extend the lifetime of the WSNs nodes and/or devices.

Apart from that, there are more vulnerability in the WSNs than the ad-hoc networks. For instance, in most cases, the WSNs are vulnerable to various sensor data faults and this vulnerability hinders efficient and timely response in the health care applications. Security is particularly important in the WSNs health care applications, where the sensor data are sensitive medical data of patients. Privacy is another major concern of patients and the greatest barrier to the WSNs health care deployment.

The health care applications normally impose constraints on the end-to-end reliability, which measures how well the health care system perform in the presence of disturbances.

A WSNs based health care system is normally consists of a number of the WSNs networks and the gateway routers; in which each of the WSNs networks is primarily used to gather the data in the specific environment such as a nursing home and/or clinic ward; while the gateway routers are interfacing the WSNs with the Internet, as shown in Fig. 1.

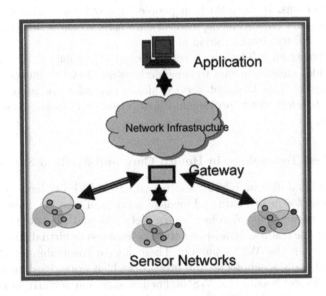

Fig. 1. The Architecture of WSNs Application

2.3   Wireless and Sensing Devices in Health Care

The primary applications of WSNs in health care include monitoring patients and checking temperature, aiming to gather patients' chronicle data and home automation. As mentioned above, the core components of the WSNs network are the sensing devices and wireless communication nodes. More and more sensing devices and wireless devices are being used in the health care systems such as the smart phones and low power devices. This trend results in the Internet of Things (IoT), where the IPv6 address schema for the IoT devices become a compulsory alternative.

3   Standards for Protocols of the WSNs Networks

In this section, we propose the protocol stack for the WSNs in health care. The proposed stack of the WSNs based health care system is shown in Fig. 2. Unlike the Internet protocol stack which has four layers, the proposed stack has five layers with an additional layer. These five layers are application layer, routing layer, and adaptation layer, IEEE 802.15.4 MAC and IEEE 802.15.4 PHY.

Essentially there are two considerations when exploiting the routing protocol for the WSNs in health care, as mentioned in the preceding section, we have to always keep in mind, that with the energy constraint and simple and cheap wireless sensor nodes, the routing protocols used in the traditional Ad-hoc networks are no longer applicable in the WSNs networks and their applications. The second consideration is the networking address schema. Since the WSNs networking nodes can be any lower power communication devices, the IPv4 schema becomes invalid but the IPv6 schema with 128-bit address spaces must be adopted.

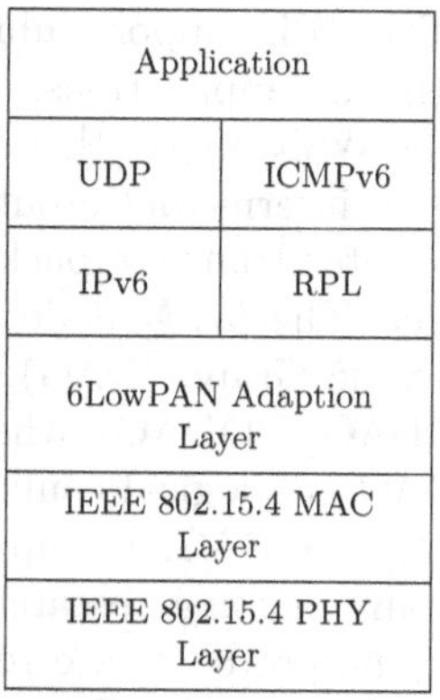

Application	
UDP	ICMPv6
IPv6	RPL
6LowPAN Adaption Layer	
IEEE 802.15.4 MAC Layer	
IEEE 802.15.4 PHY Layer	

Fig. 2. Protocol Stack

In the following sections, we discus more details about each of these layers and its protocols.

3.1   Application Protocols

For a general WSNs, the sensing nodes are used to sense their surrounding and/or to trigger a signal. Nevertheless, the applications are highly distinct in nature. The applications operate under different constraints, which are designed by application parameters. The applications generate sensor data with different patterns. For instance the application of WSNs in health care normally generate the traffic with the Poisson distribution.

The interface between the network devices in the applications is handled by the routing protocols by establishing communication paths and/or routes in the network through the mechanism of message exchanges. The application and the routing protocol parameters have to be tuned to one another to obtain the optimal behavior of a large communication network.

There are many security issues related with the application protocols. In regard to the WSNs for health care, one eminent concerns is the intrusiveness to the privacy, due to these sensing devices are susceptible to electronic interference and channel noise. Potentially, there might be some ethical issues as well.

3.2   Multi-hop Routing Protocols

There are a number of routing protocols which are based on the IPv6 addressing schema. Hence they can be adopted during the development of the WSNs applications for health care. In this section, we briefly overview a few of them that have been widely studied in the last decade.

First of all, Routing Protocol for Low-Power and Lossy Networks (RPL) is a proactive routing protocol [4]. As its name implies, the RPL is a distance-vector routing algorithm originally designed for low power and lossy networks using the IPv6 addressing schema. The RPL supports ubiquitous sensing applications such as the WSNs based health care applications.

RPL components include the WSN nodes [1], and local border router (LBR). The WSNs nodes act as hosts or intermediate routers for transmitting packets in the WSN nodes; while the router translate packets through the WSN nodes to user hosts from the Internet. The WSN node and the LBR routers apply a new concept of Directed Acyclic Graph (DAG), this DAG is separated into multiple Destination Oriented DAG (DODAG), where the root of these DODAG are normally LBRs. The DPDAG is a logical configuration on the WSN nodes, so a WSN node can join multiple DODAGs to support routing optimization.

Secondly, there are also many ongoing researches that attempt to develop the AODV-like protocols, but the protocols are relied on the IPv6 addressing schema. Unlike the RPL, the Lightweight On-Demand Ad hoc Distance (LOAD) and its successor, LOAD - Next Generation (LOADng) is a reactive routing protocol for the low power and lossy networks [2,6]. The LOAD is a derivative of the AODV and with some simplifications over the AODV, eg. removal of intermediate Route Replies and of sequence numbers. As a reactive protocol, LOAD does not maintain a routing table for all destinations in the network, but initiates a route discovery to a destination only when there is data to be sent to that destination to reduce routing overhead and memory consumption. Both LOAD and LOADng are based on the principles of Route Request/Route Reply exchanges for Route Discovery.

Lastly, we would not indent to give an exhaustive list of the multi-hop routing protocols on the IPv6 addressing. We just point out that all these routing protocols are vulnerable to the `warmhole attacks` [8].

3.3   6LoWPAN - IPv6 Routing Protocol for Low Power and Lossy Networks

In this section, we introduce an additional layer in the proposed protocol stack, which is called 6LoWPAN – an acronym of IPv6 over Low-Power Wireless Personal Networks. The 6LoWPAN is an adaption layer in the network protocol stack for integrating low-power network such as IEEE 802.15.4 into IPv6.

The 6LoWPAN network consists of one or more sensing nodes or host nodes local to the LoWPANs, which are all connected by the IPv6 addresses to the Internet through a gateway (or border router), as shown in Fig. 3. The network deals with small packet size, low bandwidth and requires resource saving for maintaining the life of network nodes.

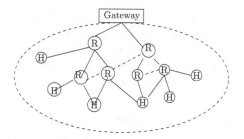

Fig. 3. A simplified 6LoWPAN network

The LoWPAN supports both star and peer-to-peer topology; the topology can be changed frequently because of uncertain radio frequency, mobility and battery drain.

The 6LoWPAN is responsible for connecting the border router node in the WSNs networks to the Internet. It fragments the packets at the IPv6 layer, then reassembles them in the data link and physical layer. There are two distinct approaches for forwarding packets in this layer: mesh-under or route-over. By taking advantage of network simulation, it has shown that route-over forwarding approach is more scalable and robust over than that of the mesh-under forwarding 6LoWPAN network [7].

3.4   IEEE 802.15.4 – ZigBee

The most relevant communication standard for the WSNs is IEEE 802.15.4, which operates in Low-Rate Wireless Personal Area Networks (LR-WPANs).

The IEEE 802.15.4 MAC specifications and IEEE 802.15.4 PHY specifications are standardized by the ZigBee consortium.

The ZigBee standard is a low-cost, low power wireless communication standard which is mainly used to create the Wireless Personal Area Network (WPAN). The ZigBee standard has provided the mesh capabilities for the IEEE 802.15.4 standard by network and security layers and an application framework. The ZigBee networks include many different areas of practical applications such as home automation, health care, lighting management and telecommunication services.

The ZigBee Alliance consists of a group of companies. These companies manufacture inter-operable products to their customers. However, all the ZigBee nodes require an IEEE 802.15.4/IP gateway to establish communication with IP networks. Three categories of ZigBee nodes are: ZigBee coordinator, ZigBee router, and ZigBee devices. That indicates the ZigBee nodes will interface with the IP networks via ZigBee coordinator.

4   Implementation of the WSN in Health Care

In the previous section, we have outlined a framework of building the WSNs for a low rate and noisy networks. We can clearly envisage the WSNs for health care just well fit in the category of application. In this section, we look at how the WSNs for health care in different settings are implemented by adopting the general approach of using network simulation.

4.1   The WSNs Network Simulator

There are plenty of network simulators for the WSNs. The NS-3 simulator is one such designed for many communication networks. The NS-3 is an open source software, virtually a model library for various communication networks. The majority of models are for the IPv4 addressing based networks; while an increasing number of researches are emerging for the IPv6 addressing based network and wireless networks. Apart from the NS-3, other network simulators such as Cooja, TOSSIM and OMNET++ Castalia have been explored to simulate the WSNs applications.

In this study, we would focus on how to apply the NS-3 network simulator to design the networking nodes including NetDevices, Interface containers and Node containers. Figure 4 show the model design of NetDevice, Interface and Node in the NS-3. The justification of choosing the NS-3, is that the RPL model, the 6LoWPAN adaptation model the LR-WPAN model (based on IEEE 802.15.4 MAC and PHY) have been developed and available to us for use.

4.2   Simulation of WSNs for Healthcare Using NS-3

Although there are many multi-hop routing protocols have been implemented such as the previously mentioned AODV, Dynamic Source Routing (DSR), Optimized Link State Routing (OLSR) on the NS-2 and NS-3 network simulators,

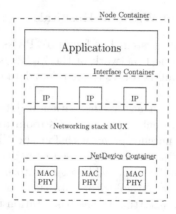

Fig. 4. NetDevice and Nodes Container in NS3

however, they are all developed for the Mobile Ad-hoc networks (a.k.a MANETs) and based on the IPv4 addressing schema. In the section, we adopt the RPL although both RPL and the AODV over IPv6 (ADOVv6) are in development stages, and have some bugs and wired behaviors that have to be fixed.

5   Configurations of WSNs for Health Care Scenarios

Normally the latency of message delivery is used as a metric to analyze the performance of the communication network. The latency is measured at the application level of the WSNs nodes, ie. difference between the time the application message was created at the source node and the time at which the application layer at receiver node, senses the the message.

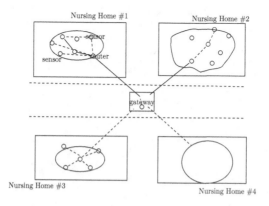

Fig. 5. A sketch of the healthcare system with four LoWPANs

5.1   The Application of WSNs in Hospitals

A WSNs based health care system has four LoWPANs and each LoWPAN in
the settings consists of a mesh network of the ZigBee sensors and one ZigBee
routers. All four ZigBee routers routes the patients data to a remote base station
within hospital.

A hospital care giver can access the patient's data at any point in time
and doesn't have to be present in the patient's room to examine the readings.
Figure 5 is a sketch of a nursing home with four LoWPANs in each patient's
room. A LoWPAN comprised of 4 or more sensor nodes (or ZigBee nodes) and
one router (ZigBee router) is responsible for monitoring the movement of the
patient and collecting their physiological data such as the blood pressure and
temperature, and then transmitting to the base station in the hospital corridor.

5.2   The Application of WSNs in Care Center

When it comes to the implementation of the WSNs applications, the overall
application of the WSNs in care center is a network of 6LoWPAN networks; Each
6LoWPAN network consists of one or more local LoWPANs. Local LoWPANs are
connected by the IPv6 addressing to the through a gateway (or border router).
The LoWPANs devices might be the ZigBee nodes or other types of low power
sensors.

Figure 6 show data transmitting through the ZigBee sensors and the gateway
within the simulated WSNs based health care system in the NS-3.

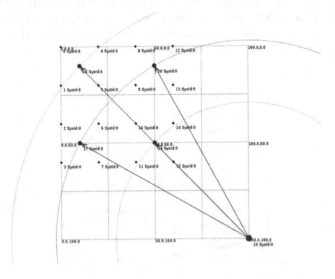

Fig. 6. The simulated WSNs based system in NS-3

The preliminary results about the performance of the WNSs based health care system have been achieved so far in terms of the latency of message delivery. A report of performance comparison with other studies will be presented shortly.

6   Conclusion

In this paper, we have proposed a framework of designing and developing efficient and low cost health care application systems based on the Wireless sensor networks.

The study has gone through from scrutinizing the requirements and characteristics of health care systems deployed in the two primarily environments. It has outlined a framework of layered protocol stack that can be applied while building the WSNs based systems to meet the requirements of health care services.

In accordance with the proposed framework, we have implemented a wireless patient monitoring and data collecting (WPMDC) system in the hospital environment. A prototype of the system has been simulated in NS-3, and some preliminary results shown that the framework be applicable to other health care related environments such as nursing home for aged care service.

After implementing the WPMDC systems, we have gained many insights into the requirements of health care services and deeper understanding of the communication protocols support the reliable communications on the wireless sensor networks with nature of low cost and noisy. In the future, we would continue the study on both the performance analysis and the security.

References

1. Agustin, J.P.C., Jacinto, J.H., Limjoco, W.J.R., Pedrasa, J.R.I.: Ipv6 routing protocol for low-power and lossy networks implementation in network simulator - 3. In: Region 10 Conference (TENCON), 5–8 November 2017 (2017)
2. Lakshmana, S.B.: A study on the impact of transmission power on the message delivery latency in large zigbee networks (2015)
3. Belhaj, S., Hamad, S.: Routing protocols from wireless sensor networks to the internet of things: an overview. Int. J. Adv. Appl. Sci. 5(9), 47–63 (2018)
4. Chen, Y.B., Hou, K.M., Chanet, J.P., El Gholami, K.: A RPL based adaptive and scalable data-collection protocol module for ns-3 simulation platform (2013)
5. Chen, F., Qin, L., Li, X., Wu, G., Shi, C.: Design and implementation of ZigBee wireless sensor and control network system in greenhouse. In: 26th Chinese Control Conference, 26–28 July (2017)
6. Clausen, T., Yi, J., Herberg, U.: Lightweight on-demand ad hoc distance-vector routing - next generation (LOADng): protocol, extension, and applicability. Comput. Netw. 120, 125–140 (2017)
7. McGee, K., Collier, M.: 6LoWPAN forwarding techniques for IoT. In: 2019 IEEE 5th World Forum on Internet of Things (WF-IoT), 15–18 April 2019, pp. 897–902 (2019)

8. Hu, Y.-C., Perrig, A., Johnson, D.B.: Wormhole attacks in wireless networks. IEEE J. Sel. Areas Communi. **24**(2), 370–380 (2006)
9. Riquelme, J.L., Soto, F., Suardiaz, J., Sanchez, P., Iborra, A., Vera, J.A.: Wireless sensor networks for precision horticulture in Southern Spain. Comput. Electron. Agric. **68**, 25–35 (2009)
10. Sadiku, M.N.O., Eze, K.G., Musa, S.M.: Wireless sensor networks for healthcare. J. Sci. Eng. Res. **5**(7), 210–213 (2018)

A New Intrusion Detection Scheme Using CatBoost Classifier

Nitesh Singh Bhati[1] and Manju Khari[2]([✉])

[1] Delhi Technical Campus, Greater Noida, India
niteshbhati07@gmail.com
[2] Ambedkar Institute of Advanced Communication Technologies and Research, Delhi, India
manjukhari@aiactr.ac.in

Abstract. Advancements in the network infrastructure have caused a positive influence in our day to day life. Many reform initiatives have been taken all over the world which are related to the digitization of the countries methodologies of handling information. The usage of modern techniques also has a drawback, which allows data theft. Hence, a secure system is required, which can detect any kind of fraudulent activity and alert the administrator. Such a system is called an Intrusion Detection System (IDS). There are many types of IDSs available at our disposal, and a lot of research has also been done on their various types. This paper presents the implementation of IDS based on CatBoost technique which is a part of the ensemble machine learning strategy. The results of the implementation have been evaluated on the evaluation metrics like accuracy, precision, recall, and F1-score. The programming environment used is Python. The implementation has experimented on the NSL-KDD dataset, and the results have been analyzed on the detection accuracy, which shows the proposed scheme has reached an accuracy of 99.46% on the NSL-KDD dataset.

Keywords: Intrusion Detection System · Intrusion detection technique · Ensemble · CatBoost · Machine learning

1 Introduction

Major reforms in the world are mostly related to digitization, and for that, machine learning has been used as a foundation to improve the situation of human understanding of the information. It has also been used to improve the network infrastructure security situation that is a necessity due to the global access of internet to the public. An effective IDS should be an automated machine. Apart from the automation of the task, high detection rate and low false positive rate is the main feature of an effective IDS. Firewalls and other security systems, are designed to prevent some attacks from occurring, but any foreign activity that is alien to their system, is completely ignored by these services. For that purpose, Intrusion Detection Systems are used which provide the service of detecting any intrusion in the system and alerts the admin through an alarm system [1, 2].

© ICST Institute for Computer Sciences, Social Informatics and Telecommunications Engineering 2021
Published by Springer Nature Switzerland AG 2021. All Rights Reserved
E. Ever and F. Al-Turjman (Eds.): FoNeS-IoT 2020, LNICST 353, pp. 169–176, 2021.
https://doi.org/10.1007/978-3-030-69431-9_13

The position of the IDS in the organization defines the types of IDS being used, and mainly there are three types of IDS based on the position,

a. Host-Based IDS, which is placed with the host, each host in the network has its individual IDS [3].
b. Network-Based IDS, which is placed between the router and the collection of the hosts connected to that router. A single IDS provides the services for the whole network [4].
c. Hybrid IDS, is a collection of 2 or more types of IDS, and can be placed wither on the host or the network, provides better security than either of the aforementioned types [5].

With the increased incorporation of technology with everyday tasks, the need for security has also increased. Every aspect of human life is being converted into a digital platform and with the upcoming smart city projects under the new initiatives of the Indian Govt., the complete world would follow, which requires a lot of security in terms of data hack and usage of data for criminal intent, which should not be allowed [6]. In order to prevent the occurrence of such activities, a system, which provides security, preferably like an IDS, but in real-time scenario is required. Aspirants of IDS should focus on building an efficient system for the IDS which works real time as well [7].

Many security systems are designed to provide protection against existing attacks like Denial of Service (DoS) but novel attacks are yet to be made more efficient in terms of detection [8]. Many times, such DoS and Distributed Denial of Service attacks can also be stopped with the help of reCAPTCHA controllers, but they are considered for bot attacks, protection against novel attacks is alien to this technique as well [9].

2   Related Work

The method of Ensemble Based learning is creating a combination of different (more than 2) models or classifiers in order to produce a single model which provides a solution with a result better than the individual models' results. This technique of amalgamating different models provides higher efficiency than individual models. The proposed method is based on a boosting technique which is a part of ensemble machine learning. It is an implementation of data's sequential modelling, which provides an improvement upon the errors and hence the performance is also improved. Boosting initiates with a weak learner, and iteratively learner is improved over time due to the reduction of errors, an analogy can be that the model is maturing over time. The advantage of boosting is that it provides a strong prediction with low overfitting, and implementation is also easy [10]. The process of boosting is further improved by implementing an extra step, which is to calculate the loss between the predicted and the targeted value, this process is called gradient boosting. It iterates to the point where the number of errors is relatively zero, and this further improves the model as it is learning on the data produced by its own self as it takes the previous prediction and modifies it based on the newly generated result [11].

Dhaliwal et al. [12] presented an implementation of a network based IDS with the foundation of XGBoost, another boosting based machine learning technology. And presented an accuracy of 98.7%. The implementation was performed on the NSL-KDD Dataset.

Chen et al. [13] presented an implementation of an SDN-IDS based on XGBoost. The implementation was performed on "TCP Dump" dataset. The main focus was on the paralysis caused by DDoS in a network. The results provide a higher detection rate with lower false positives.

Su et al. [14] presented an implementation of a network based IDS using the XGBoost approach, aimed at detecting attacks based on unbalanced data set. The implementation was performed on the KDDCup99 dataset with the results showing higher accuracy and lower missing rate.

Bhattacharya et al. [15] presented an implementation of an IDS based on hybrid principle component analysis aimed at detection of dynamic attacks. Their implementation used the classification process of XGBoost method. The results presented higher accuracy.

Devan and Khare [16] presented an implementation of an IDS by keeping a basis of Deep Neural Network amalgamated with XGBoost. The implementation was performed on the NSL-KDD dataset. The results of the implementation turns out to be better in terms of accuracy, precision, recall, and F1-score when compared to techniques like logistic regression, and SVM.

Pattawaro and Polprasert [17] presented an implementation of IDS based on the combination of feature selection with K-Means clustering and XGBoost classification model that was implemented on the KDD dataset, providing results of 84.41% accuracy and 18.41% false alarm rate.

Hu et al. [18] presented an implementation of AdaBoost based IDS for network IDS aimed at providing a solution to 'especially' low false positive rate without changing the computational complexity. The experiment was implemented on the KDD dataset, providing results of 90.4% in detection rate.

Li and Li [19] presented an implementation of a network based IDS. Their implementation is based on the anomaly technique amalgamated with the naïve Bayes classifier. They used the AdaBoost algorithm and performed it on the KDD cup dataset. Their results presented higher detection rate and lower false positive rate.

Harb and Desuky [20] presented an implementation of AdaBoost based IDS aimed at a fast learning algorithm combined with genetic algorithms to form an ensemble IDS. The removal of the redundant classifiers decreased and improved the speed of classification.

The proposed work is compared with other techniques in the Table 1 for the convenience of the reader.

Table 1. Comparison of proposed work with different techniques

S. no	Year	Author	Technique used	Accuracy
01	2008	Hu et al. [18]	AdaBoost	90.4%
02	2018	Dhaliwal et al. [12]	XGBoost	98.7%
03	2018	Pattawaro and Polprasert [17]	K-Means Clustering	84.41%
04	**2020**	**Bhati and Khari**	**CatBoost – Proposed Scheme**	**99.46%**

3   Proposed Scheme

The proposed scheme is comprised of the following steps,

i.   Dataset collection,
ii. Preprocessing,
iii. Training and Testing using CatBoost, and
iv. Decision.

The outline of proposed scheme is given in Fig. 1.

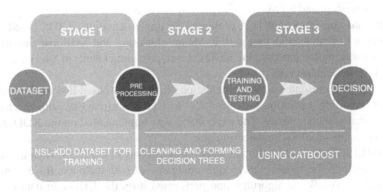

Fig. 1. Block diagram of proposed scheme.

3.1   Dataset

NSL-KDD dataset has been used as the dataset for this experiment. It is a refined version of the KDD dataset [21]. It is mainly used to simulate and test the performance of an IDS. Each record of this dataset consists of 41 attributes with each having different features of the flow and an assigned label of an attack-type, which are Denial of Service, Probe, User To Root, Remote to Local and normal attack [22].

The dataset consists of 5 million connection records for the purpose of training (24 attack types), and about 2 million connection records for the purpose of testing the said system (24 + 14 unique attack types). The dataset has been split into the ratio of 4:1, i.e., 80% for training and 20% of the dataset is used for testing the experiment.

3.2 Pre Processing

Normalization of data is a very crucial step in order to get the best results because the collection of data is from many different sources which have different file formats and hence are needed to be in a single file format for the automation process to be done. It is also done to remove the inconsistencies and remove poorly documented files and complete the databases. Python environment is used in this implementation to perform data cleaning, integration, transformation and reduction for the preprocessing purpose [23].

3.3 Training and Testing

In this implementation, CatBoost technique has been used to train and test on the dataset. CatBoost is an abbreviation of Categorical Boosting, and it is based on gradient boosting. CatBoost quickly incorporates many diverse data sources. The implementation of CatBoost is easier as it does not require a huge amount of data for training. CatBoost provides a GPU implementation of the learning algorithm and a CPU implementation of a scoring algorithm [24].

CatBoost natively performs the operation of converting a non-numerical data value into a numerical data value in an optimum way without the usage of any parametric tuning and provides satisfactory results in a single run [24].

In order to process the categorical features, CatBoost proposes a strategy of performing random permutation on the dataset. Let $\sigma = \sigma_1, \ldots, \sigma_n$ be the permutation and substitute $x_{\sigma_p,k}$ with the following Eq. 1, [25].

$$\frac{\sum_{j=1}^{p-1}\left[x_{\sigma_j,k} = x_{\sigma_p,k}\right]Y_{\sigma_j} + a \cdot P}{\sum_{j=1}^{p-1}\left[x_{\sigma_j,k} = x_{\sigma_p,k}\right]Y_{\sigma_j} + a} \tag{1}$$

The working is described in the following algorithm,

Step 1: Training the dataset.
Step 2: Converting non numerical data values into numerical data values, i.e., transforming the dataset into a single unit.
Step 3: Creation of decision trees to form rule based mechanism.
Step 4: Generate prediction of the model based on the input and the errors generated.
Step 5: Repeat step 3 and 4 until convergence is reached.

3.4 Decision

This is the last phase of the proposed scheme's process. The proposed scheme creates a classification of the attacks based on the decision trees created. The attacks are classified as Denial of Service, Probe, Remote to local attacks. The proposed scheme provides an accuracy of 99.46% on the NSL KDD dataset.

Table 2. Summarized results of the proposed method.

Attack	Precision	Recall	F1-score	Support
DoS	1.00	1.00	1.00	1825
Normal	0.99	1.00	1.00	2734
Probe	0.99	0.98	0.98	440
R$_2$L	1.00	0.94	0.97	31

4 Empirical Evolution and Results

Table 2 shows the results produced by performing the experiment on the NSL-KDD dataset, which are based on evaluation metrics like accuracy, precision, recall, and F1-score [23].

TP = True Positive
FP = False Positive
FN = False Negative
TN = True Negative

i   Precision, defines the classifier's ability to correctly identify the instance as a negative instance and not a false negative.

$$\text{Precision} = \frac{TP}{TP + FP} \tag{2}$$

ii. Recall, defines the classifier's ability to find all the positive instances, correctly.

$$\text{Recall} = \frac{TP}{TP + FN} \tag{3}$$

iii. F1 score, the result of the calculation of the harmonic mean of precision and recall, where 1 represents the best score and 0 represents the worst score.

$$\text{F} - \text{score}(\beta) = \frac{(1 + \beta^2)\text{PR}}{\beta^2 P + R} \tag{4}$$

iv. Support, the number of occurrences of class in the specified dataset.

5 Conclusion

In this paper, the research done on the similar implementation of IDS has been reviewed, and a CatBoost based approach has been proposed with its analysis. CatBoost is an ensemble-based technique. The results of the implementation have been evaluated on the evaluation metrics like accuracy, precision, recall, and F1-score. The programming environment used is Python. The implementation has experimented on the NSL-KDD dataset, and the results have been analyzed on the detection accuracy, which shows the proposed scheme has reached an accuracy of 99.46% on the NSL-KDD dataset. The main reason for using CatBoost is that it natively performs the operation of converting a non-numerical data value into a numerical data value in an optimum way without the usage of any parametric tuning and provides satisfactory results in a single run.

References

1. Bhati, B.S., Rai, C.S.: Intrusion detection systems and techniques: a review. Int. J. Crit. Comput. Syst. **6**(3), 173–190 (2016)
2. Rowland, C.H.: U.S. Patent No. 6,405,318. Washington, DC: U.S. Patent and Trademark Office (2002)
3. Bhati, B.S., Rai, C.S.: Analysis of support vector machine-based intrusion detection techniques. Arabian J. Sci. Eng. **45**(4), 1–3 (2019)
4. Kozushko, H.: Intrusion detection: host-based and network-based intrusion detection systems. Independent Study **11**, 1–23 (2003)
5. Sun, M., Chen, T.: U.S. Patent Application No. 12/411,916 (2010)
6. Ali, Z., Chaudhry, S., Sher, M., Al-Turjman, F.: Securing smart city surveillance: a lightweight authentication mechanism for unmanned vehicles. IEEE Access **8**(1), 43711–43724 (2020)
7. Bhati, B.S., Chugh, G., Al-Turjman, F., Bhati, N.S.: An improved ensemble based intrusion detection technique using XGBoost. Wiley Trans. Emerg. Telecommun. Technol. (2020). https://doi.org/10.1002/ett.4076
8. Bhati, B., Rai, C.S., Balamurugan, B., Al-Turjman, F.: An intrusion detection scheme based on the ensemble of discriminant classifiers. Elsevier Comput. Electr. Eng. J. **86**, 106742 (2020)
9. Poongodi, M., Vijayakumar, V., Al-Turjman, F., Hamdi, M., Ma, M.: Intrusion prevention system for DDoS attack on VANET with reCAPTCHA controller using information based metrics. IEEE Access **7**(1), 158481–158491 (2019)
10. Prokhorenkova, L., Gusev, G., Vorobev, A., Dorogush, A.V., Gulin, A.: CatBoost: unbiased boosting with categorical features. In: Advances in Neural Information Processing Systems, pp. 6638–6648 (2018)
11. Cestnik, B.: Estimating probabilities: a crucial task in machine learning. In: ECAI, vol. 90, pp. 147–149, August 1990
12. Dhaliwal, S.S., Nahid, A.A., Abbas, R.: Effective intrusion detection system using XGBoost. Information **9**(7), 149 (2018)
13. Chen, Z., Jiang, F., Cheng, Y., Gu, X., Liu, W., Peng, J.: XGBoost classifier for DDoS attack detection and analysis in SDN-based cloud. In: 2018 IEEE International Conference on Big Data and Smart Computing (BigComp), pp. 251–256. IEEE (2018)
14. Xiaolong, X.U., Wen, C.H.E.N., Yanfei, S.U.N.: Over-sampling algorithm for imbalanced data classification. J. Syst. Eng. Electron. **30**(6), 1182–1191 (2019)
15. Bhattacharya, S., Kaluri, R., Singh, S., Alazab, M., Tariq, U.: A Novel PCA-firefly based XGBoost classification model for intrusion detection in networks using GPU. Electronics **9**(2), 219 (2020)
16. Devan, P., Khare, N.: An efficient XGBoost–DNN-based classification model for network intrusion detection system. Neural Comput. Appl. **32**(16), 12499–12514 (2020). https://doi.org/10.1007/s00521-020-04708-x
17. Pattawaro, A., Polprasert, C.: Anomaly-based network intrusion detection system through feature selection and hybrid machine learning technique. In: 2018 16th International Conference on ICT and Knowledge Engineering (ICT&KE), pp. 1–6. IEEE, November 2018

18. Hu, W., Hu, W., Maybank, S.: Adaboost-based algorithm for network intrusion detection. IEEE Trans. Syst. Man Cybern. Part B (Cybern.) **38**(2), 577–583 (2008)
19. Li, W., Li, Q.: Using naive bayes with AdaBoost to enhance network anomaly intrusion detection. In: 2010 Third International Conference on Intelligent Networks and Intelligent Systems, pp. 486–489. IEEE, November 2010
20. Harb, H.M., Desuky, A.S.: Adaboost ensemble with genetic algorithm post optimization for intrusion detection. Int. J. Comput. Sci. Issues (IJCSI) **8**(5), 28 (2011)
21. Tavallaee, M., Bagheri, E., Lu, W., Ghorbani, A.A.: A detailed analysis of the KDD CUP 99 data set. In: 2009 IEEE Symposium on Computational Intelligence for Security and Defense Applications, pp. 1–6. IEEE, July 2009
22. Dhanabal, L., Shantharajah, S.P.: A study on NSL-KDD dataset for intrusion detection system based on classification algorithms. Int. J. Adv. Res. Comput. Commun. Eng. **4**(6), 446–452 (2015)
23. Bhati, B.S., Rai, C.S.: Ensemble based approach for intrusion detection using extra tree classifier. In: Solanki, V.K., Hoang, M.K., Lu, Z., Pattnaik, P.K. (eds.) Intelligent Computing in Engineering. AISC, vol. 1125, pp. 213–220. Springer, Singapore (2020). https://doi.org/10.1007/978-981-15-2780-7_25
24. Dorogush, A.V., Ershov, V., Gulin, A.: CatBoost: gradient boosting with categorical features support. *arXiv preprint* arXiv:1810.11363 (2018)
25. Thangaraj, M., Vijayalakshmi, C.R.: Performance study on rule-based classification techniques across multiple database relations. Int. J. Appl. Inf. Syst. **5**(4), 1–7 (2013)

Author Index

Printed in the United States
By Bookmasters